Reflection through Interaction:
The Classroom Experience
Learning Difficulties

To David and our family with grateful thanks for their support

Reflection through Interaction:
The Classroom Experience of Pupils with Learning Difficulties

Judith Watson

The Falmer Press

(A member of the Taylor & Francis Group)
London • Washington, D.C.

UK Falmer Press, 1 Gunpowder Square, London, EC4A 3DE
USA Falmer Press, Taylor & Francis Inc., 1900 Frost Road, Suite 101,
     Bristol, PA 19007

© J. Watson, 1996

First published 1996

**Library of Congress Cataloging-in-Publication data are
available on request**

**A catalogue record for this book is available from the British
Library**

ISBN 0 7507 0562 0 cased
ISBN 0 7507 0563 9 paper

Jacket design by Caroline Archer

Typeset in 10/12pt Garamond by
Graphicraft Typesetters Ltd., Hong Kong

*Printed in Great Britain by Biddles Ltd., Guildford and King's
Lynn on paper which has a specified pH value on final paper
manufacture of not less than 7.5 and is therefore 'acid free'.*

Contents

Preface

The research reported here was made possible by the Research Committee of Moray House Institute of Education. This provided the expert secretarial assistance of Angela Watson, and the invaluable research assistance of Judith Scott, whose ideas and insights were influential in the early stages.

The three authors of the reports of imaginative primary school developments in chapter 8 were more than willing to share their ideas and open up their classrooms. They are named, although their pupils are not; all are gratefully thanked.

My greatest debt, however, is to the teachers and pupils in the special schools. The value of their willing cooperation and good humour cannot be overstated. Their, and their pupils' identities are protected. It would not be realistic, however, to assume that the teachers might not occasionally recognize examples of their own talk, and incidents used as illustrations, even after the lapse of two years, and all the intervening events of their busy professional lives. Nor would it be true to claim that I never make evaluative judgments. There would be little point in undertaking classroom research on reflection in the classroom without a conviction that it is a worthwhile, valuable, activity, and without investigating ways in which it can be promoted.

1   A Framework for Reflection

Introduction

Why is reflection by pupils important? And what exactly do we mean by 'reflection'? Two of the teacher participants in the research described in this book provided unprepared and insightful answers to these two questions, referring to their own practice and their own pupils.

> I think they have difficulty following through reasoned argument, cause and effect, all kinds of things . . . and hypothesizing, which you know, can lead you on to things like crossing the road, and what will happen if . . .

> (Reflection is) thinking in depth about things, erm, just where your thinking is challenged in any way, where you are not just reacting on a superficial level, where you are thinking beyond the immediate thing to its implications and possibilities. I think!

Their words, 'depth', 'challenge', 'thinking beyond' and 'hypothesizing', encapsulate the characteristics of mature sophisticated, educated intelligence. This book, like the two teachers quoted above, is concerned with the educational experience of pupils with learning difficulties who inevitably are neither mature nor sophisticated in their thinking.

In this introduction I attempt to clarify my use of the term 'reflection' and to outline the contents to follow.

What do we mean by reflection? The term reflection involves more than thinking and has a wider domain than metacognition. Reflection includes reasoning, the creative production of ideas, problem solving, and the awareness of all these mental activities in metacognition. It embraces a wide range of cognitive activity which in Bruner's famous phrase 'goes beyond the information given' (1973).

For example, in reasoning, a person takes a mental step beyond what is initially presented, as in 'so she must have known that all the time!': in problem solving a way towards a solution is sought, 'we have to work out what time the train will arrive', and metacognition may involve such self monitoring as 'I'm finding this really hard to follow'.

So reflection is mental activity that consists of transforming given information in order to reach conclusions. This description excludes one-step mental processes such as simple memory retrieval or brief flashes of insight. It has a certain duration.

It also involves effort. In talking to pupils we sometimes asked about 'thinking hard'. 'What made you think really hard?' when talking to them about their recent classroom experience was certainly a meaningful question to them. But the term 'thinking' does not always convey the essential features of duration, extension, and effort that are involved in reflection. Further, for many teachers the term 'thinking' is associated with the teaching of specific thinking skills. The present focus is not on these important and related pedagogical initiatives, but on opportunities for reflection across the whole range of a pupil's curricular experience.

How do we recognize reflection in the classroom? Campbell and Olson (1990) emphasize the hidden nature as well as the effort of reflection, which they describe as inwardly mediated thinking, involving mental 'work' in which the individual 'forsakes its normal outward orientation on the presented world and struggles instead with a world only imperfectly indexed by a shadowy inward structure of mental symbols'.

We can and do assume that a person is thinking hard by observation and knowledge of an individual's characteristic behaviour such as absorption, stilling, silence, muttering or frowning. These, along with concentrated stare, furrowed brows and closed eyes were mentioned frequently by experienced teachers in discussion with us. One of our research project teachers said pupils were engaged — caught up in what they were doing, when they were thinking hard.

We can also ask pupils about the process of reflection, for example by asking them to think aloud during problem-solving. The degree to which this is likely to disrupt important reflective activity is open to question, and this technique was not attempted directly in the research described in this book. However, pupils did occasionally talk to themselves while working and we were able to pick up on this. Audiorecordings also sometimes recorded individual target pupils' requests and contributions which their teacher could not hear, and at least some of the pupils' feelings of frustration and triumph were expressed out loud.

Most commonly we deduce that a pupil has been engaged in reflection by its product. When for example there is some evidence of new understanding, relating ideas together in a novel way, or drawing a conclusion from given premises. Sometimes pupils spontaneously make comments like 'Now I get it' or 'that can't be right, because . . .' which show their awareness of their own cognitive advance.

We all subjectively recognize that there are times when our attention is focused, when we become temporarily less aware of time passing and of our immediate surroundings, when irrelevant and intrusive thoughts are kept at bay. And we would all probably acknowledge occasionally an accompanying suspension of breath, sense of excitement and emotional and physiological involvement which is deeply personal. Many adults if asked when they are likely to experience such attentiveness will describe watching a film where there is an element of suspense, or being involved in a game or work situation in which their expectations are confounded, and they are brought up with a jerk and forced to think more deeply.

This book concerns reflection in the classroom by pupils who have not proved to be successful learners and who are likely to have missed many of the powerfully rewarding experiences which can result from engaging with intellectual challenge. For such pupils it is especially true, as Jackson (1968) memorably pointed out, that 'no educational goals are more immediate than those which concern the establishment and maintenance of the student's absorption in the task at hand', and that 'classroom time that is wasted represents life experiences foregone'.

The same sense of irrevocable loss that can result from missed educational opportunities is particularly acute among many teachers of pupils who have difficulties in learning. One of our research study teachers described her sadness concerning the inability of one of her pupils to become fully engaged with school work: 'Even when he came to school, he was so anxious that he didn't make the most of what was there, and I really felt at the end of the year that he had made little or no progress and that was very sad. That was very depressing, because to me that was a year of his life lost, in terms of, I mean, for a young lad of ten or eleven he should have amassed an enormous amount of learning in that time . . .'

Anxiety, experience of past failures, lack of confidence and a tendency to withdraw from, rather than engage with, challenge, are very frequently found among pupils receiving special education. These additional obstacles to pupils' learning are well recognized by their teachers and clearly affected the practice of the teacher participants in the research reported here.

The book has the following plan. This first chapter presents a brief account of constructivist approaches to learning, within a framework of social interaction. From the research literature factors which appear to facilitate reflection are discussed with a special emphasis on classroom experiences. Evidence that the encouragement of reflection is of particular importance for relatively unsuccessful pupils is presented in chapter 2.

Chapter 3 describes the methodology and rationale of an investigation of reflection in classrooms of pupils with moderate learning difficulties. The following four chapters focus on the findings and implications of this research project. Briefly, a teaching style was identified which encouraged reflection by pupils: this was found to relate to other features of classrooms including their general ethos, which concludes the discussion in chapter 7.

Chapter 8 presents details of three initiatives in different settings with pupils of different age and ability levels. All have in common the aim of enhancing pupils' reflection and each focuses on a different area. Their inclusion enhances and supplements the main findings and should be a useful source of ideas for teachers.

The concluding chapter considers the implications of the research and development work for teachers' facilitation of pupil reflection, with special reference to pupils with learning difficulties.

Constructions and Scaffolds

> By helping the child to structure his activities, we are helping him to perform things he could not do alone until such time as he becomes familiar enough with the demands of the task at hand to develop local expertise and to try things alone. (Wood, 1988)

David Wood's well known book on thinking and learning summarizes important theoretical contributions towards the view of learning as activity that is socially constructed, the focus of the first part of this chapter. Very broadly it is plain that writings on cognitive development and learning have altered in their perspective over the last two decades or so to include more than the mental activity of individuals. Wells, for example, in 1981, described language development as learning through interaction, in which early negotiation of meaning and joint activity by parents and their young children was found to be associated with the most fluent and rapid language acquisition: Rogoff likewise stresses the role of a child's peers and other members of society in early cognitive development or 'apprenticeship in thinking' (1990). She means by apprenticeship guided participation in social activity in which children's understanding is supported and stretched. In referring to learning in school by such terms as 'mediated' or 'assisted performance' Tharp and Gallimore (1988) among many others view it primarily as a social interactive process.

In sum there has been a movement beyond the view of cognitive development as essentially consisting of the progressive elaboration and reorganization of mental structures by the individual. It is and must be that, but can not only be that; not a process in a single direction which is dependent primarily on that individual's activity. Constructivist theories rightly stress the crucial relationship between new experiences and what is already known. It makes absolute sense to postulate that our cognition develops through encounters with new information that is different enough to be stimulating, but not so alien that we cannot assimilate it into those mental structures that represent our present state of understanding.

Real learning must build on pupils' own existing cognitive structures, and must relate to their needs and interests. Only individuals can learn and they must construct their own understanding, but the social constructivist view is that such understanding is greatly enhanced during meaningful effective interaction with others. Teachers are constantly enjoined to start 'where the child is at', and assessing what their pupils already understand, at however informal a level, and building on it, is their stock in trade, albeit more likely to be made more explicit in early education settings and less so when syllabus constraints are more apparent.

By the time a formal academic syllabus is in force it tends to be taken for granted that pupils will have developed an idea of what is relevant or important, be aware of what they already know and have a good idea of how to relate the two in developing their understanding. This assumes a need to make sense, to learn more about the world and a satisfaction in doing so, that, as Donaldson pointed out so effectively in 1978, is obvious in very young children but seems to dissipate alarmingly fast when many children become pupils.

As Meadows (1993) says, the constructivist account implies a natural, smooth, progression towards a 'highly developed, subtle, sophisticated, intricately integrated, perfectly balanced cognitive system'. This does not seem to be an accurate description of most of us as thinkers, most of the time. What in such a theoretical model would account for our failures to get started and our willingness to cut short reflective activity?

Intrinsic motivation is high where there is a sense of personal control and growing competence, and tasks which are interesting, relevant, and present optimally challenging experiences. But to focus on the individual child in an exclusively child-centred approach is problematic, as Donaldson concludes, in a far reaching, profound exploration of her theoretical model of four 'modes' of thought (from infants' 'here and now' thinking in the 'point' mode, to mature transcendent thought with spiritual and philosophical concerns beyond time and space).

The child-centred approach is highly desirable, she says, in the sense of the teacher trying to understand the pupil's point of view and level of understanding, but not enough, if we wish to encourage the child's maximum potential. For the child's point of view is necessarily limited: teachers have a longer view of possible consequences to present action. An extreme child-centred approach runs, in her words, the risk of 'overestimating children's powers of self direction and the validity of their judgments, while underestimating not only their need for systematic well-thought-out help but also their willingness to receive this help if it is not forced upon them in insensitive ways. Young children have a remarkable fitness for the role of novice' (Donaldson, 1992). The child's tremendous aptitude for learning is apparent to all parents of infants and toddlers and it is also evident that young children are often most engaged and challenged in social contexts; in domestic activities, in play, and in disputes; in observing adults in their work roles, on the buses, in cafes and shops, in our society. Through interacting with more knowledgeable people individual children develop in social competence and understanding and this is a fundamental part of their general cognitive development, not in any way an adjunct. The extension and application of research findings on social cognition from the earliest days and pre-school years into educational settings is a welcome move to many teachers, who may feel that the recent strong emphasis on curriculum has diminished their individual and personal contribution. Social constructivism, with its view of teacher-pupil interaction as the focus for new learning, reinstates the teacher as the expert judge of what a pupil understands, and as the creator of opportunities for that same pupil to advance in understanding and eventually develop into an autonomous or self-directed learner. For novices and apprentices eventually become experts.

The view of education as enabling novices to become experts through appropriate interactions in educational settings is often described as deriving from Vygotsky's writings of more than fifty years ago, and 'Vygotskyan approaches' generally mean ones in which a more competent and knowledgeable person assists one who is less so, by providing them with the appropriate amount of help, with the important aim that eventually the learner becomes able to regulate their own activity and thinking. Vygotsky's well known phrase, 'the zone of proximal development' (ZPD), represents that gap between what people can do alone, and what they can do with the optimal degree of assistance from one who is more expert. In Vygotsky's own words it is 'the distance between the actual developmental level as determined by individual problem solving and the level of potential development as determined through problem solving under adult guidance or in collaboration with more capable peers' (1978). The zone is, of course, a hypothetical construct but the term conveys an important idea to teachers; that a pupil is often on the edge of understanding, and may be unable to advance alone. It is easy to see how attractive the term has proved, especially for teachers of pupils who clearly experience difficulties in understanding. But in its place I shall use the more general term 'scaffolding' to describe the many ways in which pupils' understanding can be advanced and clarified by appropriate assistance.

The term scaffolding avoids the unwarranted impression of precision in references to zones of proximal development. The scaffold metaphor is of a supportive structure to the child's thinking, provided by a more expert or knowledgeable person and dismantled as the child's understanding becomes better developed and the other person gradually hands over control. At different stages and levels of development and with different tasks the amount of scaffolding needed will vary enormously. Bruner illustrates this beautifully in describing in detail the responsive feedback afforded children by their mothers during the transition from preverbal to verbal behaviour. Their mothers gradually increase their demands and expectations of their children's communications in a subtle, apparently sophisticated, but largely intuitive way. For example, a precise finger point by an infant may originate in an unsuccessful reach towards a toy being responded to (scaffolded) by the mother and thus slowly acquiring cultural meaning for the baby. It has become a gesture which is understood by other adults and can be used by the child to direct their activities. The child has then internalized the meaning of pointing in this early example of socially constructed understanding (Bruner, 1983). With rather older children of four and five years Wood (1988) reports how he and his colleagues investigated the different ways in which their mothers helped them to construct a pyramid out of blocks of different sizes. The most directive mothers demonstrated how to do the task leaving the child with no responsibility and little evidence of learning. The least directive approach was to give the child verbal instructions only, without any demonstration, and again the children were able to do little on their own. Between these two approaches were mothers whose responses were sensitively adapted to, or contingent upon, their perception of their child's understanding, who offered that degree of help that was shown to be necessary, at the right time, but no more than was needed. It was this approach that resulted in the children learning to focus attention on critical aspects of the task and eventually to combine these in a sequence which enable them to complete the pyramid by themselves. These mothers were using scaffolding to help their children learn in a way they could not do on their own. The timing and nature of the scaffold provided by their mothers was contingent on the children's actions and thus their current level of understanding. Contingency is essential to effective scaffolding.

Scaffolding is easy to observe in the relaxed intimacy of successful parent-child interactions. What about the much more complex demanding and distracting setting of the classroom? Is it reasonable to even expect contingent responding by teachers to pupils in school? Can (and if they can, do) teachers help children to develop their cognitive abilities through scaffolding during classroom interactions?

Can there be effective scaffolding where curricular demands and expectations dominate and where pupil-teacher ratios are high? They are clearly radically different settings from the homes of young children, which with all their crises and distractions usually offer warm, close, predictable environments in which parents' effective scaffolding rests on their deep understanding of their child's intentions, interests and past experience.

Palincsar (1986) reported exciting results from a programme in which scaffolding techniques were used with 13-year-old students, who had poor reading comprehension, and their teachers. They worked together in groups using reciprocal teaching, with students and teachers alternating the role of leader, and in which the four processes of questioning, clarifying, summarizing and predicting were highlighted, using written texts as the focus of discussion. Gradually over time more responsibility was transferred to the students, and the teachers' role became mainly that of providing encouragement, positive feedback, and facilitating students' self-evaluation. Always, of course, they were prepared to go back to a more dominant role if this appeared to be desirable. The results showed improvements in the students' abilities to use the four processes, along with their reading comprehension, and, importantly, there was generalization in their use from students' discussion groups to the classroom setting, and transfer to similar tasks.

In a series of subsequent research studies, comparisons were made between scaffolding and different teaching methods, such as teachers modelling the four processes, and students practising them and receiving considerable feedback; it was found that only the reciprocal teaching experience was effective and that it was necessary to teach all four processes directly. A further study by Palincsar looked at the ways in which scaffolding was actually practised by eight teachers each working with a group of six students, of comparable ability and including two low achievers. Tape recordings enabled a detailed

7

examination of classroom dialogues, in which the same prose material was discussed by the different groups. After twenty consecutive school days of thirty minutes' instruction, the members of some groups were twice as able to transfer the four processes they had been taught and were also more independent.

On examination each of these groups' experience revealed some of the following features. Their teachers responded to students' ideas rather than to their words: for example they did not correct their students' own language use: secondly, the students' ideas were linked with new knowledge during scaffolding. Explicit instruction was given to the students, and the more effective scaffolding had characteristic focus and direction. Finally frequent constructive evaluative comments were given.

The scaffolding metaphor seems especially appropriate as a description of the appropriate, adjustable, but temporary support provided by the teachers to assist their pupils' understanding in Palincsar's path breaking research.

While the process of scaffolding emphasises the appropriate level of help in cognitive terms like simplification and highlighting discrepancies, it is vital to stress that maintaining pupils' interest, engagement, and controlling their frustration are also necessary components. If scaffolding is truly skilful and truly contingent it will be successful in maintaining a pupil's interest and engagement, and frustrations will be kept at a level that challenges but does not threaten.

There appear to be two major consequences of repeated experiences of skilled scaffolding from an early age; the first is enjoyment in thinking well, and meeting challenges without losing confidence and self-esteem. The second is the gradual move towards independent learning, helped by knowledge and awareness of one's own learning, and self regulation, part of the reflective domain of this book. The two are not independent and are now discussed in turn.

'Hot' Cognition: The Realm of Feelings

How can a brief account of cognitive development as socially constructed activity do justice to emotional, feeling, human beings? Reflection even in its more controlled, coolly meditative forms involves intellectual challenge and a degree of affective involvement: in more emotionally salient contexts, perhaps when attempting to grasp the complexities underlying the behaviour of one's nearest and dearest, such involvement may be very considerable, even in maturity. A flat, tired, depressed response is not one that is associated with successfully meeting intellectual challenges any more than extreme agitation. Boud *et al.* (1985) specifically include affective experiences in their definition of reflection: a generic term for those intellectual and affective activities in which individuals engage to explore their experiences to lead to new understandings and appreciations.

What more can we say about the role of feelings in reflection by pupils? It seems plain that they need to feel confident about themselves as thinkers, to feel that support is there when they need it, and that they are not diminished in their view of themselves by challenging experiences that extend their capabilities. Exactly these views were expressed in a recent Scottish study of secondary school pupils by Simpson and Ure (1994). Pupils gave 'very robust' replies to the questions of what made most difference to how well they did in school and how teachers got the best out of them. Pupils did not mention work materials or classroom organization: instead they talked of the quality of their teachers' interactions with them. They particularly valued their teachers' ability to explain, to notice their difficulties, and to respond to them without causing embarrassment. In short they needed to know that their teachers were there to help and share in their learning. One said 'it's just the way he explains everything without making you sound stupid', and another very different response was 'she says (funny voice): "if there is anyone out there who doesn't understand, put your hand up and I'll help you". But everyone feels they are making an idiot out of themselves, so you don't bother.'

This chapter began with one of the teachers in the research study recounting how a pupil of hers had been in such emotional turmoil that he got very little benefit out of a whole year's schooling, despite her concern and best efforts. Between the extremes of that young boy's experience, and the perfectly ordinary sensitivities of the Scottish secondary school pupils' comments lies a huge range of subjective experience, the result of facing challenging classroom situations in the past, and more general self-esteem. These will help determine pupils' responses to future challenge and their ways of coping with difficulties.

This is a crucial issue for pupils who have encountered repeated failure in school, who are probably extremely unself confident as learners, who are unlikely to show initiative and who are particularly prone to avoid or withdraw from any situation which, in the words of the pupil above, might make them feel they are 'making an idiot out of themselves'.

Teachers who work with such children are very well aware of their tendency to react in an emotional way to challenge, and examples of this awareness and its effect on teachers' practice are discussed with reference to our research. A pervasive tendency to low self-esteem is reported very frequently. A recent example is from work by Powell and Makin (1994) with 12-year-old pupils at a special school which was designated (as in the main research reported here) for pupils with moderate learning difficulties. The authors say 'many pupils cease to see themselves as potential problem-solvers, regarding themselves instead as being at the mercy of the world of learning that they encounter daily, and assuming that achievement is unaffected by any efforts that they make', and later, that 'many had low self-esteem in terms of academic performance and for some this extended to the whole of their 'school life' and beyond. This low self esteem resulted in attitudes towards school-work that ranged from nervous defeatism to anxious rejection'.

This quotation identifies two related factors which are believed to influence pupils' reactions to challenging school experiences; their self-esteem, and more specifically the attributions (or reasons) they give for their success or failure. Both are thought to be of particular salience for relatively unsuccessful pupils.

These two aspects of learning were highlighted by Burden (1994) in a summary of a report to UNESCO which identified trends and developments that were judged by the International School Psychology Association to be likely to influence teaching methods in the near future. Interestingly in the present context, the report takes a social constructivist approach and pays particular attention to the importance of learners' self-esteem and their attributions of academic success and failure. First, research indicates that teachers can help to enhance pupils' self-esteem, particularly if they work at the same time on helping pupils to improve their academic performance. They can, for example, act as models to their pupils, provide systematic encouragement and encourage self-monitoring, and positive self-reference.

Secondly, pupils who have encountered repeated difficulty in school are also likely to react to new challenges or difficulties in a defeatist, negative way because they are likely to attribute their lack of success to low ability rather than to the way in which they approached a problem or the effort they put into it. Some pupils attribute success to luck or chance, and failure to their lack of ability, and they may simply become passive, opt out or rely on others' judgments and not their own. It is easy to see what a vicious circle can develop for which 'learned helplessness' is really not too melodramatic a label, and when every occasion in which asking for help or admitting difficulty could lead towards a sense of competence or achievement, instead is an additional threat to pupils' fragile confidence. Increasing pupils' autonomy and sense of effectiveness is the desired end result of scaffolding and a particular need for pupils who experience learning difficulties.

The reasons pupils give for their lack of success in school tasks can be altered in more positive directions, just as their more generalized self-concepts can be improved. Craske (1988) obtained this kind of effect from a single attribution retraining experience with 10-year-olds who were exhibiting learned helplessness. In pretests they were given maths problems which were too difficult, followed by a further set of problems which, they were told, were much harder. They performed markedly worse on the later set which were in fact known to be within their level of capability. They were also found to attribute the cause of their failure to their own lack of ability, to a much greater extent than other pupils whose performance was not so affected by the 'failure' experience.

The retraining, which was designed to enable the 'learned helpless' group of pupils to view the reasons for their failure in a different light, took the form of a game, in which they competed in groups of four or five to complete sums on the board, one third of which were very difficult. On the throw of a dice the team members changed over and the game was stopped each time a sum was completed. The pupil concerned was then asked to select the reason for success or lack of it by choosing one of four alternatives: luck; difficulty; effort or ability. When they chose effort, 'trying hard', this was gently reinforced by the researcher.

After this attribution retraining pupils again worked on sums that they were told were very difficult, after having a previous 'failure' experience. This time the majority were more, not less successful, and their attributions had changed. They were now much less likely to say they were not clever enough, and more likely to say that they had tried harder. In other words they now felt more in control of and responsible for their achievements in contrast to feeling helpless. This belief was described by Craske as 'inoculating' them against the negative effects of failure.

It is probable that participation in the form of a game in which pupils saw their peers also having difficulty and heard them account for them, was important in lessening their feelings of inadequacy and increasing their feelings of competence. In a non-threatening way they were focussing their attention on their performance and reflecting on it.

Thinking about Thinking

To recapitulate the main points so far: in developing increased understanding our cognitive structures become more complex and differentiated. Experiences which are meaningful and add to our understanding are on the whole those which are congruent but not identical with those we already possess. Development of these cognitive structures is enhanced during social interaction, and contingent scaffolding enables children to make intellectual advances that would not otherwise be possible. Emotional factors also play a very important role, and these are especially likely to be prominent in educational settings for pupils who experience significant difficulties in learning.

Reflection is what this book is about. It involves thinking in depth, beyond the immediately obvious, takes time and effort and often engages the emotions. At a more cognitive level of description it consists of the development or extension of cognitive structures to enable reasoning, solving problems or producing new ideas. But reflection has another aspect, metacognition, the awareness people have of their own mental processes. An account of metacognitive development follows.

Since Flavell's imaginative and pioneering research during the 1970s the term 'metacognition' has appeared quite frequently in writings about cognitive development and possible educational applications. Acknowledged by its first user, Flavell, to be a broad but sometimes fuzzy concept in practice, metacognition refers to a variety of manifestations of thinking about cognition. Its prominence in the present discussion rests on these well supported findings: that metacognition is an important component of reflection: that it can enhance performance in a range of cognitive activities and that pupils with learning difficulties show relatively poor awareness and use of metacognition.

Flavell coined the terms 'metamemory' and 'metacommunication' to describe the knowledge and awareness children of different ages show in tasks in these domains. His studies of children's performance at different ages in memory tasks are probably the best known of these and are charmingly reported and imaginatively conceived. In one, to observe lip movements in order to discover whether children were spontaneously rehearsing a list of to-be-remembered items, they wore space helmets, and in a referential communication task designed to discover whether a listener's needs were taken into account when a child gave instruction on how to play a game, their listener was blindfolded. These different tasks both make demands that prove to be beyond most 5-year-olds, but are achievable by most 8-year-olds. If in the memory task children used a rehearsal strategy then they remembered far more items: in the second they needed to judge what information was needed from their listener's point of view. Both abilities had usually developed by the age of 8, without being taught. Flavell termed children's failure to spontaneously use helpful cognitive strategies a 'production deficiency', because they could learn and employ many of these at a younger age when explicitly taught to do so, and this did lead to quite markedly improved performance (1985). Similar research which has focussed on children with learning difficulties has found them to be very immature in their strategy use, but to show considerable advance with facilitating experiences. The questions that naturally arise include ones about the reasons for the developments that spontaneously occur with age, and the conditions under which metacognition can be facilitated and 'production deficiencies' overcome. For learning strategies to be truly of value to children's learning they need to be applied across a range of appropriate situations.

The evidence from a number of studies presenting cognitive tasks at different ages suggests that metacognitive developments occur in three areas: an increased awareness and use of strategies in particular tasks, such as the grouping of items to be remembered, and increased understanding by individuals of their own strengths, such as the ability to use visualization. There is also another kind of awareness, self-monitoring by individuals of their current cognitive state; for example that they are reading something easy and familiar, or that it is uncomfortably difficult and time to check back to earlier pages.

In a summary of recent work which greatly enhances our knowledge of metacognitive awareness in young children, Flavell and his colleagues draw conclusions from fourteen linked experiments devised for children between the ages of 3 and 8 years (Flavell *et al.*, 1995). Using characteristically imaginative tasks they have traced the growth of reflective consciousness, the aspect of metacognition which is represented by, for example, the growing awareness of thinking as a stream of consciousness, of unwanted intrusive thoughts, of events triggering off thoughts, and the realisation that other people have equally rich and complex mental lives. All these they found to be present and articulated by some 7 and 8-year-olds, and to be largely absent before that age, in their socially advantaged sample.

Before that age, Flavell and his colleagues conclude, children are not likely to imagine their parents' inner concerns, and they are less likely to know how they themselves have come to a decision or solved a problem, and less aware that they have changed their minds about something, and of the links between their thoughts.

These findings, they say, support the 'widespread view in the field that children acquire an increasingly constructivist, process-oriented conception of the mind during middle childhood and adolescence', and suggest that this acquisition is helped by maturation, role-taking, awareness of intrusive thoughts such as bedtime fears, and very important for the subject of this book, through school experiences that demand effortful mental work and highlight for pupils the processes involved in this.

The classroom research reported in later chapters was conducted with pupils who did not have such advantageous backgrounds, and who had experienced failure in academic settings. They were 11 years old, however, and were therefore potentially developing both the kinds of strategy and knowledge about their own thinking and that of others that researchers have found in many younger children. Signs of such metacognitive progress and the possibility of its facilitation by school experiences are of central importance in our investigation.

There are three major components of metacognition: strategy knowledge and use: individuals' knowledge of their own thinking, and ongoing self monitoring during thinking activity. It is easy to see that fostering these should lead to a sense of control and self reliance as well as to improved performance. The goal of independent self-regulated learning is also what scaffolding and responsive teaching approaches are aiming for.

Strategy Acquisition and Use

General strategies that are used naturally and spontaneously by young children in the busy stimulating environment of primary school classrooms include ones to do with focussing their attention, and cutting off distractions (fingers in ears), and the verbal rehearsal of items that are to be remembered. The developmental pattern of acquisition of these and more advanced strategies has been studied and documented by Flavell (1985). The years from 5 to 9 see large changes in such abilities, as part of pupils' growing awareness of themselves as thinkers, with an extending history of learning experiences which include explicit direction and modelling from parents and teachers. Piaget used the term 'reflective abstraction' to describe such pondering about cognition and believed that it is stimulated by children's awareness of the differences between their viewpoints and those of their peers, as well as by the experience of conflict in their own cognitive structures, a state of unsettling disequilibrium when their existing knowledge and understanding is challenged.

A nice example of developing strategies in the early primary years is provided by Istomina (1982), in a shopping task using a class shop. The ways in which children of different ages embarked on shopping for a list of items given them orally, changed from impulsive running to the 'shop' to carry out the errand as quickly as possible at 4 years, to (at 5 or 6 years) deliberate efforts to memorize and check what they had been told (by rehearsal or by asking the researcher to say it again). The oldest children of about 7 appeared to be forming more sophisticated logical connections between the items on their lists.

Specific thinking strategies are believed to be acquired first and then to be gradually subsumed into general ones. The specific ones develop in a particular situation and then gradually become applied in a wider context to similar tasks by the process of generalization.

Generalization of Learning

It is reported that William James said that a polyp who was able to say to itself 'Hello, thingumabob again' would be demonstrating conceptual thinking! It certainly would have recognized similarity: the ability to do this pervades the animal world, and enables it to function. But the human ability to recognize relevant ways in which situations are alike and to transfer learned strategies appropriately from one to another is of a different order altogether.

'Transfer' and 'generalization' appear more or less interchangeably in much of the literature: 'transfer' however is more often and more appropriately applied to the application of specific learning from one task to another that is similar, and 'generalization' is more often used to describe a general broadening of the application of learning into varied and naturally occurring contexts.

Since Donaldson's enormously influential publication in 1978, there has been greatly increased awareness, particularly among educators, of the power of context in influencing children's understanding and levels of performance in cognitive tasks. Such classic Piagetian tests as Number Conservation and the 'Three Mountains Task' have been found to grossly underestimate children's ability when their performance on other tasks which make apparently equivalent demands is examined. Where these use materials, language and instructions that make everyday sense to the child, then, especially in children under the age of 4 or 5, their performance is at a much more mature level. Children's cognitions are often said to become less context dependent with age, and the studies quoted by Donaldson are good examples of this. Other more everyday ones are learning to talk over the telephone in a way that is comprehensible to their listener, as children no longer assume that their knowledge is already shared, and their increasing understanding of other people's emotions and motivations (Harris, 1989). In all sorts of ways the primary school child demonstrates increasing facility with decentred, or disembedded thinking, and with this, the ability to generalize learning to new situations.

Work by Brown and her colleagues in the United States over the past decade or more has exciting theoretical and educational implications. A large research programme looked at the relationships between metacognition, the scaffolding of learning, and transfer, in a large number of pupils and students of different levels of academic achievement. In these researchers' view transfer is the test of real learning, when pupils' useful learned behaviour is no longer 'welded' to the situation in which it was acquired. This is a good description of the great difficulty many pupils show in transferring strategies that were effective in one situation to others that appear objectively similar. It is, however, always subjective experience that matters. In chapter 2 we shall refer again to the pervasive and striking difficulties that are commonly experienced by pupils with learning difficulties, in generalizing their learning.

The studies summarized by Brown *et al.* in 1983 found that initial performance on a particular test often gives a very misleading indication of learning. What really matters is pupils' ability to profit from appropriate instruction and the readiness with which they can generalize their learning. They found that weak students required more and more explicit instructions and only transferred their learning from specific training to tasks that were very similar. They were also described as being very reluctant to take risks by going beyond the information they had been given. Gifted students show the opposite characteristics. More recently Freeman's interviews of British 18-year-olds who had been identified earlier as gifted, revealed them to be very sophisticated in their metacognitive awareness, of themselves as thinkers and their general strengths and weaknesses, and of their intellectual development in specialist fields of study.

> The brightest could sometimes describe in detail how they managed their mental learning resources, and what they did to improve their learning strategies. The most successful examinees also knew about the importance of involving the whole self — intellect, emotion, and body — in their learning. (Freeman, 1991)

Brown *et al.* (1983) concluded from their extensive body of research that:

> Major differences between young and old learners reside in their ability to access and flexibly use competencies they are known to possess. Development consists in part in going from the context dependent state where resources are welded to the original learning situation, to a relatively context independent state where the learner extends the ways in which initially highly constrained knowledge and procedures are used,

and

> the entire discussion of learning to learn is really a discussion of the importance of transfer.

Students they found to be good at transfer were those who planned approaches to problem solving, sought additional information, looked for and used analogies, checked their reasoning, monitored their progress and repaired their strategies when things went wrong. In sum they used general metacognitive processing with a wide range of applicability in a wide range of tasks.

How can pupils in classrooms be helped to achieve real learning and the kind of metacognitive awareness that enables transfer and generalisation?

Curricular Infusion

For a start there are strong arguments against any attempt at fostering 'thinking' or 'study skills' through special programmes rather than across the curriculum. Nisbet and Shucksmith's (1986) very balanced discussion points out that thinking skills approaches lack clear empirical and theoretical foundations, often appear to be a set of tips rather than encouraging reflection, and most important, are unlikely to be perceived by pupils as relevant to all their work, and to be generalized. They also make the point which is pertinent to the research reported here, that, generally speaking, study or thinking skills programmes have been regarded as most appropriate for later secondary school stages, whereas older primary school pupils who are at the stage of developing a level of self-awareness and have not yet formed entrenched habits of study would appear to be more suitable candidates. Recent research lends strong support to this, as we saw earlier in this chapter. (Flavell *et al.*, 1995)

Nisbet and Shucksmith conclude that the more practical and effective approach is to incorporate the teaching of learning strategies within the general curriculum and not as ends in themselves. They advocate a combination of teaching specific skills, which are always embedded in a particular curriculum context, and can be taught fairly easily, and general ones that are applicable across broad areas of the curriculum, are transferable, and may well take longer to acquire. Both need to be included, along with the enhancement of pupils' awareness of metacognitive processes. In chapter 2 some research studies are described which have investigated these areas with pupils who have learning difficulties.

One way of facilitating the third requirement, that pupils should be helped to be more aware of metacognitive processes, is by teachers deliberately modelling reflection in their work. Although, as noted earlier, Palincsar did not find this to be effective on its own in her research, without pupils' participation in reciprocal learning, it is often advocated as potentially powerful in its effects. Tharp and Gallimore suggest that this effective means of helping pupils' cognitive development is underemployed in school, and that teachers who make use of metacognitive language will have students who do the same.

The literature on early language acquisition offers fascinating examples of long term pervasive effects of parents' interactive style with their young children. Mothers who were in the habit of explicitly telling their preschoolers that they did not understand them, and why, were clarifying and scaffolding their early communications. Later their children were relatively advanced in oral communication tasks, and in being able to gauge a listener's needs (Robinson, 1986). The same kind of role playing communication task was used by one of our research study teachers, and is referred to in chapter 7 in connection with activities which can facilitate reflection. Flavell has claimed that such activities are excellent vehicles for enabling pupils to monitor their communications by becoming aware of their own communicative goals, teaching them what is difficult for speakers in understanding them, and in their understanding of speakers, to exchange roles, and getting them to attend to feelings of puzzlement. Modelling and exchanging roles are important experiences in developing this aspect of reflection.

Thinking through Philosophy, and via Assisted Instruction

Finally two well known and radical approaches to encouraging reflection in the classroom were developed during the 1970s and 1980s in the United States. The first is philosophy-based and aims to help develop classrooms as 'communities of reflective inquiry', which introduce logic and reasoning by means of the discussion of problematic and important issues. Lipman's (1988) philosophy curriculum was designed to cover the entire school age range and comprises seven programmes which use stories as the vehicle for instruction along with extensive notes for teachers. The stories are written to highlight principles of logical and reasoning and focus on different areas at different developmental stages: thus the work for 5 to 9-year-olds concentrates on reasoning and concept development, offering a model for dialogue for children both with their peers and with adults. Through dialogue around the characters and their actions and decisions, pupils can acquire, Lipman claims, basic reasoning tools that will be generalised to many other areas of the curriculum.

Lipman's approach stresses the importance of an accepting, non-authoritarian teacher, but this does not imply passivity or non-participation. The notes make it very clear that the teacher's role is to subtly guide discussion into areas of reasoning, such as the questioning of assumptions, spelling out implications, and giving reasons for beliefs. By means of fictional models, Lipman claims, 'it is possible to show children that they themselves can think more reasonably and more creatively, for we want both to stimulate them to think and stimulate them to think better. If the reading of the text is followed by critical and interpretive discussions about the ideas hidden between the lines of the novels like treasures in a treasure hunt students will eagerly vie with one another to express their views . . .'

This may sound highly optimistic if not outright inappropriate for many young pupils but evaluations of Lipman's programmes have particularly emphasised the benefits gained by less confident, low achieving pupils.

Lane and Lane (1986) summarized some of the positive effects noted by a range of evaluations of Lipman's programme. These included significant improvements on measures of reasoning, on reading and mathematics tests, and teachers' reports that pupils had become more curious, better communicators and more considerate of each other. These authors attribute a major part of this success to the children's improved view of themselves as thinkers who were taken seriously.

Lipman (1988) makes a strong case for philosophy as a central unifying discipline which can be made available to immature pupils and can enhance their reflective ability across the curriculum. As he says, standards of logicality and rationality are the bedrock of philosophy and make the piecemeal approach of teaching isolated 'thinking skills', particularly those which emphasize non-linguistic skills like matching patterns of dots, appear somewhat trivial by comparison.

'Philosophy for children' can be described as an infusion approach because a pedagogic strategy is developed using specifically designed materials whose effect should permeate all aspects of the curriculum. Useful illustrations are provided of the application of specific reasoning processes (like providing analogies, or formulating cause and effect relationships) but there is little discussion of metacognitive awareness and learning strategies.

Tharp and Gallimore's work (1988) has also had widespread influence and aroused a great deal of interest. It represents the implementation of the pedagogy they call 'assisted performance', based on interactionist views of learning. A fifteen-year research and development project was established in Hawaii and called the Kamehaha Elementary Education Programme (KEEP). This aimed to improve the cognitive and educational development of a population they described as educationally 'at risk'. These were ethnic minority Hawaiian and part-Hawaiian children, a group who traditionally underachieved at school to a considerable extent. An entire primary school was designed to implement 'assisted performance' teaching techniques and five other primary schools were also involved. Repeated testing of the pupils in the programme and other comparison pupils showed very marked gains due to the programme, especially in reading achievement, where those in the KEEP programme performed at age-norm levels for over a decade.

The impressive results on these and other measures were attributed by Tharp and Gallimore to interactive teaching in groups, characterized by mutual participation and teacher responsiveness, alongside 'independent learning centres', where activities were designed to support and extend pupils' group experience, in which they still received assistance and also gave it to one another, while gaining more control and confidence in their own learning. A very important additional feature in this comprehensive, whole school approach, was the assistance given to teachers in the form of regular observation during classroom activities by a consultant, followed by a conference where the consultant and teacher reviewed progress and cooperatively planned the next part of the programme. The details provided by Tharp and Gallimore of teaching sessions, instructional conversations, and particularly of individual teachers' feelings and responsiveness to the programme make fascinating reading, although the emphasis given to measures of activity levels and on task behaviour as major indices of its success sometimes gives the impression that these aspects of pupil behaviour may have been highlighted rather than their deep thinking or reflection.

Both of these major research programmes, with their differing underlying theoretical approaches, offer much food for thought. Both locate real learning, the extension of pupils' thinking, within the teacher-pupil interaction, the locus of the reflective episodes described in the present research. Bonnett, another philosopher, has recently emphasized in a thought-provoking critique of current curricular trends that teachers can facilitate learning by tuning into what is in the consciousness of the pupil, what engages and occupies them at the time, and developing a process of 'empathetic challenging' (1994). The way in which we attempted to identify and investigate intellectual challenge in the experience of pupils with learning difficulties is described in chapter 3. Chapter 2 outlines the nature of such difficulties and describes some relevant research.

2   Reflection and Effective Learning

At the outset of the research reported here I had the opportunity to discuss reflection with a group of teachers of pupils with a range of learning difficulties. They were undertaking specialist in-service training and did not participate in the research. All gave very similar accounts of the particular problems their pupils had with reflective thinking.

First they talked of their pupils' poor levels and short spans of concentration. They were easily distracted and had 'butterfly minds'. Almost as common and very familiar were references to their pupils' lack of confidence, fear of being wrong, being too readily influenced by others' opinions, and being very self-critical, feeling that what they had to contribute was worthless.

Much less frequent was the comment that their pupils were not expected to be reflective and so got little experience of it, and these teachers made very little mention of specific cognitive processes apart from general comments that pupils lacked understanding.

How did the teachers' informal judgments relate to conclusions from research into the general or specific factors contributing to pupils' learning difficulties? It seems best to confine discussion now to pupils who are described as having moderate levels of learning difficulty, or as slow learners, because they are the focus of the main research reported here, and of much other relevant research.

The Nature of Learning Difficulties

Pupils described as having moderate learning difficulties are a heterogeneous group, with either predicted or actual lack of success in ordinary schooling as their common experience. They have well below average levels of intellectual functioning on standardized tests, and in IQ tests usually would score within the range 50–80, although these are now rarely used and certainly not as the sole criterion for placement by Scottish educational psychologists. Most have no known aetiology for this delay, with the probable exception of a number of pupils with Down's Syndrome. Much more obvious and common are a range of communication, social and emotional accompaniments and contributions to difficulties in school performance. The now discarded labels of psychosocial and sociocultural disadvantage were attempts to acknowledge that relative deprivation is common in their family background and home environment. It is important to note that this is much less evident with those much less able children, who are described as having severe learning difficulties, where aeti-ological factors are much more prominent.

Decades of research have been devoted to examining basic cognitive processes in this group of pupils to see whether there are identifiable causal contributions to generally low intellectual performance, in addition to those associated with social disadvantage. Those receiving particular emphasis have concerned speed of processing, memory and attention.

Poor performance could theoretically be due to overall inefficiency in these areas, or to a specific difficulty, such as in cross modal coding. Alternat-ively (or additionally) there may be higher-order processing problems, like the development and application of cognitive strategies of the kind which are identified and described as metacognitive.

First we consider basic processing and the possibility that an overall inef-ficiency of functioning could help account for poor school performance. It is possible that simple tasks such as those involving reaction time might reveal fun-damentally slow functioning within the nervous system. An example of simple reaction time is that time taken to press a button, for example, in response to a flash of light. If this is found on average to be significantly slower with chil-dren who have learning difficulties, and if it does not improve much with prac-tice, then we could anticipate that cognitive structures will also be slow to be developed and elaborated, and that much more experience will be necessary for learning to take place.

There is evidence that slower reaction times are found with pupils who have learning difficulties, but also that the gap can be narrowed quite con-siderably. Campione (1986) concluded that with some pupils, relatively slow reaction times resulted from a lack of consistency and not a basic inability to respond quickly. Even this apparently simple task (like almost anything we ask humans to do) involves a series of operations which all involve executive pro-cesses. It is quite possible that more complex processing and not speed is the main reason for slower than average reaction times.

Teachers like those quoted at the beginning of this chapter are very aware that pupils seem to be very easily distracted, and the role of attention has been investigated in several research studies. Clearly selective attention deter-mines what enters the memory system, or in the language used here, what will be assimilated into a person's cognitive structures, to form the knowledge base which in turn affects the deployment of attention. Children with learn-ing difficulties perform badly relative to their peers on tasks which have dis-tractors or are complex, whereas on simpler tasks differences may be minimal. Borkowski and his colleagues (1983) reported that they used a great deal of off-task glancing in reaction time studies and discrimination tasks, which may also be evidence of uncertainty at a processing level. There is similar evidence from Wishart (1991) with very young children who have Down's Syndrome that avoidance strategies were used very frequently when they were given object concept tasks involving searching for toys hidden in cups. The avoid-ance strategies used by the children were not produced randomly or due to boredom, but were related to the difficulty of the task. A second study involved infants with Down's Syndrome of under two years and investigated their reaction to failure in the response they obtained from kicking through a light beam, the activation of a coloured mobile. The children aged 9 months continued to kick repeatedly during two kinds of contingency schedules, one of which produced some 'free' activation of the mobile, without the child kicking. Children with Down's Syndrome who were one year older, however, almost stopped their kicking in this condition. Wishart concludes that the children, as they grew older, were coming to rely increasingly on reinforcement from others and less on their own efforts, and that this was probably fostered unintentionally by parents and others responding to the child in a non-contingent way (unrelated to the child's action), that was likely to lead to passivity and giving up soon.

Inattention and avoidance of the kind found by Wishart in very young children with learning difficulties have been described by Borkowski and Kurtz (1987) as typically negative attitudes towards problem solving and complex tasks — a pervasive negative disposition to avoid challenges. But we do not have evidence of a fundamental inability to attend: rather the explanation lies in higher level processes and in the child's early social experiences.

Researchers have also focussed on memory characteristics associated with learning difficulties. Some early studies investigating the possibility of very rapid decay in memory traces did not provide any convincing evidence for this and Kail's extensive studies, reported in 1990, found that neither short term memory capacity nor the durability of memory was associated with age or experience. Speed of processing such as accurate retrieval from short-term memory, however, is associated with giftedness. Again it is processing and the use of cognitive strategies that differentiate the less and the more able, not more fundamental deficiencies.

Metacognitive Strategies

So the conclusion from the search for factors that can help explain moderate degrees of difficulty in learning is that they do not lie in the basic inability to attend, excessively rapid decay of memory traces, or slowness of response. There is however ample support for Dockrell and McShane's (1993) conclusion that 'poor strategic processing appears to be a ubiquitous characteristic of individuals with general learning difficulties'. One reason for this poor strategic processing may lie in pupils' lack of understanding of their own cognitive systems.

Influential and informative work concerning slow learning pupils has been carried out over the past two decades in the United States and a great deal of interest has been generated concerning pupils' awareness about thinking and problem solving. Two main points need emphasis.

First, there is clear unequivocal evidence that students with moderate learning difficulties ('slow learners' generally in American studies with IQs of around 70) show marked delays in comparison with their peers in their awareness and use of what are often called learning strategies. More generally like much younger children they have shown the tendency to overestimate their memory capabilities, to fail to adopt different approaches to difficult or easy tasks, for example by devoting different amounts of study time to them, and most markedly to fail to see that similar problems could be solved by similar means.

Campione (1987) produced a lucid summary of some of this impressive, systematic, body of research. In general, direct teaching of appropriate strategies could result in quite dramatic improvements in students' performance on particular tasks, but without transfer to comparable tasks. Campione pointed out that the students in such studies were not involved as 'active conspirators'. They were not given explicit reasons as to why strategies worked. Perhaps metacognitive awareness could be fostered in such a way that pupils could learn to see connections and become more active controllers of their own learning.

In a series of studies, explicit teaching of specific strategies, plus help in self-regulation, or pupils' control of their own learning resulted in much better performance, both at the time, and also persisting over a longer period for similar tasks. The least able pupils were found to need the most explicit teaching, and there was a marked improvement in their general feelings of awareness like that of knowing something even if you can't recall it, and other monitoring activities, like knowing the time needed for studying materials. There was especially rapid development in these abilities between the mental ages of about 6 and 10 years.

The research evidence, then, strongly points to a lack of metacognitive awareness and development of useful strategies for a range of cognitive tasks, but not to fundamental deficiencies in cognition that could be more difficult to help.

Borkowski and Kurtz (1987) suggest that educational programmes for pupils with learning difficulties should be integrated approaches that focus at the same time on three important areas of known difficulty. These are, specific strategies and when to use them: general monitoring, and the awareness of the importance of deliberation, planning and effort for successful learning. These recommendations are very like those made by Nisbet concerning mainstream schools in chapter 1.

Borkowski summarizes research on cognitive strategies across the ability spectrum as showing us that 'gifted children use strategies with grace, monitor their effectiveness and believe in their efficiency in ways not characteristic of learning disabled and retarded children. Inefficient learners have striking defects in general strategy knowledge and metamemory acquisition procedures.' This stark comparison is immediately softened by the observation that there are nonetheless numerous similarities between the extremes of ability they have investigated, and the emphasis that all children can become more efficient learners and problem solvers.

Special Curricula and Special Methods?

How this can be achieved in school is central to long-standing debates within special education about an appropriate curriculum and the most effective means of its delivery. These form the background to the classroom research to be described in this and subsequent chapters.

Radical changes in expectations and aspirations concerning the curriculum have occurred during the past twenty years. Up until the early eighties the dominant view was that pupils placed in special schools because of their learning difficulties would benefit most from specially designed curricula. Time was limited: learning was expected to be slow, and to be best achieved by individualized programmes, presented in carefully planned structured sequences with specified objectives. This was thought to be most effective because it was clear that pupils did not learn so easily as their peers did in complex, busy, natural situations, often in a relatively unplanned and incidental way.

Differences were highlighted by this approach: a different curriculum was delivered by very different teaching methods, involving a great deal of individual work, with pupils following programmes of work which were carefully designed to reduce the likelihood of error and confusion. This was really special education: what were the effects on pupils' achievements?

Daniels' (1990) summary of curricular change uses the memorable phrase 'pedagogic blunderbuss' to describe what the objectives approach may become, if not used sensitively and flexibly to explore pupils' current level of skill and knowledge and devise appropriate teaching in accordance with this. In practice sequences obtained through task analysis were often treated as fixed and inflexible, allowing only one route for pupils to follow. But, as complex activities can be learned through a variety of routes, any one of them must be somewhat arbitrary. So what aimed to be helpful simplification and clarification of curricular material could easily be at odds with pupils' existing processes and strategies, and create confusion. Waiting for each step to be checked made for a fragmented experience whose meaningfulness was likely to be lost to the pupils, and an increased sense of powerlessness. Pupils' compliance and passivity could thus be reinforced by the very methods that aimed ultimately to help their independence.

Despite very many examples of excellent imaginative and impressive work in many special schools, overall the curricula composed mainly of those elements believed to be most important were in effect somewhat impoverished, in comparison with those in mainstream schools. Brennan's (1974) warning that pupils' experiences were in danger of being sterile, unexciting and inadequate for both personal richness and social competence held true in some cases. There was a restricted range of subjects and often a dearth of project and thematic work meant that opportunities for interaction and collaboration with peers were reduced. So communication, negotiation, choice and self-evaluation in natural meaningful contexts were not frequent pupil experiences. Learning acquired without such contexts did not relate to pupils' existing interests and knowledge and was unlikely to be generalized. Awareness of the difficulty of transfer and generalization meant that a series of slightly different tasks would be devised; 'building-in' generalization into more natural settings was the aim, but inevitably it tended to be somewhat contrived and controlled by teachers, not pupils.

Over time the gap between the curriculum available in many special schools and that in mainstream became more evident, and increasingly problematic with the moves towards integration and the National Curriculum initiatives.

Recently published staff development materials are helpful to teachers of pupils with special needs in advising them on curriculum development. In Scotland the 5–14 Guidelines for teachers of pupils with moderate learning difficulties stress that breadth, balance, progression, coherence and continuity are essential (SOED, 1994). All were acknowledged to be possible areas of concern when special schools had direct control of their curricula.

In England the shift away from the advocacy of a specialized curriculum and specific teaching approaches has probably been even more clear. Sebba, Byers and Rose (1993) conclude 'Future approaches need to seek a broad and balanced curriculum content delivered through flexible use of teaching approaches which emphasize the development of pupil autonomy'.

Behaviourally based, task analytic approaches are unlikely to foster pupil autonomy and are clearly at odds with the social constructivist view of learning outlined in the first chapter. For in that view learning does not automatically result from teaching, however skilfully organized and with however much appropriate repetition and reinforcement. True learning results in the restructuring and elaboration of pupils' cognitive structures as a result of their activity: this will be likely to happen when they are absorbed in a mentally challenging situation. This applies whatever the nature of the curriculum being currently used. Bennett (1991) discussing the imminent implementation of the National Curriculum in England and Wales, and its potential effect on pupils moving from a relatively restricted special school curriculum, expressed the view that curricular change in itself would have little effect on the quality of pupils' learning. What is important is the teachers' implementation of that curriculum, and especially the way in which classroom dialogue is used to facilitate their understanding.

There is some evidence that interactions between teachers and pupils with learning difficulties may differ from those with other pupils in ways that do not always help the pupil. For example some research in mainstream settings found that they were called on to answer teachers less often, given less feedback and given less time to respond (Wang, 1991). At a more detailed level Wood (1992) has reported the consistent finding that teachers wait less for responses from pupils of lower ability, and that when they are aware of this, and increase their wait time, the quality of pupils' responses is improved. Teachers of less able pupils generally use a more controlling style (asking them more questions and correcting them more frequently) and the pupils react to this with fewer initiations and contributions and very few questions. There is a marked contrast with those richly expressive conversations between parents and their children, or between peers, which are contingent on the child's activities, interests and utterances.

The present context is one of changing expectations, widening curricular experiences and increased awareness of a range of possible teaching approaches for pupils with learning difficulties. We next consider some examples of classroom research which have promising implications for teachers.

Some Encouraging Research Findings

This last section of chapter 2 considers several research studies of particular interest and relevance. All but one were conducted quite recently in British schools. All involved pupils whose low school achievements placed them within the broad category of moderate difficulties in learning, and who were receiving their education in special classes or schools or in mainstream schools with additional support.

All report promising results from applications in the classroom of social constructivist models of learning: they were chosen for this reason and because they represent a range of approaches. Some were implemented by classroom teachers and all were carried out within the familiar context of their pupils' classrooms and integrated to some degree within the usual curricular programme. This is a huge advantage in terms of meaningfulness and credibility, both for pupils and teachers, despite the inevitable disruptions and additional factors that complicate such programmes and the conclusions that can be drawn about them. The research studies to be discussed fall into the areas that, after reviewing much of the research literature on metacognition and learning difficulties, Borkowski and Kurtz propose should be included in an integrated educational programme. It should, they say:

> focus simultaneously on the interaction of specific strategies (including when to use them and when not): general implementation and monitoring; and beliefs about the fundamental importance of deliberation, planfulness and effort for successful learning.

The first two pieces of research that we shall consider report encouraging results from the teaching of specific strategies, one to help memorizing and the second a spatial planning task.

Both produced statistically significant support for the effectiveness of the teaching programme, and evidence that this was generalized to similar tasks.

Sugden (1987 (with Newell) and 1989) investigated the effectiveness of a programme which taught children to use verbal elaboration to help them remember verbal material. The overall aim was to help the children to remember new material by giving it meaning (incorporating it into their existing cognitive structures). The fifteen children who participated in the six-month programme conducted by their class teacher were found on pretesting to have the worst memories of the forty children in their groups, to make little use of memorizing strategies, and were judged to have especially passive approaches to learning. They had an average age of ten years and attended a special school for pupils with moderate learning difficulties. The programme was designed to involve the children actively, and presented increasingly complex demands over time, with a gradual handing over of responsibility to the child and a reduction of teacher support. It can be seen that the ideas of scaffolding and increasing self-regulation permeated the individual instructional half-hour dialogues between teacher and pupils. Initially the teacher used pictures as a stimulus for modelling her own verbal elaboration in the form of a simple story: the child then followed suit: the cognitive demands were gradually made more complex with the linking of two pictures, then words introduced and the pictures dropped. By the end of six months after about thirty individual sessions many of the children were generating complex stories and new information and ideas.

Sugden describes how most children had learnt to dominate the material and to place it into the framework they had constructed by the end of the programme, and that without being taught they sometimes spontaneously grouped material to be learned. Overall there were statistically significant gains over time which lasted nine months after the programme had finished, and on test materials that were much more difficult and complex than at the outset. Sugden reported that verbal elaboration in the form of story invention by the pupils was most encouraging, especially in the more complex and demanding tasks. Generalization to different materials in similar tasks was obtained for most but not all of the children, and positive overall efforts were reported by other teachers in terms of the pupils' confidence and willingness to speak.

This well designed programme resulted in impressive gains in pupils' ability to generate verbal connections, and to generalize these, although as Sugden points out, this was only achieved at considerable cost in time and effort. Moreover he emphasizes the need for explicit links to be made between the different (but similar) situations by the teacher, and direct feedback that the children's use of strategies was effective. 'It is asking too much to expect the children on their own to see the links between the various situations. It must be pointed out to them what is the aim, and why these situations are linked' and 'Reinforcement in terms of praise will also be given, but it is not a sufficient condition for this type of learning to occur'.

A second piece of research on the learning and generalization of a specific strategy in problem solving was reported by Todman and McBeth (1994). Using a Vygotskyan model they investigated the optimal level of assistance that led to generalization by pupils of their learned strategy in a different context.

They used a forward planning task that had already revealed a clear developmental sequence in young children's strategy use. The task involved bringing two objects from different spatial locations to a box, 'the quickest way'. The positions of these objects (soft toys) were varied so that judgments could be made as to whether the children used the less mature 'proximity strategy' where a near object would always be collected first, or a more advanced 'planning strategy', where objects' spatial locations in relation to the box would determine the most efficient route.

Knowledge of the usual developmental progression in strategy use enabled Todman and McBeth to allocate 35 7-year-old pupils with learning difficulties into groups after pre-testing. The children were then taught by individual computer sessions in which the instruction given was either one or two steps ahead of their current level of strategy use. Generalization of their learning was tested in the playground, and as would be predicted, those who had received instruction just one step ahead of their current level performed much better on the playground test of their ability to generalize their strategy use one week later. It was this that differentiated the groups' performance, not their learning during the computer instruction. Without the test for generalization, there would have been no indication that more appropriate levels of instruction would result in a qualitatively different, deeper, learning experience, building on the children's existing competence in an optimal way.

Both these research projects provide impressive illustrations of carefully designed teaching programmes that enabled pupils with learning difficulties to learn and adopt new and effective specific strategies. Both provided good evidence of a degree of transfer to similar tasks and Sugden's follow up tests nine months later showed that pupils' learning had lasted. Both stressed the importance of appropriate levels of contingent and specific feedback and both used individual adult-pupil instruction and testing situations.

The next studies are equally if not more relevant to the theme of this book. They describe action research which aimed to enhance pupils' general understanding of their responsibility for their learning, and their ability to monitor their own progress. They all involve pupils working in groups as well as individually in undertaking their normal planned curricular activities. This kind of study generally enables observational and illustrative evidence of a rich kind, but does not readily allow for the conclusions based on statistical evidence that are made possible by the systematic experimental designs of the kind used by Sugden and by Todman and McBeth with a greater number of pupils.

Both the experimental and the action research approach have their strengths and disadvantages, and in the present context their findings are complementary. Similarly the systematic teaching of specific skills and the enhancement of pupils' more general strategic behaviour and understanding of learning are both important means of encouraging classroom reflection. As Borkowski and Kurtz say, educational programmes for children who have difficulties in learning should include both, as the acquisition of specific skills is developmentally prior to, and the foundation of, more general metacognitive understanding.

Quicke and Winter (1994) conducted research in a Sheffield secondary school as part of the ESRC funded cognition and learning project. One phase of this included an intervention which was designed to enhance low achieving pupils' awareness of their own learning and their ability to monitor and regulate this as a means towards achieving greater empowerment and autonomy.

A sub-group of five boys was selected from a first year mixed ability class for a four week programme of discussion and work in the classroom with one of the researchers. The boys were regarded as below average in relation to the rest of the class and were regularly withdrawn for reading work with a special needs teacher. The intervention programme with the researcher coincided with class work on the Science Theme of 'materials' and the discussions or metacognitive dialogues were able to use classroom observations of these science lessons as a focus, along with a specially designed strategy card.

The strategy card was drawn up by the researchers as an aide memoire to help pupils during class activities and was also used as a reference point during the discussions. One card was designed specifically for individual use, and another similar one was for group work. This took the form of an eight-point plan and was devised by the researchers as a result of their reading, knowledge of other development work in schools, and very important, from discussions with pupils in the class studied during the research. They did not wish to use a check list of reminders, with its implied message that this is the best route or recipe for pupils to follow. Rather they wished to foster a disposition to learn in pupils, not a set of unreflecting learning habits. The language used was known to be readily understood and already adopted by many of the pupils who had been interviewed at an early stage. Group discussion was an essential element, with its potential for alerting pupils to other and different viewpoints and contributions, its promotion of democratic procedures and the fact that, as a social context, it is a natural locus for learning.

The group strategy card outlined this eight point plan:

'we must remember to:
1   Get ourselves into a learning mood.
2   Talk about what we have to do.
3   Look and listen carefully.
4   Decide who is going to do what.
5   Stop and think — work for several minutes without talking.
6   Work on the task — have a go;
                                — allow everyone to speak;
                                — listen to what they say;
                                — ask them questions.
7   Check our work.
8   Think ahead.'

The strategy card was designed to remind pupils and teachers of the language of learning, and to help them in class, as well as being a useful reference for the small group discussions. These discussions enabled the researcher to introduce issues that she had observed during the science lesson, such as the language used and pupils' misunderstandings. Emphasis was paid too, to linking their school experiences with others the pupils had, whether in or out of school, and to stressing the validity and usefulness of this. Towards the end of the four-week period of discussion the pupils evaluated the usefulness of the strategy card, and planned an experiment together, with the researcher now withdrawing from leadership of the group. Their planning went well: pupils now showed greater awareness of each other and worked well together.

The researchers concluded that the experience of discussion which was focussed on their learning, over only a short time, was beginning to change the view these pupils had of themselves as learners. At the outset they clearly regarded themselves as receivers and their teachers as transmitters of knowledge, and they also expressed ambivalence about group work. They were clearly more confident, less reticent about sharing their own ideas, and showed an emerging ability in talking about learning, after the four weeks. In this last respect the researchers emphasize their increased realization of the enormous salience of emotional aspects of school experience to the pupils. In initial discussions they spoke of learning being difficult because things got on their nerves, and of their fear of being revealed as not knowing things, and being shown up. The researchers report this highlighting of social and individual psychological elements of the learning process was the most interesting feature of their final discussions with pupils concerning what makes for good learning. It is the strength of this aspect that continually impresses many researchers into the quality and effectiveness of classroom learning experiences. Evidence of a longer term impact of group discussion and the strategy card on the five pupils concerned was provided by teachers' comments that they handled group learning better than other pupils who lacked their discussion experience.

A second paper from the same research project (Quicke and Winter, in press) explores the degree to which three teachers encouraged metacognitive awareness and pupils' self-regulation during maths, science and English classes, with the same mixed ability target class as in the earlier research, who were by now in their second year of secondary school. The three teachers all met with the researchers at regular intervals to explore their teaching activities and plans together, within an explicit theoretical framework, where the learner was defined as a 'socially constituted developing, knowing subject', and where teachers and pupils together worked to construct new knowledge by a scaffolding process.

The paper is a fascinating and detailed account of the multitude of factors, including the recently introduced National Curriculum (and changing school ethos), with concomitantly less emphasis on cross curricular activities, which were experienced as very real impediments to the teachers' efforts to adopt classroom practices which had the potential to empower pupils by helping them be more aware and more in control of their own learning.

Linking pupils' own experiences with the curriculum was one of the aims of the three teachers, but even within their classes the researchers concluded that there was still insufficient acknowledgment of the huge gap between the specialized knowledge of maths and science and what pupils brought with them to the 'interactional arena' in the way of their previous experience and commonsense knowledge.

Another recent study which attempted to enhance pupils' awareness of their learning processes, and ability to reflect on their thinking, is of particular interest as it concerns pupils with moderate learning difficulties attending a special school. Powell and Makin (1994) devised a programme for a class of ten 12 and 13-year-olds, which was implemented during the mathematics lessons taught by the second author. The pupils presented the usual mixed range of abilities and difficulties typical of a class in this kind of school, having in common low self-esteem, difficulties with academic work, and particularly in talking about their classroom experiences including their feelings.

The teaching programme designed to help pupils to talk and think about their learning occupied six hours weekly over two terms, and each of the two hour sessions comprised three elements. First were opening meetings in which pupils in a whole class group talked about their previous work or some recent experience of a broadly mathematical nature (as on their journey to school). This was followed by the mathematics work, usually undertaken singly or in pairs: on completion pupils described this to their teacher who used a word processor to record it, with the active collaboration of the pupil, before it became part of that pupil's individual file.

The final element of each teaching session was devoted to students' self-appraisals, in a group, of how they had organized their task, dealt with problems, got on with any partner, and how they felt about it. They used five point scales in an evaluation of each area. The researchers made notes in fieldwork diaries, whose analysis was supplemented by some recorded interactions. They were able to draw general conclusions over the period of their research study about changes in the pupils involved, and factors that facilitated these.

First, the verbal descriptions given by pupils of their work included more hypothetical (for example, 'what if . . . ?') and experiential ('I remember'. . . . ; or 'once I . . .') modes over the study period, using Phillips' (1985) categorization system, which was derived from group talk by 10–12-year-olds engaged in classroom tasks. Of the five modes of discourse identified by Phillips, it was these two, the hypothetical and experiential, that encouraged the pupils to 'treat remarks made at any time as remaining present for contemplation during an extended period of time'. Powell and Makin gained evidence of pupils engaging in an increasing amount of reflection and evaluation, and often these were used in response to teachers' or peers' comments. The evaluations pupils gave of their work were sometimes helped by encouraging visual depictions like drawings, and sometimes too by joint evaluations with their partner for that session. Sometimes decision making was found to be more confident when made with a partner. Teacher modelling, taking time to think, and using reflective talk also influenced pupils over the time period. Tasks had to be sufficiently challenging for pupils to put the necessary effort into reflecting on them. Finally, echoing the emphasis of Quicke and Winter, the authors remark on the significant and pervasive nature of affective aspects of their pupils' classroom experience, to the extent that 'the success or otherwise of our programme with these pupils hinged on how effectively we could deal with concerns and anxieties'.

Finally, we consider the principles and effects of a large-scale programme from further afield, developed by Ashman and Conway (1989 and 1993). Process Based Instruction (PBI) began as a classroom-based teaching and learning programme in Australia and was originally developed for pupils who attended special classes and would be roughly equivalent to our pupils with moderate learning difficulties in Britain. Since its inception many more of such students are integrated into the Australian mainstream school system and it has been introduced into mainstream schools and judged to be particularly helpful with lower ability students. It is designed to help teachers to alter their teaching in subtle but important ways that are compatible with a variety of teaching approaches, in a range of settings and across all curricular areas.

A central feature is planning, where a plan is a sequence of activities or thoughts that will lead to success on a specific task. Pupils are taught that planning helps them to solve problems and teachers initially construct plans with them on a wide range of tasks, but are advised to gradually reduce their own participation so that pupils will become more independent and automatically incorporate planning into their repertoire of learning strategies. On any specific curriculum task, the authors suggest, it is likely that there will be some learners who can work independently and without a written plan, by using well developed existing strategies, and others who will need teacher assistance with or without a plan. The model rests on task analysis by pupils and is claimed to be appropriate for any curriculum in a wide range of settings. The authors include examples of plans which are appropriate for specific tasks like the calculation of area or punctuation of a sentence, and others like the sequence involved in making a sandwich. They emphasize that the impression that may be gained of piecemeal sets of instructions is misleading and that teachers using PBI must reinforce the commonalities between plans for different activities or problem solving.

The focus on planning seems potentially very useful as part of a general awareness raising of general strategy use and self-regulation, but there is a danger which the authors acknowledge, of plan proliferation and trivialization, and of pupils failing to generalize from specific to more global planning. There is an impression from Ashman and Conway's accounts that pupils may not always feel they truly own the plans. Their own ideas and own language are not given prominence, nor the fact that many different strategic approaches are often equally acceptable and may suit different pupils.

A rare bonus is associated with PBI in the form of a very interesting evaluation of its effectiveness in primary classrooms conducted by Ashman and Conway (1993). They compared results in a range of tests taken by randomly selected 9–12-year-olds, fifty-eight of whom attended schools where a PBI programme had operated during that year, and eighty-nine from schools without

such a programme. All were receiving the standard Queensland primary curriculum. Fourteen teachers also completed a questionnaire concerning their
attitudes towards the PBI programme they had implemented. The results were
that the pupils who had experienced PBI performed significantly better than
the others on maths and reading comprehension tests and on a Porteus Maze
Test. But in a specially designed test of planning there was no significant effect
of the PBI programme.

These results highlight the difficulty of evaluating changes in pupils' approaches and thinking by standardized tests. Particularly where these involve
timed performance and a set of predetermined steps to a solution, like the
planning test in this research, they seem the antithesis of the programme's
long-term aims. The improved maths and reading scores may have resulted
from a general positive effect of teachers being involved in PBI workshops and
discussions: this seems likely as a sample of teachers expressed very positive
views about their experience of participation.

It may be that the evaluation was carried out too soon after only six
months' experience of the programme and that later testing would have shown
more impressive results. But perhaps more valuable and informative evaluation would be in the form of teacher diaries, with observations over time of
how the pupils spontaneously dealt with challenging situations. Qualitative
information rather than quantitative measures would seem to be the most
appropriate method of evaluation for this kind of development work, whose
effects are likely to be pervasive and subtle changes in pupils' and teachers'
behaviour and attitudes.

One comment in the report is also noteworthy. This is that the teachers
were directing students' use of plans rather than involving them in plan development: the authors conclude that they need to encourage teachers to have
students develop and use their own plans and to reinforce their use as early
as possible. If this happened then the pupils really would be developing useful
metacognitive expertise.

All five research projects have interesting implications for practice and
together they form a useful background to the Scottish research to be described
in the next five chapters. The following issues are of particular importance.

Were They Successful?

All reported positive results with pupils, whether in the development of specific strategies or whether in more pervasive long-term effects.

Todman and McBeth's was a short-term training intervention which was
not carried out by the class teacher. It showed a clear qualitative difference in
the acquisition of a problem solving strategy which depended on the closeness
of match between the training and the pupils' existing developmental level.
The more effective training was one step ahead of pupils' existing strategies and
was demonstrated by their ability to generalize their learned strategy to a different context one week later.

Sugden's pupils experienced two terms of individual teaching to encourage verbal elaboration and maintained the positive effects for nine months after teaching had finished, as well as in some cases spontaneously developing a grouping strategy in a memory task.

The three remaining projects were integrated into the pupils' existing curricular experience and had long-term and more far reaching aims. They also report more generalized effects from the interventions. Process Based Instruction, widely used in Queensland and New South Wales, was warmly endorsed by teachers in Ashman and Conway's evaluation. The effects of PBI on pupils' test performance allow for cautious optimism, as the authors say. Their planned longer term and more detailed follow-up studies using different evaluation methods will be of great interest. Qualitative, pervasive effects on pupils' perceptions of themselves as thinkers are to the fore in the remaining two pieces of research.

The small group discussions which formed part of Quicke and Winter's research programme only lasted four weeks, but their intensity and linking with events in the same five pupils' science classes appear to have enabled pupils' changing perceptions about themselves as effective learners and about learning within a group.

Powell and Makin documented changes in their pupils in a range of areas, from their increased use of reflective talk during mathematics classes, to their greater ability to monitor their own problem solving, and a growing sense of control over tasks, rather than feeling at their mercy.

What Contributed towards these Projects' Effectiveness?

First, whether the terms used are scaffolding, contingency or the zone of proximal development, the interaction between teacher and learner is clearly of enormous importance: the more the teacher can connect with pupils' existing cognitive structures the better the learning experience. This was clearly supported by Todman and McBeth's study within a limited area. Generalization occurred to a much greater extent with the pupils who had received the most appropriate training, best adapted to their current level.

Sugden's research aimed to challenge pupils' natural passivity and engaged them actively by using their own ideas and their own stories, and by the teacher deliberately and gradually reducing her support. Over time the pupils were taking information, elaborating it, and putting it into the framework that they had imposed, continuing to use verbal strategies with much reduced teacher support. They did not cease to need specific information, however, concerning similarities between situations and the usefulness of appropriate strategies, supporting the impression that gains in understanding were real but somewhat fragile, taking a long time to become established.

The studies which aimed to promote general strategy use and reflection used social contexts for discussions about learning, and the usual planned curricular tasks as content. However, particularly in the cases of Quicke and Winter's, and Powell and Makin's work, individual pupils' perceptions and experiences remained at the centre, particularly by emphasizing the value and validity of pupils linking their own experiences from home or elsewhere with their current classroom work. Powell and Makin's dossier of pupils' descriptions of what they had done in class showed respect for their words, their decisions and their own value judgments.

The evaluation of PBI by Ashman and Conway highlighted the participant teachers' difficulty, at least in the first year of its implementation, in allowing pupils to formulae their own plans. Perhaps the training days for teachers giving them a clear rationale and theoretical framework, and then using their own plans as examples, encouraged them to unintentionally dominate planning in their classrooms and to risk giving pupils the impression that a plan was a prescription rather than a process. The researchers conclude 'there is a need to encourage teachers to have students develop and use their own plans and to reinforce their use as early as possible'.

The Role of Talk

Several reports comment that the pupils concerned found talking about their own classroom experiences very difficult. Sugden's participants were chosen because they were not using verbal strategies in memory tasks: he reports that they became very much more fluent and eager to talk in class over time, and that they progressed from producing very sparse stories to ones that were far more detailed and complex. Powell and Makin recorded the increased use by their pupils of reflective talk, in hypothetical and experiential modes, during the course of their research. They also remark that the common characteristic of their pupils at the outset was their poor verbalization. The teacher-researcher deliberately modelled the production of reflective utterances, and other kinds of reflective behaviour like taking time to think, and planning aloud.

The discussion groups in Quicke and Winter's study enabled the five participating boys to begin to engage in talking about experiences which were very difficult for them to articulate, being emotionally laden and concerned with power and status.

The role of verbalization, whether this represented a strategy in use, as in Sugden's work, or broaching deeply felt sensitivities in the company of peers, is prominent, both as an end in itself and as a means towards deeper reflection by pupils.

Undercurrents

Finally, two reports in particular state that there were powerful emotions and feelings in their pupils that were the ultimate determinants of the success of the research programme. Powell and Makin report on their pupils' frequent anxieties, so very familiar to any teacher of pupils with special educational needs, that they might be unable to do what was asked of them, and their frequent need for reassurance, and for trust in the adults they worked with. The impression through this, and Quicke and Winter's report, is that the pupils concerned had developed very negative views of themselves over a long period, and that these got in the way of their thinking in school.

Among the general 'spin off' effects reported from the studies are references to pupils' increased confidence, willingness to speak, giving their own ideas, and sharing their difficulties; these are not incidental and minor, but may be of considerable significance in enabling pupils to begin to engage with and enjoy challenging school experiences.

In the following chapters we move to a study of Scottish pupils and their teachers in which there was no intervention and no special programme, where the interest lay in investigating reflection in the everyday experiences of classroom life.

3 The Research Focus: Reflection within the Classroom

> How then, might we set about fostering metacognitive experiences in the school? I obviously do not know but will prescribe as if I did. Try consciousness raising and training in introspection. Engage children in cognitive enterprises that should produce metacognitive ideas and feelings. Help them to understand their meanings and implications for subsequent cognitive action. (Flavell, 1981)

John Flavell, a powerful voice in cognitive developmental theory and the first to describe and investigate the 'meta' aspects of memory, communication and cognition, emphasizes the importance in education of pupils' awareness and subjective experience of having control of their own thinking. Writing in Scotland five years later, Nisbet and Shucksmith (1986) pinpoint the destructive effects of the failure to develop the kind of awareness advocated by Flavell.

> For many, especially those who have had the most frequent experience of difficulties in learning, the sense of bewilderment is never resolved. These children do not learn to use errors and false moves to diagnose or resolve problems. For them errors are destructive rather than constructive. Often the pattern of right and wrong seems so arbitrary that they begin to accept that learning is as difficult to control as the weather and that its regulation lies outside their control. It is a small step from this point to the one where the only strategies which the child is keen on developing are those which allow him or her to keep out of the teacher's eye.

This chapter describes the rationale and procedures of an investigation into reflection within four special school classrooms. The pupils are all described as having moderate learning difficulties; they will indeed have had frequent experiences of 'difficulties in learning'. But, as chapter 2 should have made clear, these are pupils for whom research findings on reflection are very promising. There is ample evidence, it is true, that reflection does not come readily and automatically as they grow older, for a variety of possible reasons. But there are also many positive indications that gains in understanding, confidence, self-esteem and independence can result from appropriate educational experiences.

What might such appropriate educational experiences be? A wide range of possibilities come to mind, from 'consciousness raising' of the kind advocated by Flavell, to specific 'thinking skills' activities, games of deduction, and group problem solving. What I as researcher most wanted to know, to establish a base line in my own thinking, was whether the small classes of special schools would emphasize thinking and present challenging opportunities to pupils who were not naturally very reflective. Would teachers believe that it was important to home in on and explore pupils' errors and signs of incomprehension? Would they deliberately arrange problematic or ambiguous situations? In chapter 2 we saw that a challenging teaching approach which views mistakes as potentially fruitful avenues to cognitive advance and resolution has not featured at all prominently in the teaching of pupils who have difficulties in learning, until relatively recently. Indeed the very different traditions of 'errorless learning' and 'practice makes perfect' have been long lasting, powerful influences in some special schools.

The decision was made. There would be no intervention, no suggestions to the teachers and no alterations to the pupils' classroom experience. This would be recorded as accurately and unobtrusively as possible. Subsequent analyses should, I thought, yield interesting lines for exploration. The research process is summarized below.

The Research Process

Date	Research activity	Participants
December	Visits. Agreement to participate and parents' permission obtained.	Four schools and headteachers.
January	Audiorecordings and classroom observations. Pupil and teacher interviews concerning sessions.	Four class teachers. Eight target pupils.
April	Transcription and analysis of audiorecordings.	
March	Interviews.	The class teachers.

In brief the aims of the research were to consider the following questions:

(i)   Was reflection happening in the classroom?
(ii) How did teachers encourage reflection by pupils?
(iii) What characterized reflective episodes in the classroom?
(iv) What were the teachers' views about their pupils' learning difficulties and the role of reflection in their educational experience?

Several principles governed the nature of the research from the outset.

(a) It was to interfere as little as possible with the normal classroom activities. The usual planned classroom experiences were to be observed and recorded in as least disturbing a manner as possible. Ecological validity (gaining a truly representative picture of the four classrooms) was a high priority.

(b) A range of curricular experiences were to be covered. Reflection might equally well occur during general 'news', discussion periods, or creative activities, as during problem solving, or mathematics.

(c) From extensive data which was representative of a small number of classrooms, features of interest would be identified and described. A pre-existing set of categories would not be used: rather, categories would be derived from the data obtained.

(d) Teachers' views about their work would not be ignored, but must not be allowed to influence the processes of data collection and analysis. They were to be obtained by interview after the period of recording, observation and analysis.

Schools, Teachers and Pupils

The decision was to confine the research project to four special schools. They comprised all the schools specifically designated for pupils who had 'moderate learning difficulties' in one particular geographical area. In common with most other special schools they all report changes in the kinds of pupil in attendance over the past few years. They say that the general level of ability has fallen, because more of the more able pupils are now integrated into mainstream schools, and the pupils remaining often present complex challenges to teachers, many having communication difficulties, and emotionally insecure family backgrounds. All classes (10–12 pupils on average) represent a range of pupils, some of whom may have had some former (but unhappily unsuccessful) attendance at a mainstream primary school.

All four schools' headteachers agreed after discussion and information concerning the aims and procedures that they would participate in the research. The focus in each school would be one class for pupils aged between 10–12 years. This range is particularly appropriate as it is an age at which children are naturally and spontaneously developing and using their reflective abilities, and additionally there are several interesting and relevant research studies of pupils of this age and with a similar degree of learning difficulty, like those described in chapter 2.

In three of the schools, in the class identified as the most appropriate and whose teacher agreed to participate, a primary type timetable was in operation, with the pupils being taught by a class teacher for most of the day with some auxiliary support and specialist help and relatively long teaching sessions. In

Table 1   The main participants

Classroom	Class teacher	Target pupil
One	Mrs Guthrie	Andrew Mark
Two	Mrs Stevenson	Johnnie Lynne
Three	Mrs Macdonald	Alastair Donald
Four	Mrs Law	Emma Samantha

All participants' names have been changed.

the fourth school the timetable resembled that operating in secondary schools, with different subject teachers and shorter teaching sessions, often of around thirty-five minutes. In this case we agreed to observe and record the regular teaching sessions of one member of staff with one class, and made arrangements for the timetabling of visits so that equivalent periods of classroom experience were recorded in all four classrooms.

Two target pupils were chosen by each class teacher as suitable for the project. They were fairly clear speakers who were not too inhibited, did not have significant behavioural difficulties and were judged to be managing quite well in their class. Parental permission for their participation was obtained by the schools. The sample of eight target pupils comprised five boys and three girls, conveniently representative of the proportions generally found in this kind of school. Their mean age at the beginning of the term during which all the recordings were made was 11.5 years.

The class teacher was told that we aimed to record their usual classroom practice and that we were generally interested in thinking in the classroom; that is, pupils' learning strategies, awareness of their own thinking and problem solving, and how teachers respond when pupils do not understand. We emphasized that normal classroom activities were being studied, and that they should not change their plans.

A timetable of visits was drawn up for each class. The target pupils alternately, and the teacher on each visit, were to wear radio microphones and the research assistant (Judith Scott) was to be present in the classroom. In all, there were eight visits to each of the primary type classes and twelve to the one operating the timetable with shorter sessions. This resulted in approximately fifty hours of classroom recording for analysis.

Classroom Recording

Audiorecording by radiomicrophone was the method of choice, as we thought it was most likely to enable natural unself-conscious behaviour in both target pupils and teachers. We considered videotaping but thought it would be too intrusive. In order to supply essential contextual information and to make notes on pupils' non-verbal behaviour the research assistant was present but unobtrusive during all the classroom recordings. She fixed up the microphone and monitored the recording equipment for each session and made a running observational record which will be described later.

Radiomicrophones were effective in securing high quality recordings of class talk in which the target pupil and teacher were almost always identifiable. Talk between them was of major interest to the research, of course, and talk between the target pupils and their peers in small group situations was another important source of information, which was not always so easy to hear and transcribe. One fascinating aspect of the data was the recorded pupils' talk to themselves, along with sighs, laughs, grunts, hums and yawns which would surely have been missed by visual observation alone.

The teachers in later interviews reported that they would have found videorecording rather inhibiting and that it would certainly have affected their and their pupils' classroom behaviour. Regarding the wearing of the microphone, they were much more relaxed:

> No, I didn't find either the observer or the tape recorder intrusive at all. We get so many people coming and going that you become very accustomed to having random others in the classroom.

and

> I think you were very unobtrusive really. I don't know any other techniques you could have really employed . . . you became part of the fabric of what was going on.

> I think that some people might have been really bothered about having someone else in the classroom being taped, but actually after the first couple of times it didn't really bother me too much, I just got on with it.

> The fourth teacher felt that she 'played safe' but that while her teaching was affected in that respect, the pupils weren't worried.

We treated the first classroom recording involving each target pupil as familiarization and did not use it in detailed analysis, although the class reaction to the novelty of the recording apparatus and procedure was of interest as noted in chapter 5.

Judith Scott, the research assistant, asked the class teacher before each session about her plans and expectations concerning the target pupil, noting these in writing. Following each session she again talked briefly with the teacher asking how she felt the session had gone, whether it was according to plan, whether the target pupil had been 'challenged' and to identify if possible any difficulties in understanding. Despite great variation in detail and the inevitable pressures of time and other demands these were potentially useful sources of information as well as being socially comfortable ways of entering and leaving the classroom.

The target pupils were also asked after each session, while the radio-microphone was removed, to recount what they had been doing, whether there was anything they had liked or disliked and what were the most difficult or easiest things they had done, and why. There was huge variation in pupils' responses, in length and detail, especially at the beginning, but a general impression of their views and feelings was gained.

We recorded a range of curricular experiences. One involved an art session with a visiting specialist with the class teacher actively involved in much practical work but little talk, so we decided to exclude this atypical session from analysis. All the other recordings were transcribed and timings were noted for checking from the audiotapes. The transcriptions inevitably were lengthy and arduous undertakings but did include all the talk by target pupils or directed towards them, for example in group situations. Contextual information from the written observational notes were added to the record of the talk experienced by a target pupil during a particular session. These transcripts form the main body of data for the analysis described in chapters 4 and 5. Their bulk and the time expended in transcription and checking were inconveniences which were more than counterbalanced by their positive aspects: representativeness and breadth of coverage. The target pupils' experience of classroom talk was now available in written form, a rich source amenable to a wide range of dissections and inspections that could be revisited repeatedly. And the tones of voice and timing captured on the audiotapes provided a vivid sense of reality and excitement and could confirm or enrich the basic written data.

Observations

An observation schedule was designed for use by the research assistant during each recorded classroom session. It was devised firstly for the essential practical reason of providing contextual information about the classroom activity which could be matched against the audiotape transcripts. Secondly it was to provide the opportunity for the target pupils' non-verbal behaviour to be described.

Summaries of each session's observation sheets were later compiled by condensing them and adding details concerning the groupings within the class, the class activity and the target pupils' talk to themselves, peers or their teacher. Within these it was possible to highlight the occurrence of reflective episodes and their context of classroom activities as described in chapter 6.

From the observation sheets we estimated the percentage of time spent by

Table 2 Pupil activity as percentage of total classroom time

Classroom	Whole class	Small group	Individual	Other	Out of room
One	36	11	38	14	1
Two	22	12	53	13	0
Three	24	13	50	12	1
Four	51	6	29	9	5

the target pupil in different settings, to provide a general picture of their activities and of the typical pattern that particular class teacher chose to operate.

We classified an activity as whole class when all the pupils were focusing on a topic together, and as small group when they did so in pairs or other subdivisions of the whole class. During individual activity pupils usually worked at tables with other pupils around, all doing their own work without any planned collaboration. Other activities included waiting at the teacher's desk, tidying up and waiting for instructions.

Further reference is made to the grouping of pupils in chapter 5.

Analysis of Classroom Talk

Teacher Talk

The richness and quantity of recorded classroom talk presents an exciting challenge to any researcher. We were to look for patterns in the teachers' interactions with their pupils which related to the encouragement of reflection in their classroom. We wanted to examine what they actually did and said, how they introduced work to pupils, how they dealt with pupils' questions or misunderstandings, how they kept things going, throughout whole classroom sessions, and across a range of classroom activities.

But it was important from the start, we believed, to not approach the transcripts with definite pre-conceived notions as to what we were going to find. We did not wish to use a ready made system of categorization but to look at the talk by teachers with an open mind. We wished to retain the richness and flavour of real talk and not to impose second order groupings like 'questions' and 'gives information' at the start. It is very easy to lose the quality of qualitative data at an early stage. In more technical terms we felt our categories had to be 'grounded' both conceptually and empirically. Conceptually they had to make sense within the overall framework embracing reflection and empirically they had to fit the evidence in the transcripts.

Henwood and Pigeon (1995) suggest that a 'grounded theory' approach requires a special openness and flexibility from researchers and that its value is to keep researchers on an analytic path while at the same time committing them to be careful not to simply reproduce their own pre-existing ideas or assumptions. Theory does not simply emerge from the data, of course. Whatever their methodology, people conducting research are inevitably influenced by their own existing concepts and theoretical positions. But the decision to allow the evidence to 'speak for itself' at an early stage, and as far as possible, does surely decrease the danger of mental foreclosure at an early stage. Another danger is of the excessive use of direct quotations without sufficient analysis and discussion. Here extensive use is made of direct quotations from the classroom transcripts, in the belief that illustrative, 'real' unedited examples have an unmatched explanatory potential. They also can convey a vivid sense of classroom reality. In general their selection and use in this study is illustrative and explanatory rather than typical or representative.

As Dey (1993) points out there is no single set of categories waiting to be discovered. There are as many ways of 'seeing' the data as one can invent. This does not mean that the categories arrived at are arbitrary because clearly they must make sense of the data.

The process of categorization forces a researcher to think about the data, in this instance teacher talk in the classroom, in detail, to become familiar with it, and inevitably this leads to the generation of ideas. Before categorisation our data consisted of transcriptions and audiorecordings. The extraction, categorization, and comparison of examples of teacher talk inevitably meant that these were removed from their context, which we know to be an important influence on our interpretation and understanding. We needed to revisit the context repeatedly and did this by means of episode identification, another means of investigating reflection in the classroom.

The category system for teacher talk

The basic unit used in the derivation of categories of teacher talk was a 'turn', an utterance bounded by a pause or another person talking. All the recorded classroom talk by the teachers was included except for purely management activities like tidying up, and talk that she addressed to visitors or other members of staff. The talk that was analyzed was all addressed to pupils and this included news time and informal chat, as well as planned class activities.

Devising a category system for the teacher talk in our study inevitably took a lot of time and involved a process of repeated refinement and adjustment, as a result of extensive discussion and recoding by the two of us. Our first system comprised fifteen categories, which were reduced to seven and later six after repeated discussion and after comparing of transcripts which had been rescored independently by us both. The system we used in the end consisted of six categories (three large ones being further subdivided) and we judged it to be comprehensive (in that all teacher talk could be categorized) and sufficiently reliable for the purpose of the study. It was derived from a total of eighteen hours of recorded teacher classroom talk.

Agreement between us on hard cases became closer after discussion, and

Table 3   Overall percentage of categories of teacher talk

Category	1	2	3	4	5	6
Mean % over all recordings analyzed	45	28	16	6	4	1

we agreed that the six categories of teacher talk that we eventually arrived at were consistent with our conceptual understanding and reading in the field of reflection. They are discussed in detail in chapter 4, and can be summarized as follows.

Category 1 concerns teachers' assessment of pupils' current knowledge.
Category 2 is where teachers encourage reflection by pupils.
Category 3 comprises teachers keeping pupils on task.
Category 4 is when teachers model reflection.
Category 5 is the promotion of pupils' independence.
Category 6 is applied to teachers' emphasis on peer contributions.

We found this categorization system to be satisfactory for our purposes, and subsequently used it to analyze all the teacher talk experienced within a number of sessions by a target pupil (that was addressed to him/her as an individual or as part of a larger group). Teacher talk which was inaccessible to the target pupil was not included. Inspection of the remaining recorded data enabled us to estimate the overall proportion of teacher talk falling into the above categories, as shown on table 3.

The teacher styles which were revealed by our categorization of their talk were found to be consistent. Different categories appeared in the same rank order for a teacher across different sessions. This rather striking fact (for sessions involved different activities and target pupils) is one of our main research findings and appears to be related in our study to the teachers' preferred grouping of pupils, to pupils' enjoyment, and to the length of classroom dialogues, all of which are discussed in chapter 5.

However, the most important determinants of teacher style and the ethos they create in their classrooms are probably, as Edwards and Mercer (1987) say, teachers' implicit beliefs about how children learn and how best they can be helped to do so. It was clearly important that we attempted to understand the implicit beliefs of the teachers in our research, but that such understanding should not affect our analysis of their classroom interactions. We were grateful that all four teachers were willing to talk at length about their teaching philosophies, their views about learning difficulties, and of the roles of reflection and challenge in their pupils' educational experience. These are discussed in chapter 7. Interviews focused on these areas one year after data collection, and thus tapped the teachers' long held beliefs, not simply those specifically related to their experience of the research project.

Pupil Talk

Target pupils talked with their peers, and to themselves as well as talking and listening to their teachers. For the purpose of this study several aspects of their talk were studied.

Reflective talk

We were interested in our pupils' use of reflective talk, in reasoning, expressing doubt, qualifications, and referring to their own thought processes, errors and difficulties, for several reasons. It would indicate a propensity to verbal reflection, of a spontaneous nature, which might relate to their teachers' own language, or be prominent in certain activities or contexts, or with peers. We made a simple record of our target pupils' reflective language, and of the contexts of its use, from samples of classroom recordings.

Self-monitoring talk

Thanks to the sensitivity of the recording apparatus pupils' talk to themselves was often audible, in addition to non-verbal indications that they were engaged in self-regulation. These might include reference to time and effort, and to maintaining concentration and keeping track of their own progress.

Classroom conversations

Conversations in the classroom comprised a sequence of turns which focused on a topic and, in our study, those we considered were always to include the target pupil, often with other pupils, and the teacher. A sample of recorded sessions provided information on the average length of such conversations in the different classrooms.

Chapter 5 concludes with information on the teachers' plans and expectations for each recorded session and their and the target pupils' evaluations afterwards. The degree of agreement between teachers and target pupils about what had been difficult, in particular, was an indication of their mutual understanding and awareness of the preceding session's activities and in particular of reflective episodes, the focus of chapter 6.

Episodes

One of our main aims was the identification of reflective episodes. We conceived of these as periods during which the target pupil was judged to be challenged intellectually. Identified primarily by what was said, and backed by the observational record, with a minimum duration of half a minute, these were times when we judged that the pupil was absorbed, puzzled, sometimes frustrated, but in every case there was the possibility of some kind of intellectual progress.

The transcripts, observational records, pupil and teacher comments and supporting information from the original audiotapes were all potentially valuable sources for the identification of such significant experiences.

Episode identification

For each target pupil, we selected complete recorded classroom sessions from the latter half of the term in which they were made. By this time pupils and teachers were accustomed to the recording apparatus and quiet presence of the research assistant, who made contextual notes and spoke briefly with the teacher and target pupil concerning each session. We were careful to select sessions which had not been judged to be unsatisfactory by the teacher, and which were representative of the activities and pupil grouping she usually organized.

We listened separately to the audiotaped recordings and examined session transcripts to identify episodes in which the target pupil showed reflection. We marked these on the transcripts and achieved consensus for the most part, particularly after the exclusion of episodes of less than thirty seconds. Periods which remained unresolved, potential episodes for reflection, are discussed separately, in chapter 6.

Our identification primarily relied on the verbal evidence of audiotapes and transcripts, and these were sometimes supplemented by the observations of non-verbal behaviour made at the time of the recordings. They include tone of voice, posture, movement, humming, yawns, laughter and singing, facial expression, mutters, grunts, moans, whispers and crying. These were a useful indication of the degree of pupil absorption, with endearing idiosyncrasies and individual differences.

1 Once identified, an episode was separately transcribed to form part of an episode 'bank', and contextual details of the activity, pupils' grouping, and links with target pupils' earlier classroom experience within the same session were noted.

2 Next a written narrative summarizing each session was made which attempted to assess the intellectual involvement and absorption of the target pupil concerned and the teacher's awareness of this aspect of classroom behaviour, incorporating her expectations before and judgments after each session.

3 Finally as a supplement to individual episode details and whole session narratives, a pictorial method of representing sessions and their reflective focus was explored, in order to highlight such features as sequence, linking and timing and to represent pupils' experience of

reflection within a discrete period of real classroom time. We hoped that this would give a rapid but clear impression of an episode representing a pupil's cognitive engagement within its context.

I believe that reflective episodes are critical learning opportunities for pupils, with potential for cognitive growth. It is important however, not to lose sight of their affective nature. They often involve expressions of elation, frustration, or anger which may be shared by teacher or peers. Words in print can only partially convey this, whereas charts or pictures can sometimes be effective in illustrating critical points in time and their surrounding context. The highlighting of reflective episodes by visual depiction is explored in chapter 6. Contexts and activities which were particularly successful in facilitating reflective episodes are described and illustrated by example, along with others which were potentially fruitful but in practice turned out to be unsatisfactory, unresolved opportunities.

We obtained a large rich and complex database from only four classrooms. All the teachers involved had different experiences, different constraints and different demands on their time and energy. But there are some features which are comparable; all were teaching, within the same area, classes of roughly the same size, of pupils of the same age who were judged on assessment to be likely to have their particular educational needs best met in this type of special school. All the teachers had extensive experience in both special and mainstream teaching and all were committed members of staff, with the confidence of their headteacher.

Teacher Interviews

The ethos or atmosphere of their classroom must indicate the degree to which the teachers felt valued, supported and motivated within the school community, and this was supported by some of their comments during the interviews. In chapter 7 this aspect of the classroom and its effect on the pupils' confidence is explored further. As part of the overall context within which reflective episodes are embedded it exerts a subtle, hard to identify, but powerful effect. It is discussed alongside information gained from the interviews which were carried out after data collection and after much of the analysis was complete. The interviews were semi-structured to allow the teachers to express their own ideas in their own way and to allow issues or ideas to emerge that had not been anticipated by the researchers. The interview guide contained questions concerning broad issues which had emerged as important and interesting on the basis of perusal of the literature, discussion between the researchers, and issues that had emerged from the research to date. Analysis involved careful reading of the interview transcripts and linking of emergent themes: similarities and differences of their views led to findings of interest, which are reported in chapter 7.

Advantages and Limitations

To make general statements about reflection on the basis of classroom interactions from four classrooms in four special schools might seem naive or presumptuous. In defence we can point to the enlightenment which has been
gained from many other detailed accounts: for example, of early language development in a very few children, or detailed accounts of classroom processes
which have yielded real insights like that of Edwards and Mercer (1987) or
more recently Woods' exploration of critical events in teaching and learning
(1993). This last is of four primary school projects and could never be accused
of narrowness or of limited interest in its relevance to other teachers. Woods
describes his research as seeking to articulate the ineffable: teachers and pupils
were encouraged to convey their feelings as well as to describe their experiences as participants in real learning, which built on 'their own needs and rele-
vancies and their existing cognitive and affective structures.' Woods' critical
events were of much longer duration than the reflective episodes reported
here, but his hopes for their potential to practitioners are the same as ours. By
reference to their own practice, experience and views, they will test the validity of what is reported in this particular research study. Evidence of generalization is often best shown by the recognition felt by experienced practitioners.
The extensive use of direct quotations from our transcripts should enhance this.
In devising the system for categorizing teachers' talk we made no initial assumptions about its effectiveness in the classroom. Rather we attempted simply to
describe the characteristics of their classroom talk in plain commonsense language within a framework of psychological and pedagogical understanding.

It was fascinating to encounter an American study of almost thirty years
ago, after our own research project was completed. It is referred to as work
that has been surprisingly neglected in a recent Leverhulme Project Report
(Wragg and Brown, 1993). Smith and Meux (1970) used the less sophisticated
audiorecording technology of the 1960s to collect a large sample of classroom
dialogues in a range of lessons, social studies, English, maths and science, with
pupils in grades 9–12. They too termed their main units of analysis 'episodes'.
These consisted of a verbal exchange around a topic. Smith and Meux used
a 'logical' rather than a psychological or linguistic system in their analysis and
categorization of their data. They agreed with Dewey's view that the rules of
successful inquiry are the rules of logic, and claimed that the forms a teacher's
verbal behaviour take during instruction are logical operations.

In attempting a categorization they initially used logical elements of a
teacher's language (such as the words 'know' and 'difference'). Finding this
unsatisfactory they moved to their method of categorizing teacher talk in
terms of what an 'ideal response' would be. Such logically correct hypothetical responses gave rise to categories with labels such as classifying, defining,
evaluating and conditional inferring. These were the processes pupils would
carry out if in practice they behaved as 'ideal listeners' in the identified episode. The categories were arrived at by a process of repeated refinement and

reliability testing as in this study and were comprehensive in applying to all the relevant recorded teacher talk.

Smith and Meux aimed simply to devise and describe their categorization system and to make no attempt to evaluate it by relating it to classroom outcomes or pupils' responsiveness. It is interesting to note the similarities between the 'logically based' categorization system they finally used and the one reported here. They comment that they were not able to produce entirely independent categories or entirely suitable criteria for them, and that any attempt to evaluate their effectiveness would have to be embedded in the pedagogical context. As Smith and Meux had anticipated they found that different subject areas resulted in different proportions of their categories in teachers' classroom talk. They did not differentiate between teachers. It is enlightening however to examine the major categories within their system, and to compare these with our own. Both studies used a large body of recorded teacher talk in a limited number of classrooms: both avoided preconceived category systems, and both derived exhaustive and mutually exclusive sets of categories.

Smith and Meux's equivalent of our Category One comprised teacher talk to which the ideal listener would respond by defining, describing, designating (by pointing or naming), and reporting (summarizing), and comprised about 50 per cent overall. Their equivalents of our Category Two included the eliciting from a listener of Explanation, Opining, Evaluating, Comparing and Contrasting, and Conditional Inferring. These categories comprised about 35 per cent of all the teacher talk they analysed. Finally, equivalent to our third large category, and forming about 10 per cent of the total, was teachers' management of the classroom.

It is fascinating that the three broad categories identified by Smith and Meux's different analytic approach have essentially the same content as our own. Many of the examples they give as illustrative material could quite plausibly have come from our own database, despite the different age and ability levels of the pupils concerned. The similarity of the overall proportions of their main category groupings and those of our Categories 1, 2 and 3 can be judged by reference to table 3. In their experience of teacher talk the pupils in our special school classrooms were not in such a radically different setting as one might have assumed. The proportions mask quite marked differences between different teachers in the present study, and between different subject areas in the American one. However, in very broad terms we can say that our special school pupils experienced similar features of teacher talk, in similar proportions overall.

A recent Leverhulme Primary Project publication, 'Explaining', has a similar focus on pupils' classroom experiences to our own. Wragg and Brown (1993) suggest how an observer can help teachers become more aware of the nature of their own explanations. 'Critical events' may occur during times when an explanation is being provided by a teacher: they are incidents when the pupils' understanding is being helped or impeded by what the teacher says. They give examples of teachers providing useful analogies, or failing to clarify confusion, and they provide a helpful outline of a simple post critical event analysis which a teacher and observer could carry out together.

This represents an entirely practical approach in which the effectiveness or failure of an explanation in enhancing real life pupils' understanding is the crucial factor, and not, as in Smith and Meux's study, a more theoretical analytic description of teacher talk. The short separate publications on teachers' explanations and questioning, however, have the great disadvantage in obscuring the fact that, as Wragg and Brown say, questions are often part and parcel of explanations.

The research reported here has affinities with each of the three research reports referred to above. All three identified segments of classroom experience which were believed to be central to pupils' progress in understanding. Woods' critical events were projects extending over time in which intellectual excitement, commitment, and emotional involvement were very apparent. Wragg and Brown used the same term to identify parts of explanations, and Smith and Meux used the term 'episode' to describe a segment of classroom discourse, as in the present study.

The present account is necessarily oversimplified. Some aspects of classroom life were not considered. There was selection and highlighting of others. There was no testing of hypotheses by intervention. Illustrative examples and excerpts of classroom talk were selected from many possible ones in the large database. We have tried to present an accurate and representative account of the place of reflection in pupils' normal classroom experience during one term of their school lives.

This we obtained by tapping pupils' and their teachers' views about recent classroom experience: by observation of non-verbal behaviour and spontaneous private speech: by observing pupils' success at their classroom tasks, and, most important in this study, by recording classroom interactions. In short, a range of converging sources of evidence of classroom reflection by pupils was explored, in the belief that common patterns might emerge. This approach is similar to that discussed and advocated by Meichenbaum (1985) as the most fruitful for the assessment of metacognition. What probably has not been adequately conveyed in this account but can be heard on the audiotapes, are the warmth, involvement and plain hard work, of all the teachers, in addition to their individual interests and other facets of their personalities. A larger sample of teachers would have disguised these, with a loss of richness that would have been no compensation for camouflage. If the teachers concerned do occasionally recognize themselves in the account that follows they are all the more assured of our gratitude in allowing us the privilege of having access to their classrooms.

The next four chapters describe classroom interactions from special schools, involving pupils with learning difficulties. Aspects of these interactions which appear to facilitate reflection by pupils are discussed, and the importance of context, ethos and teachers' expectations and views about their role emphasized.

4　The Locus of Reflection: Classroom Interaction

'The argument that the facts of greatest value to the study of education are those constituted in classroom interaction, and that they are most readily displayed in classroom talk, provides a persuasive reason for regarding classroom research as "basic" research and recorded language as its vital evidence', say Edwards and Westgate (1987), and they continue with a discussion which is very pertinent to my own experience, about the need for researchers on classroom interaction to avoid too tolerant an eclecticism, to make choices and to face dilemmas in where to focus their attention and how to record and use their evidence. For its very richness and complexity is both a strength and a source of likely difficulty and confusion. In this chapter the focus is on the evidence which is contained within the recordings and observations of the special school classrooms and relates to the encouragement of reflection. An analysis was made of teachers' classroom talk, and a teaching style was identified which emphasized reflection by pupils.

Teacher talk was the starting point and is central in its importance. Teachers orchestrate classroom experiences, and it is their talk that provides the framework for pupil activities. Awareness of the likelihood that it may assume undue centrality in a researcher's eyes because the teacher is the least difficult person in a classroom to record and interpret does not alter that fact. Later I move from the teacher focus, to look at pupils' language and thence to concentrate in more detail on reflective episodes during classroom interaction.

The first task was to examine a large body of teacher talk for recurring patterns to form the basis of a categorization system which was comprehensive and had face validity. This would enable insights into the ways in which the teachers identified and attempted to foster opportunities for reflection. They do this by other means than talking, of course, by using gestures, facial expressions, or by pausing and waiting. Here the focus is on what was the most accessible and probably the most important aspect of teaching, their classroom talk.

Categorization of Teacher Talk

The system used to analyze classroom talk by teachers and described in chapter 3 eventually comprised the six categories summarized below. They are numbered 1–6 in order of the overall frequency of their occurrence in our data.

Category 1 (Assessing) Teachers assess pupils' current knowledge, build on it, link it with other experience, and clarify the task.

Category 2 (Encouraging reflection) Teachers ask pupils for justification, explanation, ask hypothetical questions, point out inconsistency and contradiction, and suggest learning strategies.

Category 3 (Keeping on task) Teachers comment on pupils' progress, on task difficulty and provide general feedback and motivation.

Category 4 (Modelling) Teachers model reflective thinking, for example by using strategies or making contributions.

Category 5 (Promoting independence) Teachers emphasize individuality and independence in pupils' work.

Category 6 (Including peers) Teachers encourage peer contributions, peer assistance and peer judgments.

The first three categories representing the large majority of teacher talk are further divided into a number of subcategories, and discussed in detail below, with examples taken from the transcripts.

As noted in chapter 3 we used the above category system on just over 1000 teacher turns from the recordings made in the four classrooms. Transcripts which had not previously been used in devising the category system represented approximately three recorded hours of classroom experience for each target pupil. The first recordings made in each classroom were not used, in order to avoid effects of initial wariness or self-consciousness. For each target pupil two sessions were selected from both earlier and later halves of the term with a gap of some three weeks, except in the school with shorter teaching periods of forty-five minutes, where four sessions per pupil were used. In the remaining three schools the teaching sessions lasted about ninety minutes.

Percentages were judged to be the most appropriate indication of the relative importance of different categories in teachers' classroom talk because of the varying lengths of sessions in the four classrooms.

Only one untypical recorded session was excluded from analysis and replaced by another. This was a practical art lesson in which the class teacher participated but did not play a leading role. Apart from this, the sessions we analyzed were simply chosen from all those planned and recorded on pre-arranged dates.

We made the decision to confine categorization of teacher talk to that which was accessible to the target pupil, as the main focus of interest was their experience of classroom interactions with their teacher. So when a teacher addressed either a group which did not include a target pupil, or another pupil individually, this was not included. Reference to observation records was sometimes necessary to check that the teacher's talk was actually part of the target pupil's experience. As we noted in chapter 3, talk by teachers which was simply to do with classroom routines, or to visitors, was not included.

The number of teacher turns identified for analysis was quite variable from one session to another. The observational notes show that during the session with least teacher talk, almost half of the time was informal class discussion, in which the teacher encouraged pupils to ask each other questions, but did not herself probe, elaborate on or extend what pupils said.

Later in this chapter I discuss the finding that in terms of category usage the four teachers have characteristic styles. In all sessions we analyzed, both in the original derivation of the categorization system, and in the current analysis, the rank ordering of the three main categories is the same for any given teacher. Category 1 is the most frequent in classrooms 2 and 3, whereas in classrooms 1 and 4, Category 2 is predominant. Category 3 is used equally by all teachers, as are also the infrequent occurrences of 4, 5 and 6.

The nature and content of teacher talk within the different categories is now considered in more detail. Examples from the transcripts will help to clarify discussion, which at this point does not identify individual teachers or target pupils.

Category 1

This concerns pupils' understanding and knowledge of the current class activity. Teachers assess this, build on or refine it and clarify the task. They do this by direct questioning, telling, explaining, providing simple clues, making links with pupils' past experience, and summarizing. Teachers are making straightforward attempts to assess, consolidate or add to pupils' knowledge and understanding of their current activity in the classroom. In using this category, teachers are not probing and extending their pupils' thinking, drawing attention to inconsistency and illogicality, or referring to strategies. This is the important distinction between Category 1 and Category 2. Category 1 teacher talk does not demand or encourage reflection, as defined in this study. Its focus is the present task, not on extending the pupils' minds 'beyond the given'. Most of the teachers' talk in this category was initiated by them, rather than in response to pupil comments.

This large category representing 45 per cent of total relevant teacher talk is sub-divided into five, labelled A-E, in order of frequency.

1A   The teacher directly questions the pupil. Most questions are of the form who?, what?, when?, or how many? Visual materials like pictures or the blackboard are often the focus. Teachers commonly used this form of Category 1 at the beginning of sessions when they were introducing work to their pupils, in our study.
 (i)   What does it say? What is the word?
 (ii)   Does anyone recognize that creature?
 (iii) Which is the third number on the blackboard?

1B   Here the teacher builds on or modifies pupils' understanding by making corrections or contributing information. These might be initiated by the teacher or contingent upon pupils' questions or responses. Question forms by teachers rarely appeared. Teachers sometimes gave pupils straightforward clues as memory joggers, as in example (v) below, but these did not entail inferences or extended reflection of pupils.

(i)   The game is called cricket but he is trying to knock off the wicket.

(ii)   Well, that's what we call shops sometimes that belong to Pakistani people but they've got their own name.

(iii)   A trial is where they are taken to court where you have to prove somebody did something.

(iv)   The order that these letters are in is called alphabetical order.

(v)   Something that rings to tell us it's playtime.

1C   The teacher clarifies the current classroom activity, for example by outlining the procedure, summarizing progress or occasionally showing the end product, in explaining what is to be done.

(i)   The word family this week is K, curly K and kicking K.

(ii)   This is what it's going to end up like.

(iii)   So tell me the ideas we've got so far.

(iv)   You have to think about Wellington Square, so you'll have to get your DIY books and look at the story and you've got to choose the right words for the story.

1D   The teacher links the current classroom focus with pupils' previous experience, either in or out of school. Often this forms part of the teacher's introduction to the work of the session.

(i)   I think you may have heard of these letters before.

(ii)   Remember we were doing rhyming words yesterday.

(iii)   When your Mummy and Daddy were married, who was their first baby?

(iv)   When you were at the hospital, tell us, who did you see?

(v)   You know all about the roads in the city because you travel on them every day.

1E   Here teacher talk focusses on language, explaining, eliciting, or introducing new vocabulary or commenting on a pupil's usage, often indirectly as in (v) and (vi) below.

(i)   What does 'desire' mean?

(ii)   Do you know what 'winched off' means?

(iii)   That's a good word 'jamming' it.

(iv)   There's nothing wrong with 'greetin'. It's a good Scottish word.

(v)   Do you know another name for a rescue boat?

In contrast to (iv) were instances of indirectly correcting a pupil's usage by the inclusion of non-slang/non-dialect substitutions.

(vi)   Pupil: nabbed. Teacher: catch.

(vii)   Pupil: so it doesn't bash. Teacher: so it doesn't as you say get damaged.

It is not surprising that category 1A is that most frequently used by teachers. Our examples are quintessential teacher talk. All the four teachers involved in the research used a high proportion of Category 1 talk especially at the beginning of their sessions. Clearly a major concern and aim of teachers is that pupils should understand what they are to do, and gain from the classroom activity in question. So teachers' assessment of pupils' current knowledge is essential.

Teacher talk within subcategory 1A consisted almost entirely of direct questions. As commonly observed in many contexts, these did not usually result in extended responses by pupils but in brief answers or often no answer.

Talk by teachers which was categorized as 1B was less frequently in question form and appears more likely than 1A to lead to continuing discussion or to promote increased interest or understanding of the current class activity. Quite often the teacher's comments were in response to a pupil's question, like 'what's a trial?' 'what's a wicket?'

Subcategory 1C comprises talk by teachers which explained the current activity to pupils, sometimes checking pupils' understanding by asking them to repeat instructions or summarize progress as in example (iii).

In using talk in subcategory 1D teachers enhance pupils' current classroom focus by linking it with some other experience, inside or out of school. Relating new material to what a pupil already knows and finds personally meaningful and relevant makes complete sense within constructivist theories of learning, and is a frequent recommendation to teachers in such forms as 'start where the child is at'.

There were a number of occasions within 1E where a teacher gently substituted an alternative for a pupil's slang expression, and others when Scottish usage was pointed out and pupils assured that it was entirely acceptable, as in the example of 'greetin' cited here.

Analysis of teacher talk into subcategories enriches our knowledge and understanding. It is not helpful to quote percentages here as overall numbers are not large. However, all four teachers' talk was represented in all subcategories, and direct questioning was prominent, especially in the talk of teacher 2.

Category 2

Category 2 is that most directly and obviously central to the theme of this book, the encouragement of pupils to reflect. Our use of the term 'reflection' includes reasoning, as in the detection of ambiguity, inconsistency and illogicality, and the justification and clarification of ideas.

In contrast to Category 1 usage, teachers' talk now aims to extend pupils' thinking beyond the immediate classroom task. Pupils are asked to justify and explain their contributions: inconsistencies and errors are explored by the teacher, and learning strategies may be discussed. Importantly teachers were responding to pupils' comments in a large proportion of instances.

This category represents 28 per cent of all teacher talk in our sample. Like Category 1, it is subdivided into five groups, A-E in order of frequency, although there was not a large variation in this.

2A   Most frequent are teachers' exploration of pupils' errors, difficulties and inconsistencies. As the following examples show such teacher language was often quite complex, and pupils were often left to think about their teacher's remark, which was frequently in question form.
   (i)   Oh, you couldn't both have won. I don't think that's possible.
   (ii)   What does cross mean then if it doesn't mean you're angry?
   (iii)   So if you're feeling miserable you might not be too happy, but would you have to be cross if you were miserable?
   (iv)   Because it's raining doesn't mean it's winter.
   (v)   You can't get hills on a road? Have you ever driven over a hill on a road?
   In many dialogues teachers were engaging in consultation with pupils concerning ways of improving their work. The following examples came from one teacher.
   (vi)   You said 'once'. Do you want me to change that?
   (vii)   Right. Well, I don't think we put that in the story did we?
   (viii) How can we say that better?

2B   Here, teachers explore pupils' ideas, often asking for explanations or justifications. 'Why?' and 'why do you think?' were frequent questions in our data, but there was an important contrast between these and Category 1 questions. Category 2 questions were more open ended, and often did not imply that there was a correct answer. The pupil's thinking process was emphasized rather than the answer. 'You' occurred frequently in teacher talk, as in 'what do you notice?', 'why do you think?' and 'what does that tell you?'
   (i)   Why is it melting?
   (ii)   What does that mean?
   (iii)   Why would they be having eight-legged races?
   (iv)   Why have you made his face red?
   (v)   Can you tell us why you think the roads are white?

2C   2C is of similar frequency to 2B, and comprises teacher contributions which are analogical or causal in nature. Here the information was not factual, as in subcategory 1B but was more elliptical, so that pupils were encouraged to make inferences, and draw their own conclusions.
   (i)   When we are using the overhead projector we have to stand to the side because if you stand in front of it (demonstrates) watch what happens.
   (ii)   He might have got a punch on the nose. So that's the problem with this isn't it?

(iii)   We can check that. Now turn the square round and see if that side is the same length as that one.

(iv)   Your feet grow while you are growing, just like you.

(v)   What happens if you put varnish on that bit?

Practical demonstrations often accompanied teacher talk in Category 2C, as in our examples (i) and (iii), with the effect of holding pupils' attention, often in a joking way.

2D   Teacher talk concerns rules and strategies to help pupils' thinking, reminding them to check, and to be aware of other people's likely misunderstanding. Again teachers are extending pupils beyond the immediate task in a range of ways.

(i)   Just read them to yourself and ask yourself if it makes sense.

(ii)   Is that dog changing colour? Remember when you read a story they don't change.

(iii)   So when is the appointment? Check up because people don't hear things. They make mistakes so always double check.

(iv)   Have they got a magic E? No you only get a magic E when it's at the end of a word.

All four examples referred to current work and suggested specific strategies. Occasionally teachers made more general statements about remembering, checking, and discussion.

(v)   You will always be able to remember her and all the happy things you did. You'll always be able to make pictures of her in your head and that's important.

(vi)   There's always a way of working things out rather than hitting people.

Such examples are quite rare in our data.

2E   Finally an important subdivision concerns teachers' use of hypothetical questions, imaginary situations and role playing situations to engage pupils in relating the immediate classroom task to a wider range of possibilities. Examples (i) and (ii) occurred in a lively and enjoyable class discussion of how a bicycle works.

(i)   What would happen if it was made of something like string?

(ii)   They wouldn't be any good if they were made of sponge or jelly.

(iii)   Was it big? What happens if I fill the bag with feathers?

(iv)   Imagine you were moving. What would you want to do first?

One teacher frequently used hypothetical situations in role playing and communication activities to focus pupils' thinking on the likely misapprehension, assumptions, or lack of knowledge of other people.

(v)   Do we want to tell her a bit more? She doesn't know anything about him. She might think he lives in Edinburgh.

(vi)   If you were really the person who had to send out the Fire Brigade what kind of thing would you be checking up on?

(vii)   If we say 'he's a fisherman' will she know who the story is about?

The teacher talk in Category 2 differed from that in Category 1 in that it was usually occurring when teaching sessions were under way, and not at the beginning. It also tended to be in response to pupil talk or activities, and less frequently to be initiated by the teacher. It had the potential to encourage reflection by pupils in two ways, which might at first glance appear to be contradictory.

First, by focussing on pupils' reasoning, and challenging them to extend their thinking by giving explanations and justifications, drawing conclusions and making judgments, teachers were responding in a clear explicit way to what pupils said or did. This response was immediate and contingent, directly related to what preceded it. So in some subcategory 2A and 2B statements teachers challenged the logic and accuracy of pupils' remarks, and in 2C they encouraged their pupils to consider the consequences of possible events. It is notable that in the latter case these were not at all far removed from their pupils' current focus of attention.

A second way in which teacher talk stressed reflection by pupils is found in subcategories 2D and 2E. Here pupils were guided by teachers into considering in more general terms whether something made sense, or were reminded to check, and that other people were likely to misunderstand and thus would need clear unambiguous information. The language in some of the illustrative examples, 'Do we want to?', and 'If we say', give a strong impression of meaning being jointly negotiated and agreed, between teacher and pupil.

Category 3

Category 3 talk by teachers includes general references to effort, task difficulty and the need to listen hard, think carefully and pay attention. It comprised 16 per cent of the teacher talk which was analyzed in our study, and is also further divided into four subgroups, A-D, in order of frequency of occurrence. Although this category, as we have already noted, was employed more evenly between the four teachers in our study than were categories 1 and 2, there was considerable variation between individual sessions. It ranged from 43 per cent of all of one teacher's talk in one session, to 6 per cent in another: clearly as one might expect its use by teachers is dependent on circumstances, like occasions when pupils are emotionally upset.

3A Teachers give general feedback concerning their pupils' progress. This is not specifically focussed on the task as in Category 1 but is clearly intended to help pupils to keep going. The focus of teacher comments is on success, progress and behaviour.

(i) You haven't finished it. There's a difference between finishing it and nearly finishing it.

(ii) I know it's a bit difficult for you but keep trying. You're doing very well.

(iii) Right let me see. That's good. Brilliant.

3B   Here there is explicit reference to attentional aspects of pupils' behaviour, like their level of concentration, or rushing to finish their work.
    (i)   You are dreaming aren't you?
    (ii)   You can't win the game unless you are watching, right?
    (iii)   Just calm down and read carefully.
    (iv)   You weren't thinking hard.
    (v)   You want to just get on don't you, can't be bothered waiting.
    (vi)   Hey, that sounded like playground talk to me.

3C   This comprises teachers' comments on the difficulty of the activity, the effort made, time taken and general progress. Such comments were often made to the whole class and used the term 'we'.
    (i)   That's a difficult one. I think we will have to do some work on that one.
    (ii)   Right now, you have been doing that page for the last ten minutes.
    (iii)   We have only heard it a few times so it might be very difficult to remember.
    (iv)   Now that is a hard sheet but I'm sure you can do it.

3D   Teachers make explicit use of incentives to help pupils work. Several references were made in our study to points gained or lost, or to the break to come.
    (i)   Now I have to say that yesterday she worked the hardest I have ever known her to work and she got a lot of points, so are we going to try and do the same today?
    (ii)   Every word that you can read without a problem you will get to colour it in.
    (iii)   I am very disappointed in you. Maybe you will have to come in at break to do it.
    (iv)   Looking forward to those sandwiches are you?
    (v)   Those people who have finished will manage to get started on the big drawings.

Teachers' use of Category 3 talk varied from session to session, and was often high for an obvious reason, as when a pupil was upset or (as happened rarely) disruptive. The highest use of Category 3 was accounted for by a teacher giving a great deal of general rather than more specifically focussed feedback to her pupils.

Category 4

Here the teacher models reflective thinking, offering personal contributions to discussion, admitting difficulty, 'thinking aloud', and planning and checking. All four of our teachers did this from time to time although the overall frequency was small. They did not explicitly refer to strategies but showed them in practical use and several of their contributions in the examples below indicate their willingness to share their fallibility and lack of understanding.

Teachers' personal contributions were not factual but there were several examples like the following, and these were often made during group discussions.

(i)   I've not heard of that one.
(ii)   I can think of one more thing.
(iii)   I'll keep those because I can't decide.
(iv)   It's like groping in the dark working out what he means.

Thinking aloud usually took the form of wondering aloud, puzzling, often during group discussions or activities.

(v)   I suppose they will have to change the rules.
(vi)   I wonder what some of those things could have been.

There were a few examples, too, in our data, of teachers modelling the use of simple strategies in comments like:

(vii)   I don't really understand that, do you? Shall we check and see what it says?
(viii) Let's see what's next on my list.
(ix)   It's all terribly complicated for me to take in. Do you know why? It's because there's so many people.
(x)   This word looks a bit strange to me because I think you've got it the wrong way round.

Category 5

Talk by teachers in this category emphasizes the value of individual contributions, pupils' own ideas, personal references, and thinking for themselves. Examples in the recordings are fairly infrequent but occurred in all sessions that were analysed and are of interest to the study.

(i)   You like these ones, the five minute thrillers do you?
(ii)   It's got to be something different. You can't use the same ideas.
(iii)   Do you never get angry then?
(iv)   What do you like? Do you like being in a team or do you like being the one who has to go and catch people?
(v)   There's no right or wrong answers. It's what you think.

Category 6

Teacher talk which concerns peers helping, explaining or evaluating other pupils' comments or work occurred rarely, in only 1 per cent of all teacher talk considered here.

(i)   Do you think what he did was a good idea?
(ii) Could you explain to him what we are doing.
(iii) No, it's a soft sound. Listen to her.
(iv) She knows how to do it. She'll tell you.
(v)   Is she right? How many do you think, Sandy?

Within the present limitations of examining only teacher talk there was very little evidence of pupils' explanations or discussion with peers as an integral part of classroom life, planned and encouraged by the teacher. Role play activities in one class are discussed in chapter 6. These were the general exception to the finding that teachers' encouragement of peer contributions was infrequent.

Teacher Style

We now turn from the characteristics of the six categories and their distribution within the recorded teacher talk considered as a whole, to a consideration of their use by individual teachers.

A major interest in the research was whether the classroom talk of our four teachers might show consistent patterns of category preference. An early impression that this might be so was gained from the research assistant's classroom observations, and this was reinforced by the experience of initial transcription of the audiotapes. Further evidence of consistent teacher styles in category usage was available in the analysis of their classroom talk.

Once the category system had been decided upon, we confined its subsequent use to classroom talk by teachers which was accessible to the respective target pupil for that session, as noted in chapter 3. This meant it was either addressed to that pupil or to a group of which he/she was a member. There were two reasons for this restriction. First it enabled a judgment to be made concerning the possibility that a teacher might pay special attention to the target pupil during the session in which he wore a microphone. This would have meant a departure from her usual classroom practice and an unrepresentative atypical experience for the target pupil. This was not in fact found, as we show below. Secondly it was important to maintain the focus on the target pupils' experience within the classroom, to clarify our thinking about the reflective episodes in which they were involved, which are described in detail in chapter 6.

The four teachers wore radiomicrophones for every recorded session, and almost all their talk was clearly audible and relatively easy to transcribe. The large body of teacher talk which did not involve or reach the target pupil was not lost but remained available in the transcripts for later inspection if we so wished.

Table 4 shows the proportion of talk by the four teachers within each of the six categories. Percentages are more appropriate than raw figures because session lengths did vary around the average of three hours which were analyzed for each of the eight target pupils. These consisted of two sessions each, selected from earlier and later parts of the term, for three classrooms, and a total of four shorter sessions for the remaining one (that of Mrs Macdonald). Overall more than 1000 teacher utterances were categorized, and these were distributed fairly evenly across the sessions.

Table 4 shows, quite strikingly, that the proportions of different categories used by the four teachers remained surprisingly similar, across different sessions, with different target pupils and a range of curricular activities. Moreover the rank order of frequency of category use by the four teachers was the same both in the data originally used to derive the category system, and in teacher talk which directly affected the target pupil and is summarized in table 4. These are the findings that justify the claim that the teachers used consistent styles in their talk with pupils.

The evidence that a teacher uses a particular style in classroom interactions rests, in our research, on identifiable characteristics which are found during different curricular activities and on different occasions. A particular style is believed to represent something consistent and fairly basic to a particular teacher. It must have developed as a result of experienced teachers' judgments of what is effective, as well as from their feelings of what is comfortable and appropriate for them. Later, chapter 7 suggests that teachers' long-held, deep seated, perhaps never fully articulated beliefs about pupils, education and learning, are related to their style.

One would also anticipate that teachers' styles, in mirroring their deep seated beliefs and values, will be associated with their classroom's ethos and their organizational and curricular preferences. These will also be explored later.

As shown in table 4 the same category remained dominant for all four teachers across different sessions. The main difference lay in their use of Categories 1 and 2. Mrs Guthrie and Mrs Law used more than twice as much Category 2 talk as Mrs Macdonald and a great deal more than Mrs Stevenson. Correspondingly, Mrs Guthrie and Mrs Law used much less Category 1 talk than did the other two teachers. The percentages in the remaining categories did not differ greatly, and Categories 4, 5 and 6 together made up less than one-tenth of the total talk that was categorized.

Henceforth, for clarity and simplicity, the teacher style which uses a lot of Category 2 talk, is described as encouraging reflection, because that is what the teachers using it are trying to do. It makes no claim at this stage regarding effectiveness. This is discussed in chapter 6.

The target pupils' classroom experiences are the subject of chapter 5.

Table 4 Teacher talk categorized (as % of total)

Category	1	(mean)	2	(mean)	3	(mean)	4	(mean)	5	(mean)	6	(mean)
Teacher / Target pupil												
Mrs Guthrie Andrew	32		50		6		9		3			
Mark	36	(34)	36	(43)	17	(11)	4	(7)	7	(5)	2	(2)
Mrs Stevenson Johnnie	57		6		26		8		1		2	
Lynne	69	(63)	4	(5)	17	(22)	4	(6)	4	(2)	1	(2)
Mrs Macdonald Alastair	53		21		21		4		1		1	
Donald	62	(57)	16	(19)	10	(16)	7	(5)	5	(3)		
Mrs Law Emma	33		47		8		7		4		1	
Samantha	23	(28)	44	(45)	19	(14)	7	(7)	5	(4)	2	(2)
Mean		(45)		(28)		(16)		(6)		(4)		(1)

5   The Locus of Reflection: Pupils' Classroom Experiences

> Efficient learners bring to bear on typical learning situations a number of resources that facilitate learning in new domains: they have learned to learn. They tend to profit more — learn more rapidly and transfer more broadly — than poorer learners from objectively identical learning situations because they know more about learning and supplement for themselves the information afforded. They apportion effort appropriately, continually monitor progress, know when and how to ask for advice and so on. (Brown *et al.*, 1983)

The 'efficient learners' described in Brown's classic paper appear very different from those who were described in chapter 2 as opting out of learning with a deep sense of failure and bewilderment. After examining evidence of reflection in pupils' language use, this chapter considers several aspects of the eight target pupils' classroom experience which are associated with their teachers' emphasis on reflection. First we examine the pupils' use of reflective language in class: the spontaneous and appropriate production of terms like 'know', 'wonder', 'understand', 'remember', and logical connectives such as 'if', 'so' and 'because', are evidence that these are accessible and familiar. Many studies of these areas of semantic development conclude that the early primary years typically see marked changes towards mature understanding and use. Our target pupils would be expected to be developing along similar lines, if perhaps rather slowly.

Powerful contextual effects on their use and understanding of reflective language would also be expected, like that reported by Phillips (1985). He found that 10–12-year-olds used very different talk in teacherless peer group discussions from that in groups led by a teacher. Hypothetical and experiential talk by the pupils was almost entirely confined to the teacherless situation. Yet such talk (for example, the use of 'what about . . . ?' and 'I remember when . . .') provides the ideal framework for reflection, encouraging pupils to go beyond the immediately present 'given' context, and to become actively involved, as Phillips says, in their own learning.

I referred in chapter 2 to the research by Powell and Makin (1994), with 12 and 13-year-olds attending a school for pupils with moderate learning difficulties. Their production of hypothetical and experiential language was encouraged and increased in group situations where they described their work to their peers and teacher, who provided constructive feedback. These pupils were found to need a teacher's specific focussed feedback to help them move towards more independent learning, but this was effective in a group context.

Evidence that our target pupils had access to a basic reflective language was an encouraging sign that the facilitation by teachers of their reasoning, problem solving and metacognition would be appropriate. At this point the contexts of pupils' use of such language were not examined, and there was no attempt to differentiate between particular target pupils and classrooms, but to obtain a general picture.

Three aspects of our target pupils' classroom experiences are also explored in this chapter and related to their teachers' style of classroom talk. First is the proportion of time pupils were engaged in individual or group activities: second, the nature and length of the classroom conversations in which they took part, and third, their response to a new situation.

Finally, the brief post-session comments made by both target pupils and their teachers illustrate their respective satisfactions and frustrations and the degree of agreement between them.

Target Pupils' Reflective Talk

This section describes target pupils' talk which was recorded in a limited sample of classroom sessions, all of them judged to be satisfactory by the teacher concerned, and to be representative of that particular classroom. All took place towards the latter part of the term, when the recording equipment and observer had become familiar to both teachers and pupils.

The recorded sessions whose transcripts for target pupils' talk lasted between sixty and ninety minutes. There is no attempt here to quantify the different types of reflective talk, or to identify particular target pupils. The interest lies in answering the following questions:

(i) Did the target pupils use the language of reflection? Did they talk of knowing, thinking, understanding, or of being unsure? Did they spontaneously make links with related experiences?

Did pupils' talk show signs of 'going beyond the given', providing explanations, predictions, hypotheses and inferences during problem solving and reasoning? Further, did pupils' talk indicate their awareness and use of specific strategies such as checking and planning, and adjusting their communication to the needs of their listener?

(ii) Did pupils monitor, evaluate and sustain their own current mental activity? This would be the pupil equivalent of the Category 3 talk by their teachers, which referred to progress, effort, interest, attention and occasionally to rewards or sanctions.

The following illustrations from our target pupils provide answers to these questions. The person to whom the pupil spoke is indicated by T (teacher), P (peer) or S (self), and there is no detailed discussion of the context, because this is considered in relation to the reflective episodes in chapter 6.

What is significant here is the evidence of some reflective talk being used in the classroom by all eight target pupils. It is more prominent in some classrooms, but all the pupils at some time used reflective talk spontaneously and appropriately. We can infer that they were confident and comfortable with this usage, whether they were initiating, responding or talking to themselves.

The Language of Thinking

All the pupils talked frequently of knowing, and not knowing and some of thinking, doubting, wondering and forgetting, mainly in answer to teachers' questions:

for example   I forgot to say . . .
                I recognize . . .
                I was wondering . . .
                I dinnae ken . . .
                I doubt it . . .
                I think . . .

Pupils' talk often also expressed their hesitancy, speculation and uncertainty. This was usually in direct response to a teacher's question or Category 2 type utterance like: 'Why do you think that?'

for example   Maybe going duck shooting (T)
                I was going to say eight there (T)
                That might be the sister in the family (T)
                It looks like, mince, spaghetti and sauce (T)

Often, but not always in response to a teacher's Category 2 prompt, there were explanations and justification by pupils:

for example   Because the twelve's pointing that way (T)
                So the germs won't spread (T)
                You're on the red book, that's why (P)
                and (picking up on a work sheet error). They must have forgot to put another word there (P)

Hypothetical statements, predictions and inferences were quite common, and were often addressed to peers in the sessions we sampled, as in all the following examples:

for example   I wish I could hear everything Tony is saying in his mind (P)
                You'll get a point if you do extra (P)

You can poke someone's eye out doing that (P)
You wouldn't catch either of them (P)
Better move that in case anybody stands on them (P)

Evidence of our target pupils' awareness of strategies to help their problem solving or communication was present in remarks such as the following:

How can you count that much, Miss? (T)
I've not got a number line. I just use a ruler (T)
That's what we say 'on the blink' (T)
How could I put it? (T)

and with their peers

Does that make sense? (P)
We're missing something (P)
Let me see how you've wrote 'balloon' (P)

There were many occasions when pupils' talk indicated that they were having difficulty, but they only infrequently asked for help from their teacher, and this when it happened was in general, not specific terms. Pupils' remarks about their difficulties were much more likely to be addressed to themselves or to their peers:

for example   I don't know how to do it (S)
I need help here (S)
Still make it wrong (S)
We're in a little bit of a muddle (P)
What do you do here? (P)

Pupils' Self-monitoring Talk

Pupils in all the classrooms made frequent comments about their general progress, the difficulty of their work, and occasionally about the points they hoped to gain. This is the pupils' equivalent of Category 3 talk by their teachers, and is similar in not being specific, not truly conversational and not usually responded to. Its function is, surely, self-regulation and self-monitoring, a means of keeping track of what one is doing, maintaining attention and motivation.

Such talk was occasionally addressed to teachers, but more often to other pupils or to the speakers themselves. Much of it would have never been heard but for the radiomicrophones.

There were references to general progress:

I'm whizzing through my maths (T)
I've only got one left (T)

I've made it before they came back (T)
Which one are we at? (S)
Where was I? (S)

Comments on task difficulty:

Dead easy (T)
Nae bother (S)
Getting a bit harder now (S)

Surprisingly perhaps we found no complaints that work was too hard, but at times about the difficulty in attending:

I can't hear myself doing it (T)
That was boring! (S)

The few comments about rewards were made to peers:

I've not got much points because I've been off (P)
You'll get a point if you do extra (P)

As might be expected self-monitoring talk occurred most frequently when pupils were engaged in individual work, when they appeared relaxed and were not under time pressure. In classroom 3, which was the most time conscious with shorter sessions and frequent reminders from the teacher to hurry up and to finish the work, there were very few examples. One perhaps significant remark from a target pupil in that class after a session in which he had played a game may illustrate this point. He said that he hadn't been able to hear his friends when they were playing a card game because the teacher had talked too much. The teacher in question felt the session had gone well and that the target pupil was relaxed and participating well. On another occasion the same pupil said that the most difficult thing he had to do was to listen to his teacher, and several times he said he didn't know what he was doing.

His teacher said that he found it difficult to keep on task, and didn't have the zest and enthusiasm of the others. The pupil appeared conscientious and anxious although the tasks were not challenging. With very little opportunity to talk, to pace himself and to monitor his classroom activity he was unusual in expressing his unhappiness and dissatisfaction at the close of each recorded session. His teacher believed him to be overconfident and her constant reminders to keep working were designed to maintain his attention but may well have increased his obvious anxiety, and feelings of lack of control.

In summary, from only a small quantity of the total recorded pupil talk we have obtained some affirmative answers to the questions posed in this section.

Target pupils did verbally monitor their own progress and had access to useful reflective language. The illustrations show how this was used in appropriate situations, often informally with peers.

As already noted in chapter 3 there was overall little planned work for small groups which required cooperation and shared goals. Target pupils' talk with peers was often confident and helpful in tone and was sometimes relatively complex, as in those examples which were conditional or hypothetical in form. In this respect there was often a contrast with their very terse, uninformative, and inhibited talk to their teachers. The potential of working towards more planned peer collaboration is considered later in this chapter.

In addition to the reassuring presence of some reflective talk by all target pupils are some striking omissions. During the sessions recorded there were no instances of pupils relating the current focus of activity to their previous experience either in or out of school, whether in terms of factual information, procedures or strategies. Their teachers all frequently did make explicit connections, but none of the sampled target pupils' talk included examples like:

'that reminds me of . . .'
or 'it's like when we . . .'

which would be described as experiential language by Phillips (1985).

This may be strong evidence of the difficulty and rarity of spontaneous generalisation, so frequently described in pupils who experience difficulties in learning, and underlining their need for explicit reminders and instructions. Our teachers made such links with pupils' experiences both in and out of school. The fact that pupils did not do so may suggest that links could be highlighted by different means. There could be more emphasis on pupils explaining procedures, or giving instructions to each other, for example, thus learning from personal experience how important it is to build on and cooperate with another person's current knowledge and understanding. Group discussions could facilitate pupils' search for similar relevant experiences.

Another feature of note is the rarity of specific requests for their teachers' help by pupils. Although they were sometimes heard to say to themselves that they were stuck, or didn't understand their work they tended to wait for the teacher to check on their level of understanding and identify their problem. Where pupils did admit to difficulties they were very unspecific, rarely verbalizing where their working had led them or identifying for themselves the source of difficulty. In some but not all one-to-one situations pupils tended to say things like 'I canna', or 'I dinnae ken how to' . . . with a rather helpless sounding, extremely unconfident, wary tone of voice, which sometimes contrasted markedly with that they used with their peers. One-to-one teaching might be assumed to be ideal situations for enabling teachers and pupils together to identify and resolve difficulties in learning. But early indications from our data were that this was not often happening. Further examination of pupils' group experiences follows.

Table 5   Pupil grouping as % of total time

Teacher	Group	Individual
Mrs Guthrie	47	38
Mrs Stevenson	34	53
Mrs Macdonald	37	50
Mrs Law	57	29

Classroom Grouping

As shown in table 2, earlier, one of the noticeable features of the classrooms of the two teachers whose styles most emphasized reflection was the comparatively small amount of time spent on individual teaching. Table 5 summarizes information concerning this averaged over all the recorded sessions and expressed in percentage terms.

These percentages mask considerable variation between individual sessions, and for the sake of clarity only two major groupings are distinguished here. Individual work involved pupils working in their peers' presence but without any explicit cooperation, usually tackling their own work at their own pace. Group activity comprised whole class and smaller groupings, which might involve discussion and cooperative activity to a greater or lesser extent. Waiting for the teacher, for instructions, doing nothing and time out of the classroom made up the remaining time of between 12 per cent and 15 per cent.

It is immediately clear that in both classrooms where there was a high proportion of Category 2 teacher talk, there was also considerably more group activity and correspondingly less time when pupils worked as individuals.

Complex talk from some target pupils in the form of predictions and hypotheses, was only found (and that was rarely) when they spoke informally to peers, as were also their admissions of difficulty. This partly results from opportunities being very reduced in the short sessions of classroom 3 with a strong emphasis on completing set, rather undemanding, curricular tasks, but there is additional evidence of a degree of pupil inhibition in one to one teaching situations. A striking example comes from classroom 1 where there was a notably cheerful and relaxed ethos, when Mrs Guthrie moved her chair close to the target pupil to see his writing, something he found difficult because of poor motor control.

> *TP:*   I've done it Miss. Now go away.
>
> *T:*   You surprise me. I'm not going away just yet. I want to just be sure.
>
> *TP:*   Dinnae look.
>
> *T:*   One more . . . you've written it beautifully . . .

> *TP*:   Go away Miss. I'm not doing this until you go away. Take your
>   damn chair.

(T moved to other pupils, returning briefly to TP after he had calmed down.)

Such a sense of exposure in pupils is not usually so clearly expressed by our
target pupils but is conveyed by their flat tones of voice and terse replies in
this situation in several sessions. Individual teaching offers teachers many opportunities for promoting reflection by means of appropriate contingent responses, but only if their pupils are sufficiently engaged at the time, and only
if they feel emotionally secure. Pupils will then be able to make progress in
episodes which challenge and 'stretch' them. However such episodes may
occur less frequently during individual teaching for other reasons in addition
to pupils' vulnerability to feelings of exposure like that shown in our example.

Alexander (1992) neatly expressed an inherent dilemma for teachers in
primary mainstream classes.

> The more accessible teachers seek to make themselves to all pupils as
> individuals, the less time they have for direct extended and challeng-
> ing interaction with any of them: but the more time they devote to
> such extended interaction with some children, the less demanding on
> them as teachers must be the activities they give to the rest: and the
> less demanding an activity is of their time and attention as teachers,
> the more the likelihood that the activity in question will demand little
> of the child.

Teachers often report that they feel more relaxed with a group because they
are less aware of the need to allocate their time between individual pupils who
are waiting their turn, and thus feel more able to dwell on topics and to follow
up pupils' ideas. This is supported by two of our teachers' views on grouping,
which are more fully reported in chapter 7.

> A lot of work is whole class, just differentiating by my expectations,
> of, you know, expectations of what is to come from each child, either
> in terms of pace or quality.

Mrs Macdonald pointed out that in her experience one-to-one teaching of
pupils was very difficult, as:

> Even with ten pupils they are all very demanding, and they all want
> to have their say, and they all want a bit of you, and to have even five
> minutes to hear someone read and not be interrupted by other people
> is near on a miracle.

This teacher described how she was 'on call' during the extensive periods in
which pupils did individual work in her class. She worked hard to keep pupils'
attention on their task, and monitored this during their periods of individual

work. Her vigilance and diligence in this respect, however, could be counter-productive as continual reminders and responses to all pupils meant that her attention to any one of them was fragmented and interrupted by responding to the 'calls' of others.

For example, in one session, during ten minutes of reading to the teacher the target pupil was interrupted more than twenty times as Mrs Macdonald spoke to other pupils. An illustrative excerpt follows:

T: . . . So what are these men doing?

TP: Moving.

T: (to another P) Steven, two seconds, if you've got a problem. Right, now don't interrupt other people, cos they're busy.

TP: They're moving the furniture in.

T: Right, they're moving the furniture in. (To another P) Could you get me a pen, love? They're moving the furniture into the house and can they get it in easily?
      (To P) No, one of the felt-tipped ones.

P: Someone has the rubber.

T: (to another P) Right, stop it. Close your folder and put it on the floor. I said put your folder on the floor. Now, the next step is I move you. Is there a problem?
      (To TP) Now, what's happening in this picture?

Such fragmented interactions were not the norm during pupils' individual work, but similar examples of teachers' endeavours to respond to a range of different pupil demands did occur at other times, and are reminiscent of the well known work of Bennett *et al.* (1984). Here one of the most salient findings was that teachers who were committed to individualized teaching certainly addressed most of their talk to individual pupils, but that it was very often of brief duration and likely to be frequently interrupted by the teacher's perceived need to correct, advise or remove other pupils. Encounters that were directed at exploring the level of pupil knowledge, skill, or understanding, they reported, appeared to mainly consist of checking or giving the pupil the correct answer. It is perhaps surprising to observe the same tendency in the much smaller special school class. Our observations indicate that opportunities for pupils to think deeply will not be fostered where the pupil's intellectual focus is not shared by the teacher and where adequate time for concentration is not available.

During the interviews described in chapter 7 the teachers gave many good reasons for the relative infrequency of collaborative group work in their classrooms, and generally they agreed that this was a loss, of what, under good conditions and with unobtrusive adult assistance and monitoring, can be a very productive experience. Pupils can learn so much from negotiating interactions, learning to repair breakdowns in understanding and to consider their peers' ideas in what Edwards and Mercer (1987) call an 'unrehearsed intellectual adventure', and one of our teachers called 'learning to be a social being', through working in collaboration.

Classroom Conversations

Our discussion now moves to conversations between our target pupils and others within their classrooms. Reflective episodes, periods of particular significance for pupils' cognitive engagement are discussed in detail in the next chapter. Here we outline more general features concerning classroom conversations in our study and make links with the teacher talk described in chapter 4.

An enormous amount of classroom research has concluded that pupil-teacher conversations are often disappointingly brief and dull, and unrewarding to both partners. Researchers such as Wells (1985) have contrasted the same children's talk at home (fluent, challenging, more complex) and at school (limited, safe, terse). Wood (1992) and others have shown what dramatic changes can result from teachers' deliberate alteration and monitoring of their way of talking to pupils, by cutting down on questioning, for example. Wood says 'I have found that youngsters will respond to speculation with speculation, hypothesis with hypothesis, and suggestion with interpretation.' And more recent work by Wood within special schools has found that teachers there are particularly prone to adopt controlling pedagogies, and especially with those pupils who have the greatest learning difficulties.

It was clearly of interest to examine the nature and length of classroom conversations and to relate these to the teachers' style of interaction. My aim here was not to conduct a quantitative exercise, but to sample a limited number of recorded classroom sessions, and to identify and describe the classroom conversations occurring within them. Conversations for this purpose consisted of sequences of speakers' 'turns', focused on a topic. Turns are utterances which are bounded by a pause or by another speaker. Both turns and the conversations they composed were readily identifiable from the typed transcripts of the single recorded session selected for each target pupil from the latter half of the term in which classroom recordings were made. The teacher concerned had judged each to be satisfactory.

All the conversations involved the target pupil, the teacher or helper and sometimes other pupils. As extended sequences of talk were the main interest, only those of three or more turns were included. The number of turns in each identified conversation was counted, and an average calculated for each session.

Table 6 shows the mean number of turns in the conversations the eight target pupils took part in, in the randomly selected sessions.

Conversations were longer on average in classrooms 1 and 4, where the teachers' style was more focused on reflection than in the remaining classrooms, although extended dialogues did occur at some time in all four. It is also immediately obvious that the commonly observed 'typical' three turn teacher-pupil dialogue consisting simply of initiation by teacher, response by pupil and (terminal) feedback by teacher is not the norm in these classrooms. Such sequences, often abbreviated to IRE or IRF, standing for initiation (by teacher), response (by pupil) and evaluation or feedback (by teacher), have

Table 6   Mean length of classroom conversations (in turns)

Teacher	Target pupil	Mean number of turns	Overall % Category 2 in teacher talk
Mrs Guthrie	Andrew	8.1	43
	Mark	11.6	
Mrs Stevenson	Johnnie	7.3	5
	Lynne	7.4	
Mrs Macdonald	Alastair	7.0	19
	Donald	7.0	
Mrs Law	Emma	16.0	45
	Samantha	30.1	

Table 7   Categorized teacher talk in classroom conversations, expressed as percentage

	Category of teacher talk		
	1	2	3
Longer classroom conversations ≥ 9 turns	39	49	9
Shorter classroom conversations < 9 turns	51	14	30

been called the 'essential teaching exchange', and this quintessential classroom talk has been found in many observational studies of educational settings to be overwhelming in its dominance. In this respect in our special schools are very different from many mainstream settings where pupils are not experiencing such marked difficulties in learning, and where class sizes are much bigger.

Table 6 indicates that where teachers emphasized reflection by pupils, conversations tended to be longer on average. Length in itself is not a guarantee of quality. Such judgments can only be made by examining the content and nature of conversations as well as the number of participants. If a few very long conversations for example, in classroom 4, had involved only one pupil and the teacher they would have effectively prevented other pupils' participation. However, in this class, long focused discussions included several pupils and so were more likely to be cognitively enriching experiences for all of them.

The importance of the teachers' style of classroom talk was examined further, by grouping all the conversations from the sessions into longer and shorter ones. The convenient cut off point of nine turns was used to differentiate conversations, and the percentage of teacher turns falling within the three main Categories 1, 2 and 3 was calculated.

As table 7 shows, longer classroom conversations contained proportionately much more Category 2 talk by teachers, and this was relatively infrequent in shorter dialogues. So not only do we have the rather general finding, that in the two classrooms whose teachers habitually used more Category 2 talk, conversations are longer on average, as shown in table 6, but we also have more specific evidence that this category of teacher talk is prominent within such sustained classroom conversations. There is clear evidence that the more challenging teaching style is not inhibiting pupils, but appears to encourage their sustained participation in classroom dialogues.

The lack of Category 3 talk in longer conversations is an interesting sign that general feedback and encouragement from teachers did not have this effect. Category 1 talk was prominent in all sessions, especially towards the beginning, when teachers were engaged in assessing pupils' knowledge and their understanding of what they were to do. Longer conversations including more challenging talk by teachers tended to appear later in the sessions, especially in classrooms 1 and 4.

The following two episodes illustrate some of the characteristic features of shorter and longer classroom dialogues. Longer sequences contain a high proportion of Category 2 talk by teachers, more pupil participation, and longer pupil utterances. Shorter classroom dialogues often contain monosyllabic utterances by pupils and a high proportion of teachers' Category 1 questions.

The first comes from classroom 2, where Lynne, the target pupil (TP) is sewing with the classroom helper (H), and another pupil (P). In this classroom such long conversations were very infrequent, so this is an important exception.

H: Is your Mum coming to the sale and coffee morning?

TP: I think so. It depends if my Dad doesn't get called into work.

H: Oh I see, where does he work?

TP: At the sewage.

H: Oh, at the sewage, I see.

TP: In (place name).

H: If he's on call he's got to stay, has he?

TP: My Mum cannot come cos it's my Dad who'll drive.

H: Oh, that's right. Where is it you stay?

P: Ask your Dad to take you then.

TP: How can I?

H: That's what she's saying if you listen. She's saying if her Dad's got to be on call for his work then . . .

TP: Who could take me?

P: It's your Mum.

TP: My Mum doesn't drive.

P: Why?

TP: Because . . . I'm not telling you.

P: She can drive if she's a lady.

TP: All women don't drive.

H: Lots of people don't drive.

P: My Mum can drive.

This episode, in a relaxed informal setting of a practical activity, is an excellent example of reasoning, explanation and the correction of misapprehension. The helper continued the conversation and unobtrusively clarified possible misunderstandings. Lynne's logic is impeccable when she says that the fact that some women drive, as P has said, does not mean that all women do.

A typical short interchange in classroom 3 occurred when the teacher (T) was testing pupils' memory for a story.

T: What's that picture of?
P: Leaves.
T: You were right the first time. What's that a picture of?
TP: A pile of leaves.
T: Good.

This extract comes from a tightly organised lesson using discussion of reading material which is focused to the extent that there is little opportunity to 'go beyond the information given'. The story does refer to the protagonists' feelings and motivation but the pupils did not seem to be engaged or to identify with the story events.

In the absence of such engagement and identification, classroom conversations were short, desultory and unchallenging for both pupils and teacher.

Class Response to Novelty

Situations which are not part of the usual curricular experience can provide a useful indication of pupils' reaction to challenge: in our four classrooms there was a new situation at the outset of the research project with the potential of arousing pupils' interest and curiosity. This was the introduction of the audio-recording apparatus: radiomicrophones to be worn by the teacher and a target pupil, and the presence of the researcher.

Naturally this was a considerable change in the normal routine, and it entailed a brief explanation by the teacher and research assistant to the class and target pupil concerned. The initial recorded session with each target pupil was considered likely to be unrepresentative and was not used in the research for detailed analysis. However audiotapes of the first sessions provide interesting examples of spontaneous questions and comments, hypotheses, explanations and practical experimentation by some pupils. The following classroom dialogues illustrate some of these.

Classroom 1

The class was involved in practical science for much of the term, and pupils were practised in predicting what would happen, in testing their ideas, and giving explanations. There was a relaxed but lively atmosphere, and the frequent bursts of laughter on the tape convey a flavour of the pupils' enjoyment. Andrew, the target pupil, said in a brief discussion with the researcher (R) after the session that he had liked talking into the microphone and hearing the voices over the tape.

> *P.*   Andrew's not to touch them, eh?
> *TP.*   Are you recording them now?
> *R.*   Yes, it's working nicely.
> *TP.*   Are these on?
> *R.*   Yes.
> *TP.*   (examining dials) There's another two. That's the one that I've got, eh?
> *R.*   That's the one that's linked to you and that's the one that's linked to Mrs Guthrie. In fact do you know why it makes that buzz? That's because they're very close together.
> *TP.*   If you stand near that one it'll buzz will it? Is it all right Miss? Stand near that one. Miss'll have to stand near that one, eh? Cos if I stand near that one it'll buzz. Miss it's awful big that taperecorder.
> *R.*   It is a big one.
> *TP.*   What are these?
> *R.*   That's for the headphones.
> *TP.*   Does a light come on, on this Miss?
> *R.*   No there's not a light on that one. It's a different sort.
> *TP.*   Miss, is there a light on your one?

Classroom 2

Lynne, the target pupil and the rest of her class initially showed mild curiosity concerning why she was given the microphone. When the second target pupil wore it, two weeks later, they asked a number of questions.

> (TP Makes noises into the mike, blows and sings.)
> *TP.*   There's no holes in this. How can they hear?
> *T.*   You're speaking into the mike.
> *P.*   When you speak in it your voice goes down there into the box. Goes down there into the thingummy.
> *P.*   But that's broken.
> *R.*   No, that's the aerial. It's like your radio.

Classroom 3

This was a brisk task oriented classroom with relatively short teaching sessions. It was noticeable that pupils rarely asked other than basic procedural questions during class. They showed no curiosity about the recording but the target pupil appeared slightly apprehensive.

TP: Miss is that on. Miss?

T: I don't know.

This was the only reference to the novel situation in the classroom which because of time constraints had not been explained more generally to the class, either by the teacher or by the research assistant.

Significantly perhaps, Mrs Macdonald commented in the interviews one year later. 'No one asked when you left, actually, about the research assistant or recording apparatus. I mean they never ever said 'why haven't you got that?' It was just accepted that that was it.'

Classroom 4

In this classroom many group activities including much role play occurred. Pupils showed considerable interest in the reason for the target pupil (Emma) wearing the microphone and proffered their own hypotheses.

P: Why do you need that on you?

P: If she didna she wouldna hear us.

T: Is there something wrong with her ears?

P: Aye, she willna hear us through that.

P: Aye, if you talk she'll still hear.

T: She doesn't hear through that. She hears with her . . . ?

Ps: Ears.

T: It's not for listening. It's for the machine to listen.

P: So she willna hear us.

P: When we've finished can we listen to some?

T: Well, we'll have to talk about that later. There's some people who haven't given any news this morning.

Pupils' responses to their early encounters with the new situation in their classroom exhibited curiosity, spontaneous questioning and conjectures in those classrooms where explanations, problem solving and the encouragement of reflection were part of their everyday experience.

Teachers' and Target Pupils' Views of their Classroom Experiences

This final section considers teachers' and target pupils' opinions of the classroom sessions which were recorded and observed.

As described in chapter 3, immediately after each recorded session target pupils and teachers had a brief discussion with the researcher. Prior to each session the teachers had outlined their general plans and their expectations concerning the target pupils. Afterwards they were asked for general comments about how things had gone: they were asked about any difficulties they had noticed in the target pupils, and the degree to which they (the target pupils) had been challenged. As always the teachers were wonderfully cooperative and tolerant, and only two unexpected disturbances meant that such discussions could not take place.

Our target pupils were also seen separately by the researcher at the end of each recorded session. They were asked what they had been doing, what they had liked or disliked, and whether there was anything they had found really hard or easy and why. This met with variable success. Most of the pupils' comments were brief and general. This was clearly not simply due to reticence and the imminent playground break. Alastair from classroom 3 gave inconsistent judgments on two occasions, citing for example, the same activity as really easy and really hard. Such anomalies support the general impression that reflecting and talking about their classroom work was difficult for the pupils and somewhat alien to them. Inconsistent replies are omitted from the summary from thirty recorded sessions which follows. Despite their brevity the pupils' judgments are of interest. First, our knowledge of their reflective ability is enhanced through their identification and description of salient aspects of their classroom experience. Second we can investigate the match between the judgments made by target pupils and their teachers of the session in which both had just participated. This provides a valuable framework for the more detailed discussion of reflective episodes which follows in chapter 6.

Pupils' Comments

First, consider the pupils' accounts of what, if anything, had been specially easy or difficult for them and their reasons for this. Responses concerning what was easy included several which implied or directly stated that no effort or thinking was required, often because they were told very directly what to do.

For example writing was easy, 'because it was already written down', and 'because the teacher tellt us what to write and we had to copy it down'. Watching TV was easy 'because you just sat there watching it'. Two pupils cited an activity as easy because it was familiar to them: sewing 'because I do lots of sewing at home' and reading: 'because I've done it before'.

Occasionally pupils said that an activity was easy because they liked it. Concerning computer work: 'I like pressing the keys'.

Andrew gave a metacognitive answer in connection with his enjoyment of sums, when he said 'I like adding them up. Sometimes, I add them up in my head. Some are hard, some are easy.'

There was not an invariable connection between liking an activity and finding it easy. Pupils might well refer to different activities in response to the two questions. The last pupil's explicit enthusiasm for hard sums was however unusual.

Pupils' references to things that had been difficult for them included some which were quite specific, and these were often of a practical nature; model making; 'difficult trying to fit paper clips', and drawing; 'trying to draw a fish was hard', making steering; 'difficult to get the bits to fit together'. One pupil's disagreement about her teacher's judgment still rankled. She felt she had provided a good alternative, 'but the teacher didn't want me to write that'. Sometimes the source of difficulty lay in the effort entailed, as in making a boat, 'because I was knackered', and some pupils expressed more complex difficulties in understanding. For example, reading was difficult for Alastair 'because there were different words', and for Donald the alphabet was difficult 'because of jumbling all the letters up'. 'Understanding what to do', and 'listening to the teacher, because I didn't hear what she was doing' were comments from two pupils who were clearly engaged in self monitoring during classroom activities.

Finally, pupils also referred to the intellectual effort involved in activities they cited as difficult. Writing was difficult 'because I had to think about it' and drawing 'because I had to think what pattern to do'.

There was no evidence that pupils disliked activities that they found difficult. In seven of the twenty-two sessions for which data are available pupils liked everything and had experienced no difficulties, and in twelve sessions they liked everything although they mentioned something that had been difficult for them. In the remaining three sessions the pupils said they had not enjoyed anything and one clearly still resented having been corrected for something she felt was unwarranted. In one session Johnnie had been very confused and the confusion had not been resolved. He also commented that he had liked nothing on one occasion but nothing had been difficult for him.

In chapter 6 we discuss some of the main reasons found in this study for the occasional frustration expressed by pupils, and also for the few times when they said they had not liked anything they had done. These are, work that was too simple and therefore boring, confusion which was not resolved, and disagreements about their work with their teacher.

Teachers' Comments concerning their Target Pupils

Did the teachers' post session comments identify the same difficulties as the target pupils themselves? Clearly it would be naive and unrealistic to expect a perfect match here. The pupils may not be very aware of their difficulties; they may not be willing or able to talk about them, or they may describe them in very different terms from those used by their teachers.

Teachers were responsible for a class of ten–twelve pupils. Interruptions and unexpected happenings were inevitable from time to time. Any one pupil might be demanding most of their time and attention during any particular session. Moreover although there were many of the non-verbal cues to pupils' engagement that experienced teachers pick up with great sensitivity, it is what pupils say and do that provides most evidence of difficulty. Many pupils who do experience difficulties in understanding become adept at camouflaging this and keeping it from the notice of their teacher.

A selection of the teachers' comments are presented alongside those of their target pupils to indicate the correspondence between them. Teachers sometimes made reference to difficulties they believed the pupil to have experienced and sometimes to unexpected achievements.

Classroom 1

Comments by teacher	**Comments by target pupil Andrew**
1 Understood after explicit instructions.	Understanding what to do (was difficult).
2 Can't get over steering mechanism he designed, he did his own problem solving.	Making steering: difficult to get pieces to fit.
3 Doing maths in his head — really unusual.	Like adding up sums in head.
4 Finds drawing difficult.	(Easiest part) was drawing motorbike.

	Target pupil Mark
1 Quicker on maths than sounds.	Difficult writing. Had to think about it.
2 Clocks need basic attention. Not aware of time passing as such.	Difficulty with 'half past'.
3 Imaginative area difficult because of no structure and no right answer.	Nothing difficult.
4 Could recognise square and rectangle but not say why.	Sums were easy.

Here understanding of the target pupils' difficulties by the teacher is fairly accurate. There is consistency between the reports of each in the activity selected for comment despite the fact that these were relatively long sessions with a range of varied activities. Both of the target pupils were able to talk about their own achievements in the classroom at a specific and at a more general level.

Classroom 2

Comments by teacher	**Comments by target pupil Johnnie**
1 'Before' and 'after' difficult sequencing difficult — not resolved.	Nothing was easy. Doing my work was difficult.
2 Learned new word, 'wicket'.	Liked rhymings and that.

3 Sequencing was difficult. He tends to look at something and say he can't do it.

Writing them — the sheet was difficult. (Had to convert dates words to numbers — confused throughout.)

4 Able to share ideas.

Nothing was difficult.

Target pupil Lynne

1 Didn't know what a border was.

I was doing a border, making a pattern, like dots. The teacher wouldn't let me do it so I had to change and do the red one.

2 Writing her own ideas; lifeboat was difficult.

I had to go on dotted lines — keeping hand steady was difficult.

3 As soon as she had to think she didn't get it, but with perseverance she did.

The seventh one, that's the one I'm stuck on. Just because I wrote down 'the anchor' the teacher didn't want me to write that.

In classroom 2, Lynne was specific in her comments, two of which took an aggrieved tone because she resented the teacher's direction. With Johnnie the confusions were of comprehension and in two sessions both he and his teacher knew they had not been resolved.

Classroom 3

Comments by teacher

Comments by target pupil Alastair

1 I didn't feel he should have had a problem with beginning and end, first and last. Felt he was playing on it.

Letters difficult because of jumbling them all up.

2 Reasoning is impossible. He believes his own answer. It doesn't bother him that his world is different from others'.

Difficult doing the jigsaws on the floor.

3 No difficulties.

There were difficult words.

4 Switched off — not in a working mood — no matter how often prompted.

Nothing difficult. Pictures were easy to colour in.

Target pupil Donald

1 Coordination problem with clips.

Trying to fit paper with paper clips was difficult.

2 Seemed worried that he had not listened.

Difficult listening to teacher.

3	Thinks he knows more than he does.	Difficult trying to get the same colour.
4	Chose highest level on computer. It was difficult for him.	All really easy.
5	Very relaxed, taking turns talking to others.	I couldn't hear what my friends were saying (during game). Teacher was talking too much.

There is considerable mismatch between what the two target pupils have to say about their classroom experiences and the judgment of their teacher, except in the very specific examples of the jumbled alphabet and the paper clips. Almost half of the teacher's comments are negative in expectation and pessimistic in relation to the possibility of helping the pupil resolve his difficulty. This is particularly marked with target pupil Alastair.

Classroom 4

Comments by teacher	**Comments by target pupil Emma**
1 Emma's difficulty is transferring ideas onto paper. Doesn't plan ahead.	Counting money difficult.
2 Making boat. All were her own ideas. She resolved the difficulty herself. She never quit.	Making boat was difficult because I was knackered.
3 No serious difficulties in understanding, but she didn't justify what she said from the picture. There's an evidence and opinion gap.	All easy.

	Target pupil Samantha
1 Finds it hard to identify what audience needs to know.	Typing out story was easy. It (computer) tells you what to press.
2 She hadn't worked out classes of effective questions in the game. No idea of collecting information, then sorting and selecting what's needed.	To draw a fish was hard.
3 It's always challenging for Samantha to verbalize what's in her mind. She's unable to fill in what a person needs to know.	Difficult putting words in.

Table 8   Sessions judged by teachers to have challenged target pupils (expressed as percentage)

Classroom 1 Mrs Guthrie	100	Challenged imaginatively. Enjoyed the power over all that he could do. Very challenged. Really thought through problems. Yes, stimulated rather than challenged.
Classroom 2 Mrs Stevenson	20	He was challenged. He tends to look at something new, and say he can't do it. With encouragement he will look again. Easy but couldn't have done more. He has been prompted to think and to discuss his ideas.
Classroom 3 Mrs Macdonald	50	Challenged, managed to complete sheets, really confidence boosting for him. No, he was switched off. Not in a working mood. Anagram challenged him. Rest familiar.
Classroom 4 Mrs Law	85	Yes the game stretched her. She disagreed with the others who were wrong, so very pleased. Don't think she was challenged. She dashes things off if left to her own. She never quit so met challenges but needed the teacher's interest to keep her going.

Here Mrs Law's comments are specific and detailed and focus particularly on the cognitive difficulties she has identified in both girls.

In these examples the teacher is using the same reflective language that she used in pre-session discussions. The two target pupils' comments in contrast were very pragmatic. In most cases they do not share their teacher's focus in their comments, and they do not show any effects of this teacher talk in terms of their own understanding of her aims, to do with planning, writing or talking for an audience, justifying their opinions, systematically narrowing down alternatives or producing ideas, all of which were emphasized in the sessions' planned content and procedures followed by the teacher, but perhaps not made as explicit as they might have been.

A striking feature of the teachers' comments is the degree to which they believed their target pupils had been challenged by the session they had just participated in. Eighteen sessions were judged by teachers to have been challenging, out of twenty eight. Table 8 shows the percentage of sessions judged by each teacher to have been challenging to the target pupil concerned.

This small sample of teachers' comments on their target pupils' experience of challenge contains revealing, rich descriptive terms which may be preferable to our use to 'challenge' with its slightly confrontational sense. Our teachers talked of stimulation, and of pupils being prompted to think, being stretched and not quitting in relation to intellectual challenges. They also referred to their pupils' lack of confidence, expectations of failure, being switched off, needing their presence and interest to maintain their motivation, and their tendency towards impulsive behaviour when left alone.

A range of material, audio recordings, observations, and discussions with teachers and pupils provides different perspectives on pupils' classroom experiences relating to reflection. It seems useful at this stage to note significant points arising form this evidence.

First, all the target pupils were found to have access to and to spontaneously use some reflective language, and to show evidence of self monitoring. However, much of this language was not occurring in task-related pupil teacher dialogues, or task-focussed discussion with peers, but in chat. Self-monitoring was very general in nature, and no examples were found of pupils linking current and previous experiences, or of their spontaneous use of analogies and generalizations, in the absence of teachers' prompts. Just as striking was the infrequency with which pupils made explicit requests for help to their teacher, although many quiet indications of such a need were recorded. When pupils did say that they were having difficulties, it was in general terms like 'I'm stuck', 'I don't get it'. They tended not to identify the source of their difficulty, and the strong impression that this was foreign to them was reinforced by their discussions with the researcher following each recorded session. Here mild prompting did not elicit from some pupils more than very general descriptions of the work they had just engaged in.

In the two classrooms where pupils heard the least Category 2 teacher talk, observations showed them also to spend less time in group activities, and to take part in shorter classroom conversations on average with their teachers and peers. The teachers in these classrooms were less likely to believe that their pupils had been positively challenged by their work, and there was more divergence between their judgments and those of their target pupils about their difficulties and achievements.

In the next chapter the pupils' experience of intellectual challenge in their classroom is examined in more detail.

6   Reflective Episodes and their Context

How else can we know when pupils are thinking except by what they say? (One of our teachers)

Brief segments that are a 'fine line between order and chaos' are — to both teacher and observers — the intellectual high point of the lesson. These observations point to the importance of infrequent events, ways of talking that have special value at specific moments, ways that would be lost in analyses that combine frequencies from the lesson as a whole. (Cazden, 1988)

This chapter describes the identification of 'segments of time', when we judged that target pupils were challenged intellectually. The contexts of these 'reflective episodes' are described in the second part: definitions and examples are the focus of the initial discussion.

The term 'reflective episode' applies to a period of time, when target pupils showed evidence of being cognitively engaged, as when, for example, they asked for help, explained to others, noted errors and contradictions. The evidence lies in the tape recordings and in the observations made of classroom sessions.

We judged the word 'episode' to be appropriate because duration is necessarily entailed by reflection. We believe it to be a period of time within much longer teaching sessions when the quality of pupils' learning experience changes, becoming more intense, involving mental absorption, and being accompanied by emotional feelings. Subjectively we experienced and could recognize such states ourselves. But was the attribution and identification of similar essentially private experiences to our pupils fruitful?

I decided not to rely on behavioural indications that pupils were thinking hard, although these would complement and support other evidence. In discussion with a group of teachers with a wide range of experience of pupils with learning difficulties I had asked how they knew that pupils were thinking hard. Silence and stillness were most frequently cited. The absence of signs of distraction is often taken to indicate pupils' 'on task behaviour' by teachers. But while it seems obvious that reflection would not be compatible with a heated argument with fellow pupils, it is certainly possible for teachers to be misled by quiet and apparently attentive behaviour. This study concerns much more than compliant application, or even assiduity, in pupils: it involves the identification of at least some occasions when pupils' interest was held, their minds taxed and cognitive advance possible.

The main evidence for this was verbal, obtained from a sample of class-room recordings for each target pupil. These averaged eighty minutes per pupil, comprising one entire session for all except Alastair and Donald, for whom two sessions each were used. All the sessions chosen for this part of the investigation took place in the latter part of term and none had been used earlier in the teacher talk analysis. The use of different samples as sources for different kinds of information must have increased the reliability of any findings and enabled greater confidence in their representative nature. The degree to which coherent conclusions could be drawn would depend on consistency between sessions within any one classroom.

It would be presumptuous to claim that pupils were not engaged in think-ing hard at other times which were not obvious, particularly when they were working alone. But the continuous nature of the audiorecordings and obser-vations enabled a fairly accurate judgment of the pupils at these times, and there are several examples of extended episodes or linked episodes of reflec-tive activity by pupils in which verbal interactions between teacher and pupil were interspersed by concentrated individual effort on the pupil's part. These were in marked contrast to the busy but otherwise undemanding activity observed for much of the time.

Identification of Reflective Episodes

What were the criteria necessary for a segment of classroom time to be iden-tified as a reflective episode?

First, it involved the target pupil interacting verbally with the teacher or classroom assistant, or with peers, over a topic which was in some way pre-senting an intellectual challenge. This occurred when target pupils expressed puzzlement, gave an explanation, justification or correction, spontaneously commented on difficulty or used strategies like checking their work. The term reflection is here being used in a broad sense and can be seen to resemble what teachers were apparently aiming for in their use of Category 2 talk. Target pupils' talk indicative of their cognitive involvement figures therefore in every reflective episode identified.

This is supplemented by evidence from observations of pupil behaviour made at the time. As noted in chapter 3 these included many notes of pupils' yawns, sighs and groans and more positively laughter, excitement and signs of pleasure. Such indications of accompanying emotions were very helpful.

Episodes also must have a certain duration. Reflection takes time, and our view of it did not include brief flashes of insight or intuition but something more extended, sustained over a time period. In practice a minimum period of half a minute was judged to be appropriate. This could be when a target pupil was working alone, with their teacher's support, or within peer discussion, or dialogue with the teacher. The actual duration and incidence of reflective episodes within the selected classroom sessions were of course of great interest.

A judgment was also made concerning the resolution of each identified reflective episode. When pupils' thinking appeared to have advanced,
their confusion been reduced or resolved, self-awareness increased or ideas
acknowledged, this was judged to be satisfactory: both the observational notes
and taped vocalizations lent support to this. On other occasions, however, the
target pupil met with an intellectual challenge which was not resolved: in this
case there was often accompanying behavioural evidence of frustration and a
tendency for this to be followed by signs of detachment or opting out.

After discussion of effective and facilitative reflective contexts the second
part of this chapter includes examples of both satisfactory and unresolved
reflective episodes, from the whole body of recordings. A number of reasons
for unsatisfactory outcomes are given.

The episodes were initially identified separately by the two researchers.
The standard observation sheets were condensed to provide an outline summary of each recorded session, and one of us used this to identify reflective
episodes involving the target pupil, checking these against the transcripts. The
other researcher identified episodes by listening to the original audiorecordings:
where we both agreed on the same incident this was transcribed in detail and
became one of the items in an episode bank. No doubt, some periods of
reflection by pupils were missed by this somewhat conservative approach.
However the reassuring consistency of the nature of the identified episodes
within the different classrooms means that useful conclusions can be drawn.

Incidence of Episodes

We now turn to the incidence and quality of the reflective episodes involving
each of the eight target pupils.

Table 9 summarizes the classroom sessions for the target pupils in which
reflective episodes were identified and highlighted. These might be satisfactory or unresolved. What is of particular interest is the nature of the involvement of both teacher and target pupil, the extent and pattern of episodes of
reflection, and their context, for example the ongoing classroom activity and
pupil grouping.

The sessions described in detail in this chapter occupied about eleven
hours in teaching time, and the total duration of the episodes identified was
almost three hours. For the individual target pupils this period of time varied
greatly. As table 9 shows the teacher rather than the individual target pupil
determined the frequency and total duration of reflective episodes.

Episodes in which pupils appeared to advance in their thinking occurred
both in group and in individual teaching. They were not more prominent
when a class size was reduced, for example by half doing something else,
although group size, as teachers commented later in interviews, was an important factor in teachers' planning in the first place.

Great variation in the proportion of time occupied by reflective episodes

Table 9 Summary of reflective episodes in sample of classroom sessions

Classroom	Target pupil	Activity	Grouping	Outcome	% of session time
1	Andrew	Number, Science	Individual Group	Satisfactory	46
	Mark	Craft, Maths	Group Individual	Satisfactory	30
2	Johnnie	Date	Individual	Unresolved	15
	Lynne	Spelling	Individual	Unresolved	5
3	Alastair	Computer, Colouring	Individual Individual	Abandoned	5
	Donald	Computer, Phonics game	Individual Group	Unresolved	<1
4	Emma	Phonics, Reading game	Group Individual	Satisfactory	62
	Samantha	Role play, Discussion	Group Group	Satisfactory	37

is shown in table 9. We need to examine more closely their nature and contexts within individual classroom sessions, in order to explore some of the reasons for the large differences in the target pupils' experience of intellectual challenge.

Episodes in Context: Some Illustrations

Pictorial summaries can be effective in highlighting target pupils' experiences of involvement, providing samples of pupils' and teachers' talk, and of the context. A sample are included here for illustration. The summaries enable comparisons to be made between pupils' experiences of reflection in different sessions, without always reading lengthy descriptive accounts. Their content as always requires selection from many possible alternatives.

The examples which follow highlight features judged to be of interest and significance in our study. These are the duration and linking of episodes, brief extracts of teacher-pupil verbal interactions, and behavioural observations which give the flavour of pupils' intellectual engagement and accompanying emotional experience, in a succinct, and easily comprehensible format. The white bands in the following depictions of classroom sessions represent identified episodes, in each of which the target pupils' reflective activity is described.

This small number of illustrative examples cannot show what simple visual inspection of them all reveals to be a striking feature. This is the consistency shown by the teachers. We have already seen that their style in classroom talk as defined by their category usage applied in different curricular activities and with both target pupils. Naturally the four teachers also had a well practised, preferred style of classroom organization. Mrs Law in classroom 4 planned

Figure 1   Target Pupil: Andrew

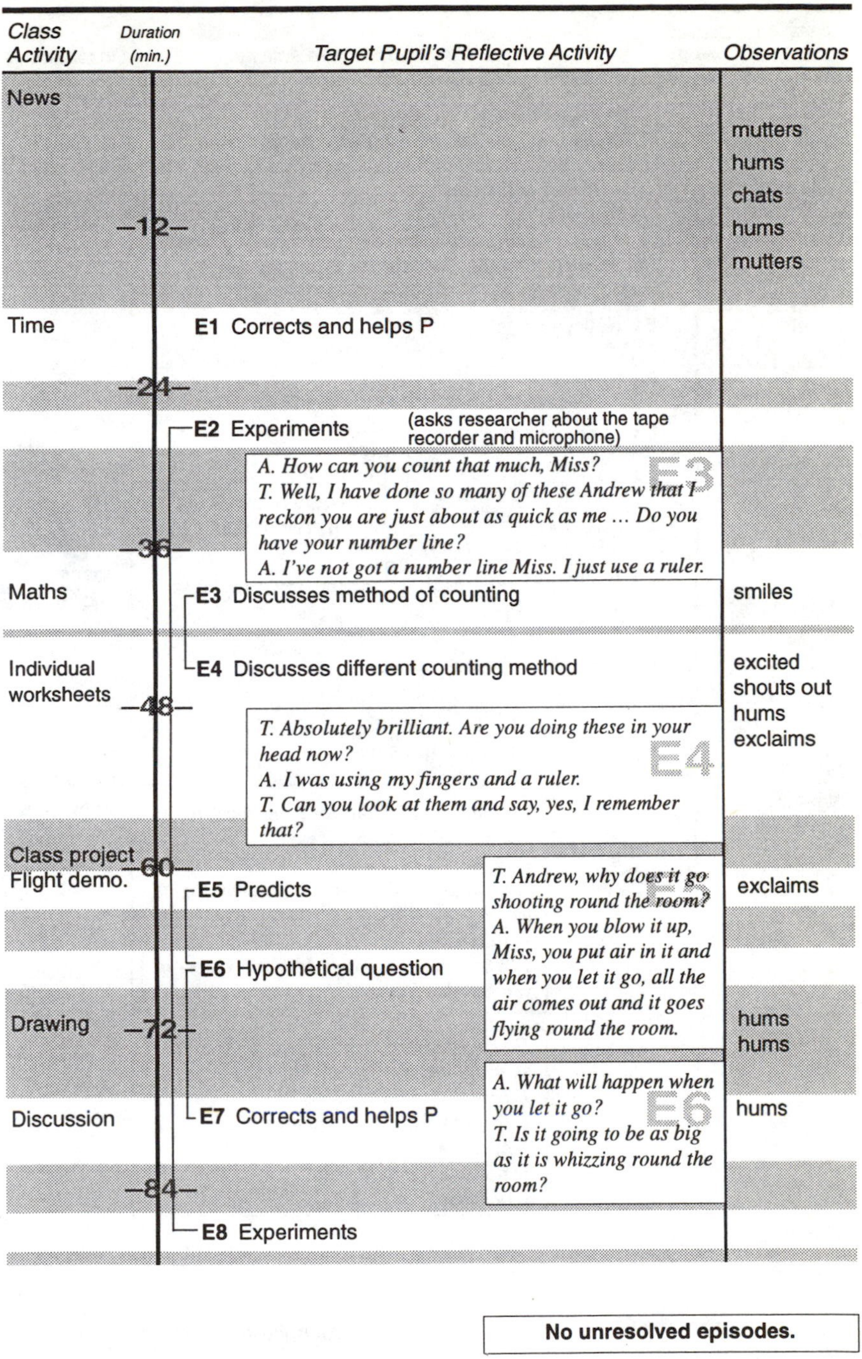

Class Activity	Duration (min.)	Target Pupil's Reflective Activity	Observations
News			mutters hums chats hums mutters
	—12—		
Time		**E1** Corrects and helps P	
	—24—		
		E2 Experiments (asks researcher about the tape recorder and microphone)	
		A. How can you count that much, Miss? *T. Well, I have done so many of these Andrew that I reckon you are just about as quick as me … Do you have your number line?* *A. I've not got a number line Miss. I just use a ruler.*	
	—36—		
Maths		**E3** Discusses method of counting	smiles
Individual worksheets		**E4** Discusses different counting method	excited shouts out hums exclaims
	—48—	*T. Absolutely brilliant. Are you doing these in your head now?* *A. I was using my fingers and a ruler.* *T. Can you look at them and say, yes, I remember that?*	
Class project Flight demo.	—60—	**E5** Predicts	exclaims
		T. Andrew, why does it go shooting round the room? *A. When you blow it up, Miss, you put air in it and when you let it go, all the air comes out and it goes flying round the room.*	
		E6 Hypothetical question	
Drawing	—72—		hums hums
Discussion		**E7** Corrects and helps P	hums
		A. What will happen when you let it go? *T. Is it going to be as big as it is whizzing round the room?*	
	—84—		
		E8 Experiments	

No unresolved episodes.

sss
Reflection through Interaction

Figure 2 Target Pupil: Johnnie

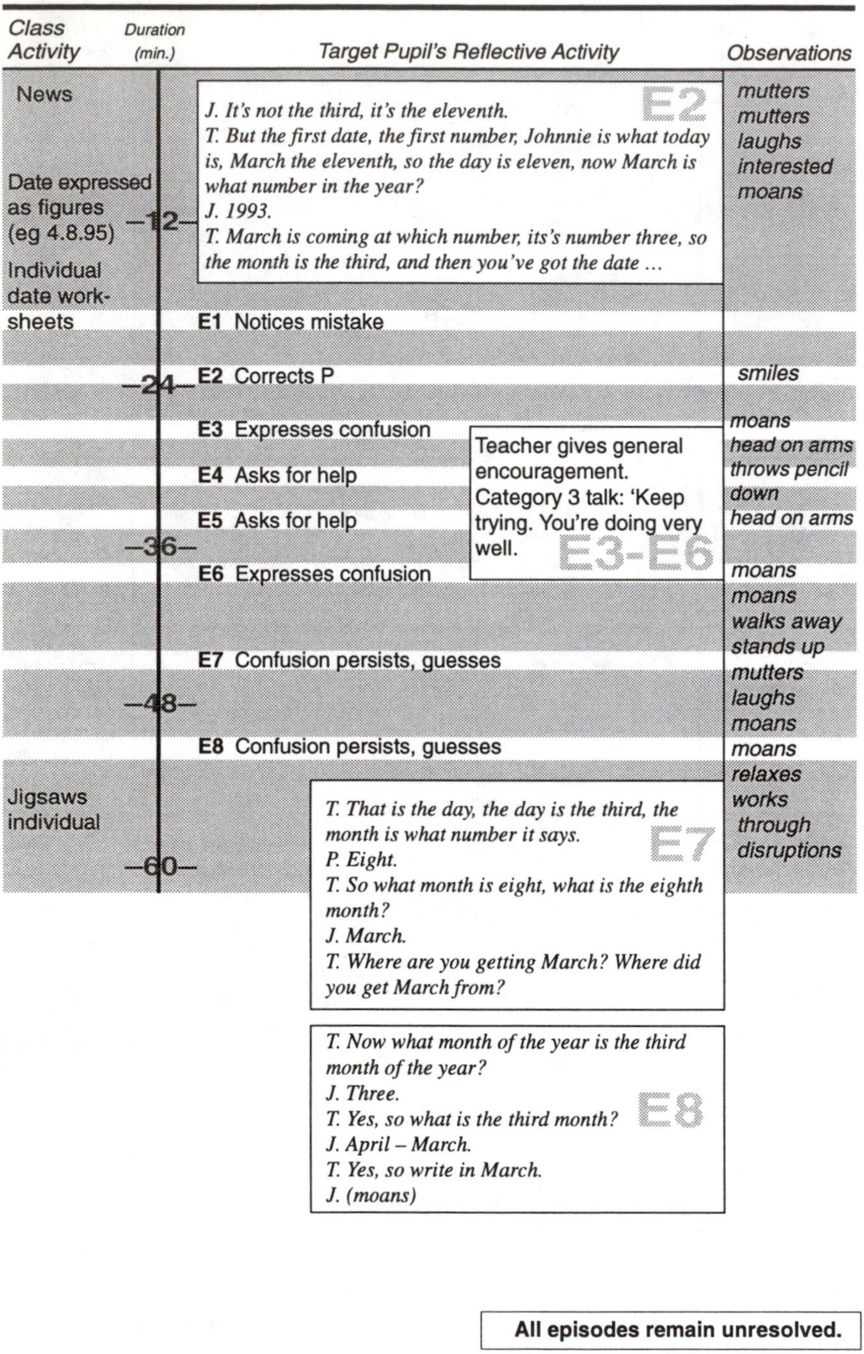

Class Activity	Duration (min.)	Target Pupil's Reflective Activity	Observations
News Date expressed as figures (eg 4.8.95) Individual date worksheets	—12—	**E2** J. It's not the third, it's the eleventh. T. But the first date, the first number, Johnnie is what today is, March the eleventh, so the day is eleven, now March is what number in the year? J. 1993. T. March is coming at which number, its's number three, so the month is the third, and then you've got the date …	mutters mutters laughs interested moans
		E1 Notices mistake	
	—24—	**E2** Corrects P	smiles
		E3 Expresses confusion	moans head on arms
		E4 Asks for help	Teacher gives general encouragement. Category 3 talk: 'Keep trying. You're doing very well. **E3-E6**	throws pencil down
		E5 Asks for help	head on arms
	—36—	**E6** Expresses confusion	moans
			moans walks away stands up
		E7 Confusion persists, guesses	mutters laughs moans
	—48—		
		E8 Confusion persists, guesses	moans
Jigsaws individual	—60—	**E7** T. That is the day, the day is the third, the month is what number it says. P. Eight. T. So what month is eight, what is the eighth month? J. March. T. Where are you getting March? Where did you get March from?	relaxes works through disruptions

T. Now what month of the year is the third month of the year?
J. Three.
T. Yes, so what is the third month? **E8**
J. April – March.
T. Yes, so write in March.
J. (moans)

All episodes remain unresolved.

92

Figure 3 Target Pupil: Samantha

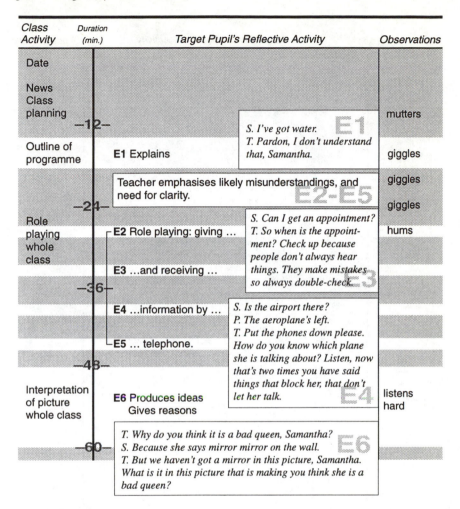

Class Activity	Duration (min.)	Target Pupil's Reflective Activity	Observations
Date			
News Class planning			mutters
	—12—	S. I've got water. E1	
Outline of programme		E1 Explains	T. Pardon, I don't understand that, Samantha.	giggles
		Teacher emphasises likely misunderstandings, and need for clarity. E2-E5	giggles
	—24—		giggles
Role playing whole class		E2 Role playing: giving …	S. Can I get an appointment? T. So when is the appointment? Check up because people don't always hear	hums
		E3 …and receiving …	things. They make mistakes so always double-check. E3	
	—36—		
		E4 …information by …	S. Is the airport there? P. The aeroplane's left. T. Put the phones down please.
		E5 … telephone.	How do you know which plane she is talking about? Listen, now
	—48—		that's two times you have said things that block her, that don't
Interpretation of picture whole class		E6 Produces ideas Gives reasons	let her talk. E4	listens hard
	—60—	T. Why do you think it is a bad queen, Samantha? S. Because she says mirror mirror on the wall. T. But we haven't got a mirror in this picture, Samantha. What is it in this picture that is making you think she is a bad queen? E6	

No unresolved episodes.

93

Figure 4 Target Pupil: Lynne

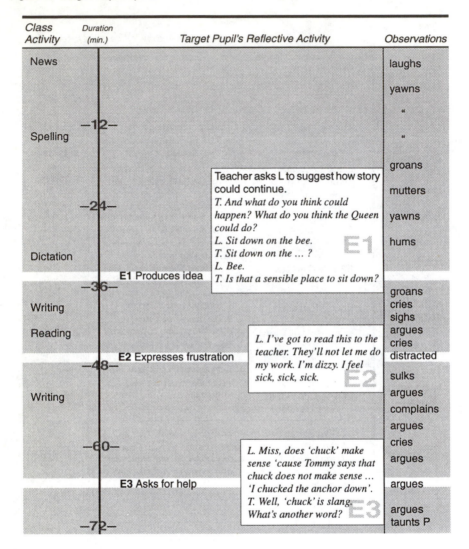

Class Activity	Duration (min.)	Target Pupil's Reflective Activity	Observations
News			laughs
			yawns
			"
Spelling	–12–		"
			groans
		Teacher asks L to suggest how story could continue.	mutters
	–24–	*T. And what do you think could happen? What do you think the Queen could do?*	yawns
		L. Sit down on the bee.	hums
Dictation		*T. Sit down on the … ?*	
		L. Bee.	
		E1 Produces idea *T. Is that a sensible place to sit down?*	
	–36–		groans
Writing			cries
			sighs
Reading		*L. I've got to read this to the teacher. They'll not let me do my work. I'm dizzy. I feel sick, sick, sick.*	argues
			cries
	–48–	**E2** Expresses frustration	distracted
Writing			sulks
			argues
			complains
			argues
	–60–	*L. Miss, does 'chuck' make sense 'cause Tommy says that chuck does not make sense …*	cries
			argues
		E3 Asks for help *'I chucked the anchor down'.*	argues
		T. Well, 'chuck' is slang. What's another word?	argues
	–72–		taunts P

All episodes remain unresolved.

94

group activities for a large proportion of each session and was herself a very active participant in these, whereas Mrs Guthrie was very involved herself in lively news discussions which began each morning session, and she then gave very clear outlines of the work, often with demonstrations. She played a less prominent role during subsequent individual or group work, leaving pupils to work alone but in the knowledge that they would be revisited at regular intervals, as shown in figure 1.

In classroom 4, as figure 3 shows, reflective episodes often occurred during relatively long periods of whole class involvement when the teacher made considerable efforts to keep up pupils' interest and activity, whereas in classroom 1 they were more likely to be stimulated by the introduction, linkage and demonstrations provided by the teacher before pupils worked quietly alone with shortish episodes in which their teacher participated.

These different approaches appear to be equally effective in ensuring that the pupils engaged with work that was challenging to them and capable of extending their thinking for a considerable proportion of the time available.

In the remaining two classes, for different reasons, pupils did not experience such a challenging learning environment.

Johnnie and Lynne, the target pupils in classroom 2, both tended to be restive and to complain about their work. The behavioural observations in figures 2 and 4 show how frequently they yawned and moaned. There were several possible reasons for this, but prominent among these must have been their teacher's wish for them to avoid difficulties in their work which she feared were likely to render the classroom tense if not explosive. However these pupils felt frustration anyway. There was a tendency, perhaps because the work was not very demanding and did not fully engage their attention, for pupils to react to very small criticisms which might only be implicit (like a rephrasing of what they had said, or a substitution for their slang, or a suggestion that their answer could be improved upon) in a forceful and emotional manner. Added to this was the lack of precise, explicit, contingent feedback and an insufficient knowledge of what they were expected to do. They had little idea of where each session was leading apart from the general 'doing ma work' which was the comment frequently made by the target pupils after sessions had finished. This contributed to the tense classroom atmosphere, so very different from the calm explicitly wished for by the teacher. One way she tried of achieving this was during the long discussion news periods at the beginning of each day. Mrs Stevenson did not talk very much in these, but when she did, diverted the conversation towards didactic ends rather than making contributions herself, as well as inviting other pupils to ask questions of the speaker. Those in our data tended to be rather uninterested routine questions, like 'what is your friend called?', and 'what colour was it?', and did not convey an impression of interest, and did not build on pupils' original contributions.

Observations and recordings of classroom 3 were very different again. The curriculum material used is discussed in the second half of this chapter.

One effect of the short teaching sessions was probably to reduce initial discussion of an informal level and to increase the teacher's desire for an end product of some kind. There was a rapid pace of teacher talk, a lot of checking, monitoring and commenting on pupil behaviour, and generally passive compliance by the pupils who were usually assiduously occupied. Unfortunately there was no evidence of inherent difficulty in the material, or of pupils having to think hard, and there was little of interest to stimulate discussion had there been time. Doing the work and finishing the task were the criteria employed by the teacher for a successful session. The pupils apparently gained their main satisfaction from the atmosphere of their teacher's jokes, teasing and minor badinage, but not from the work they were engaged in. There were no significant satisfactory reflective episodes involving either of the two target pupils, Alastair and Donald, in the sessions we sampled.

Our discussion now moves to classroom activities and their effect on pupil reflection, using the entire body of recordings as evidence.

Classroom Activities and Reflection

A basic assumption in planning and undertaking the classroom research described in this book was that reflection could occur in all sorts of classroom activities, right across the curriculum: the episodes selected for detailed examination in this chapter occurred during a variety of individual, small group, and whole class work, and many more occurring in a wide range of contexts are to be found in our episode 'bank'. However it became clear at an early stage that we were identifying very few reflective episodes in one of the four classrooms in the study. As indicated in table 9 this was in classroom 3 where the teacher chose to work through a curriculum package in the form of a well-known reading scheme. This had already been planned by Mrs Macdonald prior to the research and she was confident that it would provide a suitable context in which to identify reflection by her pupils.

The scheme in question was designed for pupils with learning difficulties who were in the 'interest age' range of 7–13 years and in the reading age range of 6–9 years. It was of an appropriate level of difficulty therefore for the pupils in classroom 3. The publishers claim that its street credibility, realism, and characters with whom pupils can readily identify, guarantee its inherent interest to them. Pupils progress systematically from wordless pictures to full pages of text, with supplementary well-produced back up reading material which does not introduce new vocabulary but rather enables consolidation of what pupils have already encountered.

In addition, many practical activities such as model making, glueing, colouring and associated games were provided.

What the package seriously lacked in practice was a stimulus to pupils' imagination and thinking. The target pupils we observed carefully completed associated practical tasks, and played the games, and they were usually able on request to recall the names of the main characters in their reading book. They were frequently reminded that these characters should be coloured in consistently, and this was emphasized as being very important. But the story events in our recorded sessions were of everyday familiar activities, getting wet, dirtying the kitchen floor, demolishing piles of leaves: in short mundane everyday incidents in which no new complex ideas were introduced and the pupils' imagination was unlikely to be fired.

There was pressure on time in the sessions concerned and the teacher clearly wished to achieve her planned objectives by the end of each available forty minutes. The result was a strong emphasis on finishing, and very little on any aspects of the curriculum materials not directly related to the final product. Among the very few occasions we could identify in which there was any extension beyond the immediate task were two very brief dialogues involving the teacher and a target pupil. Both linked Alastair's personal experience to an aspect of the story he was reading: he referred to his own dog's illness and possible reasons for this, and on another occasion he talked about his feelings of anger. Significantly afterwards, in discussion with the research assistant, he commented that he had enjoyed 'talking to the teacher and that' about himself. This contrasted with his usual negative, uninvolved, attitude.

What only rarely occurred in this classroom were examples of pupils' questions or expressions of interest or indeed of difficulty, and the taking up of these opportunities for encouraging pupils' reflection by the teacher. A combination of factors probably accounts for the almost complete absence of such episodes. There was pressure of time, and there were curricular constraints in the form of clearly specified end products whose achievement was sometimes quite fiddly and complex. The classroom task of the teacher thus became focussed on managing the practical activities and keeping pupils working. Her aims for each session for a given target pupil were quite often of the form 'that he finish what he has to do'. This emphasis contrasts very strongly with the expressed views of the other three teachers, who all to a greater or lesser extent, expressed the belief that they should capitalize on any opportunities which arose in their classroom to extend their pupils' thinking. They all felt that too much reliance on ready made curriculum packages could inhibit this process.

Mrs Law spelt out the idea of taking up pupils' interest when she said in a later interview:

> You have to strike when the iron is hot with any child, and if something is going well, stick with it.

Mrs Macdonald, the teacher who had used the reading scheme throughout the term in which recordings were made gave her opinion of it one year later in interview.

> I think it is still quite a success with them. They are still enjoying it, and again, they're older pupils with learning difficulties and a lot of

them haven't managed to learn to read so . . . if that's working and they've still got enthusiasm . . . it's worked for them. It wouldn't necessarily work for anyone else.

Mrs Macdonald repeatedly emphasised that her pupils' concentration span was extremely limited and that to focus on something for even a short period of time always proved to be quite difficult. She advocated helping to extend pupils' periods of concentration by activities such as using taped instructions with workbooks, and headphones. Her approach throughout appeared to assume that the curriculum package chosen for the pupils was appropriate for them, and that her job was to help them to use it, rather than to explore and extend their understanding through interaction. She described her job as being 'on call' for her pupils. Implicitly, the onus was on the pupils to ask her for help. This helps explain our finding that, although Mrs Macdonald's talk included a number of Category 2 utterances there were very few reflective episodes with satisfactory outcomes. On examination of the data it was clear that most Category 2 talk in classroom 3 was in the form of general reminders about strategies to the whole class rather than responses to individual pupils. Our observations were of vigilant monitoring and frequent reminders that time was getting on, rather than responsive, contingent, interaction.

Among many interesting features of this teaching approach one distinguishing characteristic emerged on the observation sheets for classroom 3. This was the evenness of the distribution of the teacher's comments throughout each recorded session. This contrasts with the variation and clustering of teacher talk observed in the three other classrooms which were usually associated with a change of activity. In classroom 3 sessions were quite short and were occupied by the reading scheme, whereas in the other classrooms they lasted over one hour and involved two or three main activities.

Changes in the amount the other three teachers talked were clearly related to a change in activity. For example in classrooms 2 and 4 teachers talked only half as much during 'Newstime' as when pupils were engaged in individual work, whereas in classroom 1 Mrs Guthrie spoke three times as much during preliminary discussion as during her pupils' group activity. Ebbs and flows occurred as the teachers handed over more responsibility during interaction to their pupils, or took a more directing role themselves. There were spaces where the teacher could 'home in' on potentially fruitful opportunities with the whole class or with individual pupils which were not observed in the regular and rapid 'monitoring' style of classroom interaction that was typical of classroom 3.

It is ironical that in classroom 3 Mrs Macdonald was very concerned to keep her pupils' concentration levels high and in her later interview spoke of her pupils' need for a bright lively classroom atmosphere, and yet the stimulus of intellectually challenging, truly engaging experiences for pupils was largely absent.

The other three teachers in their later interviews all stressed the importance of flexibility and expressed their doubts about using ready-made packages or schemes much of the time.

> I've never ever found that there was a scheme, or anything that you could just lay hands on and use — it just doesn't work. You have to look at material and say 'can I do this with these children who are in front of me', and the answer is usually no. In preparation I always have at least three times more materials than I ever use — because once you put it into operation, you find you think 'oh heavens above, how did I ever think this was going to work', and you jettison it, you do something else. You think, 'well, I'm not sure about this,' and suddenly it takes off, and you end up developing that. (Mrs Law)

Another said that she tended to set up her own materials although she found there were now a lot of very good materials in science and technology, but

> most of the material is designed for a primary, you know mainstream primary, and you end up having to adapt them anyway, so you tend to pick and choose from what's available, rather than take it as a whole. Use what's appropriate. (Mrs Guthrie)

Mrs Stevenson advocated presenting situations and deliberately organising material as a way to encourage pupil reflection,

> but the best have been spontaneous, child centred, when they raise the questions . . . the teacher should be the facilitator to encourage their thoughts from discussions.

She said that open-ended discussion and stories encourage imaginative ideas.

The remainder of this chapter concentrates on activities which our teachers believed to be particularly useful in encouraging their pupils to think more deeply. While any area of the curriculum can in principle provide pupils and teachers with many opportunities to develop reflection, in practice we found that the published curriculum package as used in one classroom did not do so, and classroom 3 is not considered further in this context.

Three activities we observed did appear to be especially fruitful in providing sustained classroom experiences of challenge and involvement, and had been planned by teachers to do just this. Their equivalents can be used across different curricular areas, and they have a promising research history. Our examples illustrate problem solving, reasoning and communication tasks.

Problem Solving

As long ago as 1890 William James defined problem solving as a search that occurs when the means to an end do not occur simultaneously with the establishment of the end. In other words during problem solving there is a known goal and no routine way of reaching it. Two illustrative examples come from our classroom 1 data. First, small groups were set the task of building a safe, strong and comfortable go-kart from a set of parts; in the second example a whole class solved a hypothetical everyday problem situation through role-play.

Model construction

This session was remarkable for the responsiveness of all the pupils to the challenge of their task, and particularly for the way in which Andrew, the target pupil, rose to the occasion. The buzz of excitement and laughter is a striking feature of the audiotape.

Mrs Guthrie, the teacher, had anticipated that Andrew would be interested but thought he might lack initiative and imagination, and that working within a group could frustrate him if the others did not cooperate well in the task, which was to build a go-kart which was safe, strong and comfortable and would be able to carry an 8-year-old from another class.

The teacher structured this long session very skilfully, organizing the pupils to work in groups of three to make their go-karts. The topic was introduced by the teacher asking a pupil to bring in a bicycle from the hall. She reminded them of a recent visit to a museum where they had seen a 'boneshaker' and introduced the concepts of safe, strong and comfortable in a lively amusing way, with vivid visual imagery to make her points:

T:	I wonder why they make this part of the bicycle out of hard, strong material.
P.	They've done it hard for people to ride on.
T:	What would happen if it was made of something like string?
P.	It would break.
Andrew:	It would snap and break.
T:	. . . and another bit that's strong?
P.	The pedals.
T:	They're strong, they wouldn't be any good if they were made of sponge or jelly.
Andrew:	(Laughs) Sponge or jelly!

Mrs Guthrie's remarks were amusing, imaginative and drove her points home effectively.

She referred to her own driving experience when talking about brakes and reminded the class several times of their task.

You have to think, how can I make it safe, strong and comfortable.
And we're going to test it.

In groups of three the pupils worked with enthusiasm, helped by the occasional participation of the teacher or classroom assistant. For most of the model making time they both withdrew, coming back with occasional assistance, reminders

Figure 5   Target Pupil: Andrew

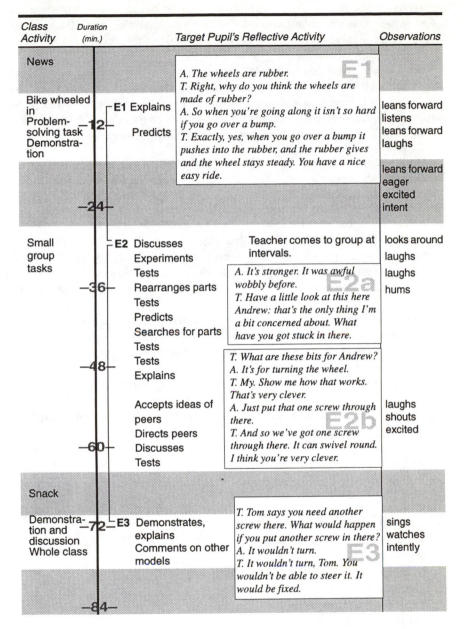

Class Activity	Duration (min.)	Target Pupil's Reflective Activity		Observations
News			*A. The wheels are rubber.* *T. Right, why do you think the wheels are made of rubber?* **E1**	
Bike wheeled in Problem- solving task Demonstra- tion	**12**	**E1** Explains Predicts	*A. So when you're going along it isn't so hard if you go over a bump.* *T. Exactly, yes, when you go over a bump it pushes into the rubber, and the rubber gives and the wheel stays steady. You have a nice easy ride.*	leans forward listens leans forward laughs
	24			leans forward eager excited intent
Small group tasks		**E2** Discusses Experiments Tests	Teacher comes to group at intervals.	looks around laughs
	36	Rearranges parts Tests Predicts Searches for parts	*A. It's stronger. It was awful wobbly before.* **E2a** *T. Have a little look at this here Andrew: that's the only thing I'm a bit concerned about. What have you got stuck in there.*	laughs hums
	48	Tests Tests Explains	*T. What are these bits for Andrew?* *A. It's for turning the wheel.* *T. My. Show me how that works. That's very clever.*	
		Accepts ideas of peers Directs peers	*A. Just put that one screw through there.* **E2b** *T. And so we've got one screw through there. It can swivel round. I think you're very clever.*	laughs shouts excited
	60	Discusses Tests		
Snack				
Demonstra- tion and discussion Whole class	**72**	**E3** Demonstrates, explains Comments on other models	*T. Tom says you need another screw there. What would happen if you put another screw in there?* *A. It wouldn't turn.* **E3** *T. It wouldn't turn, Tom. You wouldn't be able to steer it. It would be fixed.*	sings watches intently
	84			

No unresolved episodes.

and appreciative comments. Andrew the target pupil was especially active, and rapidly took on the role of chief designer in his group. He made a discovery which was significant and exciting for him, that a go-kart's back wheels have to be fixed, and do not steer. He explained this repeatedly to other pupils who did not understand.

By repeated trial and testing he devised an effective steering mechanism, cooperated well with other pupils, accepting and acknowledging their ideas, and offering helpful suggestions to solve problems encountered by the other pupils in the whole class demonstration and discussion at the close of the session.

Mrs Guthrie afterwards commented on Andrew's work.

> He surpassed himself. He's really coming out of his shell. Can't get over the steering mechanism he designed — the fact he could do his own problem solving and get on himself helped him.

She commented that she had been tempted to show the class a ready made go-kart to start with, but now realized that might have inhibited their production of ideas. She believed Andrew had been very challenged, and really thought through problems and was still trying to think through the steering. She felt that he was perhaps not 'stretched' by the group situation, being immersed in his own bit.

Our observations and recordings showed what his teacher could not have been aware of, that Andrew did gain a lot from his discussion and demonstrations to his peers and that his acknowledgment of their help and contributions was both positive and genuine.

In sum, this session demonstrates that small group problem solving can be very successful where there is a clear goal, where this is clearly spelt out and where there is unobtrusive help available to pupils in small groups.

Within the group Andrew's activities included:

trying parts
testing
rearranging parts
testing again
pointing out others' misapprehensions
searching for different parts
testing again
helping other pupils, acknowledging help
giving instructions
explaining the problem
demonstrating to the group

and his language included the following reflective comments:

So we don't need one on that end.
How're we going to make it turn?

Watch what happens when I put it up like that.

When somebody sits on it they're not going to fall right through are they?

It's not daft, but it'll just look funny with a green bit sticking up at the front, eh?

We've decided to make it stronger.

Had you noticed the back was turning, right, and the front was turning and they were wobbling all over the place and falling off?

Sam's just gave me an idea.

No, I don't think this is going to work somehow.

Role play

Mrs Law planned two problem-solving activities during the same morning. The first one presented a practical everyday problematic situation and was introduced by the teacher to the class through a picture of a boy who is locked out of his home. The class had the task of interpreting the pictured situation and then of miming alternative solutions.

In contrast to our first illustrative example, this role playing activity lasted less than thirty minutes. The use of mime engaged the pupils' interest and probably taxed their powers of communication to a greater extent, their teacher felt, than a verbal approach.

Mrs Law modelled a solution first and then worked to encourage consistency, commonsense and the production of pupils' own ideas, as in the following extracts:

(i) She pointed out that the target pupil Emma's suggestion was not consistent with the evidence of the picture.

'Is there anything that tells you it's cold? No, I don't think so', and 'What makes you think that?'

(ii) Pupils' answers had to be sensible and realistic: 'Now, I want you to think hard. If this was really Martin and really outside his own door and he couldn't get in and there was nobody home . . . what do you think?'

(iii) The teacher encouraged pupils to produce their own ideas, counteracting quite vigorously their tendency to rely on minor variations of their peers' suggestions.

'Has anyone got a different idea? Something that's not been done before? That's the same idea as Ken's. Never copy someone else — that's boring.'

Reasoning

During reasoning given information is transformed to reach a conclusion. Often the distinction is made between formal reasoning where logical rules apply and there is an agreed correct answer, (as for example, in analogical reasoning), and everyday reasoning such as that involved in decision making, testing hypotheses, and evaluating the strength of an argument. Both kinds are frequently involved in classroom activities. Reasoning does not include inspired guesswork, flashes of insight, or simple remembering.

An illustrative example is of a game played by two pupils in one of our classrooms.

Logical game: guess who?

The object of the game is to ask questions which eliminate possible answers systematically. The pupils ask questions in turn. Answers are limited to 'yes' and 'no', and the object is to identify the partner's chosen card.

This is one version of very many similar kinds of game which pupils often find difficult. Their memory for previous answers is being stretched, and their understanding of the systematic, efficient reduction of possibilities is being developed.

In the session from which our example is taken the teacher was aware that Emma was having difficulty in understanding the role of questioning, and she gave a lot of contingent but tactful feedback about 'good questions': for example:

> Did you ask if it was a boy or a girl, or a man or a woman? That might be a good one to ask next time as you're left with an awful lot to choose from', and 'Can you make that a better question? If you got another chance what would you ask?

Mrs Law commented afterwards that Emma had not yet grasped wider classifications, and tended to ask questions that were too specific, asking about a green hat, for instance, instead of a hat. Her teacher felt games like this could reveal unexpected gaps in pupils' understanding which she would work on in future. This particular skill was, she felt, an important one, and once acquired would be transferable to other reasoning tasks.

Emma herself was definite in her view that to win the game 'you have to think very hard'.

Communication Task

Tasks which involve the conveying of information to another who does not share the same knowledge are often called referential communicative tasks and are said to involve metacommunicative knowledge. Research studies have found these activities to be especially difficult for pupils with learning difficulties, but to be greatly facilitated by practice, role play and modelling, along with explicit, contingent feedback.

In the example, one of several among the data, the class helped Mrs Law to write instructions for their neighbouring class to follow. They had just made edible 'boats' with sardines, before the teacher introduced the task:

> Well I think some of the other boys and girls in the school would be really pleased to make boats like these as well. I wonder if you could help me to write some instructions so that another class could make them, 'cos some of the wee ones would enjoy this wouldn't they? They could do it.

The task involved conveying precise information which was sufficiently explicit to enable a listener (or reader) to replicate quite a complex sequence of actions. Mrs Law highlighted the important aspects by enacting the class's verbal instructions before writing them down, reading them out and putting them to a practical test. This began a process of repeated correction and refinement with the recurring question, 'will they know what we mean?' Testing of the amended versions both focused pupils' attention and amused them. This is a very effective procedure in alerting pupils to the need for explicit communication with others who lack their direct experience.

Unresolved Episodes

In contrast to the successful episodes described in the first part of this chapter there were a number of occasions when pupils' puzzlement, expressions of difficulty and explicit requests for help were not resolved in a satisfactory way. Chapter 5 indicated that our target pupils' enjoyment of sessions was associated with their experience of working hard, but was not evident when they had experienced unresolved confusion or when their initiatives had been misinterpreted or not followed up. There are a number of unresolved episodes in our data, lost opportunities for the extension and clarification of pupils' thinking. These are, of course, part of busy classroom life in any school, for any pupil, and many will be inevitable and will usually pass unnoticed. The use of radiomicrophones gave us privileged access to pupils' talk, some of which was not heard by their teachers, and some not responded to appropriately.

Inspection of such unresolved episodes in our data revealed a range of reasons for the failure of teachers to take up the learning opportunities they provided, in addition to the obvious one of pupils' inaudibility.

(i) Teachers usually worked through talking to identify and help resolve pupils' difficulties, when they were aware of them.

Only once in our data did a teacher completely abandon the activity of a pupil when knowing he was floundering. This was when Alastair had been working at an anagram exercise on the computer. When the teacher was with him he appeared anxious, resorting to random-seeming letter pressing and wild guessing, so she told him to leave it to do something else. Shortly after he paired up with another pupil at the same task and relaxed visibly (our observation sheet shows 'sings', and several 'laughs' during the three minutes this occupied), and appeared to be on the verge of understanding, when he was again told to leave it and go and sit down.

Significantly perhaps, before the session started Mrs Macdonald had said she didn't expect much of Alastair because he was being slow. Afterwards she commented that this had been for him a typical 'thrown off key' day. Because of a change of routine due to staff absence she believed he was 'not prepared to take anything on'. Alastair himself said afterwards that doing the letters on the computer had been difficult but that he didn't know why.

In this example the teacher's low expectations of the target pupil reduced the likelihood that he would be able to meet any challenges he encountered in his work.

(ii) Cases when a teacher did not develop opportunities for reflection were much more frequent. This sometimes appeared to result from a teacher's failure to follow up on a pupil's line of thinking because of the dominance of her own goals as in the following illustration:

The target pupil Johnnie had an arm injury and had been X-rayed. Class 'newstime'.

Johnnie: We went back and there was a crack in my bone, and there was some fluid in it.

T: What does that mean, do you know, fluid? (No pause for a reply). It's swollen is it?

Johnnie: Yes.

T: What is the cure? What did he give you? Anything?

Johnnie: Gave me a sling.

T: A sling. Did he give you any medicine?

Johnnie: It was a she who gave me the sling.

T: It was a. . . . ?

Johnnie: A she.

T: A lady doctor. And did she give you any medicines? I remember on Friday it was very sore. Did it get worse or did it get better?

Johnnie: Better a bit.

Every single statement by Johnnie had potential interest and possibilities for development. Both are lost in the teacher's focus on medicine and her kindly concern for the pupil feeling better.

Medical and dental events frequently aroused pupils' interest in this classroom. A second example of a lost opportunity happened when two pupils returned from the dentist.

Lynne: What did you get?

P: Cement.

Lynne: Cement. What's that? (amazed tone)

T:	Hello. Did you get a sticker?
P:	Yes.
T:	What does the sticker say?

Here the teacher was willing to use the dental incident as a learning opportunity for reading, but did not clarify the obvious puzzlement of the target pupil.

(iii)   Teachers could easily misinterpret a pupil's contribution.

During 'news' Johnnie picked up on what a pupil had said, saying that it was 'not news, that's a diary'.

T:	Now Johnnie asked a question. He said — what did you say Johnnie? What is a . . . ? What is a . . . ? You've forgotten the question you asked.
Johnnie:	Diary.
T:	Now that's a good question.
P:	It is a thing, it's a diary that you write the things about you.
Johnnie:	No, I was meaning that's a diary. It's meant to say news.
T:	Well it's like a news book.
P:	And you write things in it that you do and everything . . .
T:	Everyday when you're here, you write something about your news, don't you. So that means you are keeping a record of what you do everyday, and that's your diary. Look Gill has got one . . .

In retrospect the teacher said that Johnnie's mention of diary was not expected, but that she had taken it up and perhaps spent too long discussing it.

(iv)   There were occasions when pupils picked up errors in work material, or made by the teacher, which could have been highlighted more and pupils praised for their alertness and accuracy.

Lynne:	Is that a W? That's a W but the teacher put L (on board) Miss, it's will. It's WILL but you put LILL.
T:	(changes it) My brother will . . .

On another occasion pupils read aloud from a chart naming seasons. Winter, spring, summer, autumn, winter.

T:	Now have a look carefully. How many seasons does it give there?
P:	Five.
T:	But there are only . . .
P:	Four.
Johnnie:	Why has it got winter there?
T:	There is one month that is repeated again.
Johnnie:	I'll scribble it out.
T:	It's winter, quite right. No need to rub it out. When it's January it's all cold and there is snow and frost . . . (No explanation).

Pupils were quite exercised when they perceived an inconsistency in worksheets.

Johnnie: I dinnae get this.

T: You do. You're doing it very well.

Johnnie: Whenever it says October here it says 'j'.

T: That's on its own and this is a different exercise.

Johnnie: Why do they have to do October? It doesn't say.

T: They want you to do it both ways . . .

(v) On other occasions the teacher did not believe the pupil had a problem:

T: What does this say down here Johnnie?

Johnnie: I don't know what to do.

T: Right, Johnnie, I know it's a bit difficult for you but keep trying. You're doing very well. What's that? The 23rd . . .

Johnnie: It never tells you how to . . .

T: The 23rd so write rd.

and later again with the same target pupil.

T: Johnnie I'm sure you've written the date like this before haven't you?

There was no take up of the opportunity the teacher was given to ask Johnnie to explain why he was confused.

(vi) Opportunities for pupils to comment about their own progress and feelings about the work were sometimes missed:

T: Here's the scissors.

Lynne: It's boring.

T: Is it boring? Well why is it boring? Have you read it yet? What does it say? It's boring when you don't do anything but when you start reading then it becomes interesting. Come on Lynne, what does it say here?

The teacher's comments and questions about the work were not given in such a way as to enable an answer and reflection by Lynne about her own work. As comments like those made by Lynne appear infrequently this seems a pity.

(vii) Occasionally teachers gave feedback or instructions to pupils that were ambiguous or contradictory. In the following instance the pupil's initial confusion was exacerbated.

Alastair, the target pupil, was engaged on a simple colouring task. He asked the teacher what colour something should be, was told it was for him to decide, but then immediately after it was pointed out by the teacher that his choice was incorrect.

T: Alastair, who decides what colour things ought to be?

Alastair: Concrete is brown.

T: Have you coloured the concrete in brown? Alastair, I just said, if you colour that in brown will you be able to see . . .

Alastair:	How about red concrete?
T:	You can have any colour . . .

(viii) Sometimes the teacher's responsiveness appeared open but concealed the determination/goal of eliciting a certain concept from pupils. This sometimes diverted discussion and led to confusion.

T:	And think about why his back was bent. Right Johnnie, what's the word? What do you need?
Johnnie:	Cos the bag was too big and it bent his neck.
T:	Was it too big or what else could it have been? Too . . . ?
Johnnie:	Too big.
P:	Too small.
T:	No, you could have a big bag on your back but it doesn't mean to say it could bend your back . . . What happens if I put lots and lots of books into a bag?
P:	It'd be heavy.
T:	That's right so why did the man have a bent back?
Johnnie:	Cos his bag was full of clocks.

Teachers' attempts to explain were sometimes puzzling to a pupil, as in the following long digression when the pupil had actually correctly read 'ticket'.

T:	Now when you go on the bus, what do you get?
Lynne:	A bus pass.
T:	A bus pass but also a . . . ?
Lynne:	Ticket? (puzzled)
T:	A ticket. You're quite right. Some people don't get tickets. They just have to show their . . . ?
Lynne:	Bus pass.
T:	But when you go on the bus Lynne?
Lynne:	I have to pay.
T:	You have to pay.
Lynne:	Twenty pence.
T:	And what does the bus driver give you?
Lynne:	What?
T:	What does the bus driver give you?
Lynne:	A ride.
T:	Yes, but when you give him the money, what does he give back to you?
Lynne:	A ticket.
T:	A ticket.
Lynne:	Why, why a ticket? Why, what's a tick . . . ?
T:	He gives you a ticket doesn't he?
Lynne:	Why, why? It doesn't do anything.
T:	Well, cos if somebody, if any inspector . . .
	(Does not finish, and turns attention to another pupil).

This long effort on the pupil's part to guess what the teacher wanted from her (particularly mystifying in this example because she had already read and said the right word) contains a genuine question concerning the function of tickets which was not taken up at all.

The above dialogue is one of several similar examples where a teacher probably felt she was encouraging a pupil to think. But it can be seen to be unsatisfactory from the pupil's point of view. She had already read the word, one of many with ck in the middle, in its sentence. She had no difficulty at all in knowing what a bus ticket is, but she did find it hard to understand her teacher's questioning. When she finally asked an intelligent question this was unanswered.

(ix)   Finally at times a teacher's focus was on a pupil's language rather than on what was being communicated, and this could lead to curtailment of the discussion and the implication to pupils that what they said was not acceptable.

During class 'news'

Lynne: Laura's going to come across and watch it at my house cos her telly's on the conk.

P: On the blink.

T: You mean it's broken.

Lynne: Aye, on the blink.

T: It's broken. I see.

P: That's what we say, on the blink.

T: You're going to get it repaired?

Lynne: No it's Laura's telly what's on the blink.

T: Oh, I see. Broken, all right.

The pupils involved were aware of the alternative phrases they used and that it might be necessary to explain these at times. But the teacher's response in effect failed to take the opportunity of talking about usage and effectively curtailed communication.

Our illustrations are selected from a larger number of unresolved episodes which almost all occurred within two of the classrooms studied. A few came from classroom 3, where evidence of challenging episodes was very sparse as we have noted: overwhelmingly the remainder occurred in classroom 2. Pupils in this classroom regularly expressed their failure to understand, or asked for explanations which were not taken up by the teacher. We have already noted that their teacher used very little Category 2 talk, encouraging reflection by pupils, and that she typically gave pupils a lot of rather general encouragement and feedback. More Category 2 talk by Mrs Stevenson, specifically responding to the many pupil initiatives, questions and requests which occurred could have sometimes turned inconclusive and sometimes rather desultory classroom dialogue into challenging, enriching, learning episodes. We have already noted that the teacher's own 'agenda' of desired outcomes for her pupils often appeared in practice to restrict her responses in a manner reminiscent of Edwards and Westgate's (1987) analysis of classroom discussions. They describe teachers as inadvertently inhibiting fruitful pupil talk by asking too many questions, reformulating pupils' ideas, and limiting pupils' expression of alternative ideas by seeking 'right' answers.

Mrs Stevenson was very aware of the volatility of pupils' emotions and this awareness seemed to lead her to play safe for much of the time, and not to fully capitalize on the many challenging opportunities which naturally arose during their everyday classroom experience.

Discussion

How reliable are these conclusions? There are many behavioural indications besides pupils' talk of their engagement in class activities. A combination of recorded and observational data gives a picture of pupil involvement which both researchers used to identify episodes of reflection with consensus. It may be that reflection was happening at other times, unobserved. However, many of the behavioural observations made in the classrooms where episodes rarely occurred were of pupils who were chatty, distracted, sleepy, or mildly disruptive. And in the exceptionally busy classroom 3 there seemed little likelihood of serious reflection by pupils because of the rapid pace at which lessons were conducted and the intensity and dominance of the teacher's talk. Here there were few periods of thinking time and the emphasis was on doing, finishing 'our work' and 'concentration'. Unfortunately quite often what had to be concentrated upon was undemanding and unengaging to the pupils. There was also a serious mismatch between one set of observations concerning a target pupil and his assiduity, albeit at an undemanding task, and his teacher's insistence that he had not been working satisfactorily and that she was 'very disappointed'. Such findings if frequent are bound to give rise to concern.

Radiomicrophones are invaluable aids to analyzing classroom interactions because of the clarity and sensitivity of the recordings. Not only did they pick up pupils' yawns, moans, humming and singing but also occasional *sotto voce* comments and quiet answers to teachers' questions addressed to others. This talk provides evidence of times when pupils are alert and making contributions although sometimes these were ones which any teacher would be extremely unlikely to detect.

Perhaps more surprising were teachers' failure to respond to pupils' explicit statements of incomprehension or requests for help. As noted these occurred with both target pupils in classroom 2. Both persisted in asking for explanations concerning their work and were often to remain unsatisfied. Here the teacher tended to give them general advice or reassurance, like:

'Read the passage again and it tells you', or 'You do understand and you're doing very well' where they had expressed a need for more explicit, direct, feedback or instructions.

There was an uncertainty and ambivalence of approach, with the teacher apparently so concerned to not upset her admittedly fairly volatile pupils that she inadvertently increased their level of frustration with general (sometimes vague) directions and an air of detachment from the work itself on occasion. This is illustrated by references to worksheets as 'they want you to do it both ways'. Class discussions were lengthy with very little teacher participation, but when she joined in, it was to direct the news items towards didactic ends as in 'what is a liquid — is it something that flows?' in the context of a potentially absorbing account of a pupil's hospitalized sister on an intravenous 'drip'.

The likelihood of lengthy reflective episodes was consistency high in the two remaining classrooms. They occurred both during individual work and in whole class activity, and unresolved episodes were never observed. As the depictions of sessions show episodes of reflection were often linked within sessions. Mrs Guthrie in particular would return briefly to an activity which had been explored earlier, in a naturally contextualizing way, such as asking the target pupil the time as break approached, after he had earlier worked on time work cards, and leaving him alone with an instruction to 'think about it' when engaged in shape, and revisiting him over a lengthy period of some eight minutes. The atmosphere is confident, relaxed, and pupils' frequent chuckles are evidence of their enjoyment.

Mrs Guthrie and Mrs Law referred to their pupils' cognitions and strategies in an unforced way. They talked of the processes of planning, checking, and noticing, and asked pupils for their ideas and explanations, and predictions of likely consequences. They frequently asked whether things 'made sense', and referred to different people's interpretations and likely misunderstandings, sometimes using themselves as examples. Mrs Law in particular used role play as a means of reinforcing the fact that messages can be ambiguous and are liable to misinterpretation. In short their interactions with pupils were evidence of their expectations concerning their pupils' ability to reflect during class activities. They engaged in quite lengthy dialogues to this end, as we saw in chapter 5's examples.

The evidence from this study is that pupils' enjoyment was greatly enhanced in those classrooms whose teachers had greater expectations and made greater demands. Often when pupils were engaged in practising skills using individual worksheets and with one-to-one teaching, they appeared frustrated and bored and gave the impression of low ability, in contrast to the enthusiastic participation by the pupils in the more cognitively demanding classrooms. This is not to claim that the latter pupils found learning easy. They experienced many obstacles, were sometimes emotionally upset, and found it quite difficult to work together in groups. But there was also clear evidence of episodes of engagement, interest, and a sense of achievement.

In this chapter the process of reflection has been located within episodes when pupils were challenged intellectually. The episode bank from which our illustrations were drawn was built up by rather conservative means and there may well have been some omissions. However at this stage the following points can be made with confidence.

First, in order to make reasonable judgments about pupils' experience of intellectual challenge it is essential to examine the roles of both teachers and pupils during verbal interaction. Simply identifying a teacher style that potentially encourages reflection by pupils as described in chapter 4 is not enough.

At the risk of oversimplification our evidence suggests that in classroom 2 satisfactory reflective episodes were rare because the teacher did not respond contingently and specifically to her pupils' focus of interest, but gave general encouragement of a Category 3 type. There was in addition the pervasive influence of predetermined goals which resulted in many lost opportunities, in the form of pupils' ideas being curtailed or undeveloped, or substituted by those of the teacher.

In classroom 3 a number of factors are believed to have inhibited reflection: pressure of time, set materials that failed to ignite pupils' interest, emphasis on finishing an end product, and fiddly practical activities. Most important, however, was the lack of pupil interest and initiative which was exhibited in a variety of ways, so that the teacher's talk which could potentially have enabled productive reflective episodes to develop was ineffective.

From the remaining two classrooms comes ample evidence that reflective episodes were frequent, satisfying, experiences for pupils and their teachers. Both necessary components were present: pupil interest and teacher responsiveness concerning work that was sufficiently but not excessively challenging. 'Empathetic challenging' is an appropriate descriptive phrase of this teacher style coined by Bonnett (1994) in his philosophical discussion of thinking in education.

In the following chapter our teachers' educational philosophies, feelings, and expectations concerning their pupils illuminate these findings on their classroom practice.

7 Behind and Beyond Reflective Classrooms

The teacher styles described in the preceding chapters have developed over the years, and will be affected by a variety of influences including practice within their current school. They will also 'reflect teachers' implicit beliefs about how children learn and how best they can be helped to do so', as Edwards and Mercer (1987) comment in their detailed classroom observation study. This chapter first describes some of the beliefs held by the teachers and relates these to their styles of teaching, and then considers the broader issue of the prevailing ethos of their classrooms.

So the focus of our discussion on classroom reflection is broadened in this chapter. There is a move away from detail to larger issues, those of teachers' differing views and philosophies, touching on values and beliefs about human worth, their theories about how pupils learn and how best to help them learn, and their own feelings about their job. This is a rich enlightening data source and we are privileged to have access to it. The four teachers are very different individuals with varied experiences who work in different schools. But important themes emerge from discussion with them which have relevance for most teachers of pupils across a wide ability range.

Investigation of Teachers' Views

The views and perceptions of the teachers themselves are the focus of this section and the words of the teachers, in the ultimate form of transcripts, are the basis for exploring and analyzing these views and perceptions. Information was obtained by semi-structured in-depth interviews. First the researchers chose broad issues to be covered in the interview and developed a guide containing questions to encourage the teachers to discuss them. The questions, and the interview schedule as a whole, were carefully screened to make sure that the teacher was not led into a restricted discussion which only reflected the researchers' values and agenda, and that interviewees would be able to express their own ideas in their own way, and there would be the opportunity for unexpected issues or ideas to emerge.

The interview guide was developed on the basis of a review of the literature, from issues that had emerged throughout the research and from discussion between the researchers. It was in four sections which covered the teachers' background in teaching, the learning environment, reflective thinking and the research project itself: the teachers had been sent the reports so far written up on the project, and their reactions and views on these were sought.

The interviews were conducted individually with each of the four teachers, who were all very generous with their time. Interviews lasted between one and two hours. Three were tape recorded and one interview was conducted over the telephone and recorded direct.

Analysis involved careful readings of the transcripts making notes of interesting points. Contradictions, similarities, themes, developments and approaches were noted and after several readings it was possible to link these.

Findings

The teachers' experience

All four teachers had from fourteen to eighteen years of actual teaching experience, three of them having taken breaks to have a family. Three teachers had a variety of teaching experience with infants and primary posts before going into special education. One teacher had taught for a year after training but not enjoyed it: she then became a residential social worker but found herself teaching as part of the job:

> So I went back into teaching, through the back door as it were, but into special needs. I think my interest had always been there, and I think that was why I found teaching so difficult, because my interest has always been with the children who are failing, showing problems, and I felt very frustrated in my probationary year not really being able to address their problems sufficiently. (Mrs Guthrie)

So apart from one year's probationary teaching this teacher's experience has been all with special educational needs including support teaching within mainstream, and has ranged from pupils with hearing and learning difficulties to behaviourally and emotionally disturbed children. The other three teachers had spent varying lengths of time in special education. Mrs Macdonald had been in her present school for eleven years having previously done learning support for two or three years. Mrs Law had been in special education for fourteen years and had taught for eight years in her present school. Her previous experience included four years supply teaching with special education, some time with hearing impaired children and a post within a support unit that was a resource for psychologists that catered for primary and secondary children. Her description of this experience gives a flavour of her approach to her teaching and to her career:

> . . . there were primary and secondary, and a lot of acting out children, but some withdrawn and some with specific learning difficulties, and

the added dimension to the job was that we were involved with other professionals to a far greater extent than I ever had before, in meetings with psychologists, social workers, whatever. And working with a psychologist who believed very much in family therapy, and who involved us in achieving her ends and working towards specific aims with a family and with children. And that was very professionally developing, and I really enjoyed that.

Mrs Stevenson had spent the least time within special education with four years' experience, two within her present school and some time as a home-based teacher with excluded children, but she had had longer experience in mainstream education that included secondary, junior and infant teaching.

Teachers' views about reflective thinking

The four teachers' responses to the question 'What do you understand by the term reflective thinking?' are given below and this section of the book shows that it appeared that the two teachers who used the greatest percentage of talk that encouraged reflective thinking had a qualitatively different approach to reflective thinking from that of the other two teachers.

> Encouraging children to probe deeper into what they have said and how they think.

> Well, what exactly your responses are, how you take in what people are saying to you, what you feel that they are saying, how your understanding of it, and how you respond back. I think that's an example of reflective thinking, because you've taken in information, churned it around in your head, done your processing and then . . . back.

> I should have read that (report) again, shouldn't I. (Laughter) You're challenging yourself, it's that process that goes on, that you know, how am I doing, what, how can I deal with this, what can I bring to this, how is this affecting me. That internal self challenging that goes on.

> Oooof. Ehm, thinking in depth about things, ehm, just where your thinking is challenged in any way, where you are not just reacting on a superficial level, where you are thinking beyond the immediate thing to its implications and possibilities and extensions. I think!

At this stage both Mrs Guthrie and Mrs Law bring in the element of 'challenge' and the idea of depth, where you are not 'reacting on a superficial level'. Mrs Stevenson also introduces the idea of depth in the first quotation, but this is not expanded on, and Mrs Macdonald in the second seems to be describing the cognitive process more than the metacognitive process.

When discussing the role reflective thinking played in education, all four teachers felt that it was an integral part of education. They emphasized how easy it was to underestimate their pupils, that they needed to be challenged and 'stretched'. Even with their extensive experience and very small groups two emphasized how they had to be constantly on guard against low expectations and how,

> Suddenly you get a flash and you think 'gosh' especially with other people working with them. They don't know the child so well and they make a demand you wouldn't have thought of making and it gets results sometimes . . . (Mrs Law)

and

> I have found that expectations can be very limiting because they surprise you . . . just stun and amaze you if you give them the opportunity. (Mrs Guthrie)

The role of reflective thinking within education was expanded on in very different ways by three of the teachers.

Mrs Macdonald, who had defined reflective thinking more in direct cognitive terms, seemed to believe that her pupils did not think reflectively and linked this apparent inability to 'concentration' in a way that implied that this was the whole problem:

> I don't think they would consciously think about what they are doing, I mean a lot of the time the responses you get, well, I don't think they think about it, if the information's there they will tell you, but sometimes they just open their mouths and anything comes out. And whether there's been some thought process in there is debatable, because it might not be anything to do with what you have actually asked them. Although I suppose that says that they've been thinking about something else other than what you've been thinking about, or what you were trying to get them to think about. But that's concentration, as opposed to, you know, anything else.

In contrast Mrs Guthrie immediately accepted the teacher's role in developing what she called 'this critical awareness' in pupils and linked this to the value of a more open-ended approach to teaching:

> . . . I mean children do need to . . . ehm . . . need to be helped to develop this critical awareness in the way that other children seem to pick up quite naturally. They are relating to their environment and what goes on there, they are learning those lessons naturally. Whereas our children need to have it pointed out to them, the fact that . . . it's

got to be pointed out when it happens and they are doing it, and what to do, are they benefitting from it. In fact there's that overlap too, from one situation to the next, they are not good at that . . . This is where that more open-ended approach to teaching gives much more value to them because without having to make explicit the road we were taking, there would be a natural progression from one situation to another, rather than this compartmentalising that we are doing. Life's not like that, not made of compartments, of specific bits of learning.

She recognized that this approach sounded very 'airy fairy' and 'idealistic'. But as she said:

> . . . I'm experienced enough a teacher to know that (things) have got to be organized and arranged and with thought behind them, but I do believe that it's a much more fruitful way of learning, if it can be achieved . . .

In an interesting aside, it was at this point that this teacher linked a teacher's ability to take this 'creative learning' approach to the wider school environment and the fact that there was greater scope to take this approach where there was a:

> . . . sense of value all around, everyone felt that what they had to say was of value and worth, and that there was a great deal of respect for one another, in all areas — teacher, children . . .

In a similar manner Mrs Law accepted the teacher's role in developing reflective thinking in pupils and again linked this into a broader approach to education:

> I think it's (reflective thinking) important: if you just do things and don't think about them, well they may as well never have happened. Things don't get processed into the computer that is the brain unless there is reflection. And I think good teaching provides structures that enables pupils to reflect on what they have done, whether it be a picture or a story or just a discussion that helps them to go over it again, and extrapolate what is important to them or what they enjoyed or what they might do next time. Generally enrich what they actually experienced, and as I say, enabling them to go over it in a mental way, as I say if they just go through things and never have an opportunity to reflect then I think very quickly that experience will, unless it was all the more exciting, will just disappear and slip out the back, and I think the more reflection and the more different forms of reflection you put on to any experience, then the deeper the impact will be.

In Mrs Macdonald's approach there is the implication that thinking should produce a 'correct' answer, and instead of acknowledging that what pupils think may be built on in a constructive way, the implication is that they are not concentrating if they are not following the same line of thought as the teacher. In contrast the other teachers have a constructivist approach where the starting point is the pupil, the pupil's thinking and the pupil's experience, and the aim and skill of the teacher is to identify where the pupil is and to draw out and build on this experience.

Identification of reflective thinking

In looking at how teachers recognize that their pupils were thinking reflectively, Mrs Guthrie simply says that it is when they are 'engaged' and that it is 'absorption', which is a very broad, subjective approach. She was not able to define precisely how she recognized reflective thinking, but she was prepared to accept and to read into pupil behaviour the implication that thinking was taking place, rather than seeing it as an explicit, precise process. She had the confidence to do this, confidence in her own judgment and also confidence in her own professional expertise:

> It can be communication, — they're talking with each other or the teacher, but yes, engaged is the word. Caught up in what they are doing.

Mrs Law also takes a broad, subjective approach to judging whether pupils are thinking reflectively, and is prepared to use her judgment and intuition:

> Only really, by their utterances or by what they produce, in terms of, as I say speaking or pictures or what they ask you to scribe, if that's appropriate. I mean you can also learn what they are thinking by their errors, by what they are not able to do. When you see them failing you realize the point that they have reached, and you realize what your next input must be. So you can see where their thinking has taken them, and where they now need support.

Here there is an interesting contrast. This teacher is prepared to use 'errors' and 'what they are not able to do' to judge where the pupil is in the thinking process, whereas Mrs Macdonald sees the process as being more clearcut:

> *Interviewer*:   To what extent can you tell if a pupil is thinking reflectively?
> I suppose if you gave them a question, if you asked them something that would mean that they had to think about something — and they responded with a correct answer then you would know. (Mrs Macdonald)

By implication an 'error' would mean that thinking (reflective or otherwise) was not taking place, and there is no apparent use of the teacher's intuition or judgment.

In answer to the same question Mrs Stevenson does not elaborate beyond saying,

> By what they say or write, how they act. How else can you tell what is going on in children's minds?

This uncertainty is also expressed later on when she says she 'finds it difficult sometimes, in knowing what they think'.

Teachers' approaches to reflective thinking

Mrs Stevenson's comments frequently referred both to her pupils' need for success and their emotional vulnerability, and her classroom practice showed some ambivalence. Pupils were, she said, assessed very closely to determine what they could do and the idea was to build on that and to avoid frustrating experiences. Situations were carefully presented and material deliberately organized. But this teacher also said that she had noticed incidentally that the best situations were spontaneous and child centred, with the pupils themselves raising the questions. She often felt that the teacher should have more of a facilitator's role, encouraging pupil's thinking, often as it arose in discussion. She advocated group discussions, practical activities in groups, drama, and sequencing games, like predicting what happens next. There was evidence of some conflict between what she actually did, and what she would perhaps have liked to do. In practice the constant awareness of desired outcomes (for example, certain concepts) apparently sometimes inhibited discussion.

The following example is taken from a class news time. Johnnie's sister was in hospital, and had been given an intravenous infusion.

Johnnie:	What is liquid food Miss?
T:	What do we mean by liquid food Johnnie?
	Good question. What is liquid food?
Pupil:	It makes it go through the tubes and then into the person.
T:	Yes it's something. What is a liquid?
	Is it something that flows or is it something that's solid?
Pupil:	It goes for your brains.
T:	It's opposite to solid isn't it? It's a liquid . . . it moves. Think of something you would drink.

General chatter follows with the loss of an opportunity to explore a promising and interesting line. The teacher's restricted use of discussion appears bound by implicit curricular goals and there is conflict between following these and a more open-ended discussion following pupils' interest.

The classroom practice of Mrs Macdonald was clearly strongly influenced by her belief that the pupils' difficulties were a result of failures in concentration.

To focus on anything for any length of time, sometimes even a short time can be difficult for them. You have to try to work in areas of trying to develop their concentration span.

She liked to use aids like television, tape-recorded stories with headphones and workbooks with audio-taped instructions to help pupils to focus attention, and emphasized that they would switch off without bright and interesting materials and a lively approach.

> You can't compete with the cartoon characters or something that's bright and colourful on a television . . . so I mean if you can get their attention onto something that's educational and it's on the television I think it's a wonderful thing.

The sessions we recorded were conducted at a brisk pace with frequent reminders to pupils to attend and the use from time to time of deliberate mistakes by the teacher with the same aim.

The following example is taken from a session on phonics:

T:	Right. You will have to check that I read those words right. Are you ready? Roll, yell, bell, shell.
Pupil:	That's right.
Teacher pauses	meaningfully.
Another pupil:	Miss, can you say that again?
T:	Well, yell, bell, shell. I said 'roll' and you said that's right. You'll have to listen.

Mrs Macdonald swiftly moved on, so that pupils did not have the satisfaction of noticing and drawing attention to her 'mistake'. There was little opportunity for pupils' initiations, or production of ideas. This seemed to stem directly from the teacher's view that they needed to be kept busy concentrating on teacher-directed activities, prepared in detail beforehand.

Mrs Law agreed that 'the learning environment has to be rich and stimulating', but pointed out that:

> Because it's rich and stimulating doesn't necessarily mean that the children will learn or take from it because they won't. You can put up displays for all you like but they will very often never see it, just walk past.

She emphasized that teachers need to engage in 'challenging and asking them to examine what it is they are saying and doing and what the consequences will be because often they never go that far'. She stressed that teachers' responses to pupils must be clear, unambiguous and immediate: 'Strike while the iron is hot', but that teachers also needed to 'weigh up' when it's time to say 'what do

you think?' and 'I am much more now inclined to throw it back at them and
see what they come up with', and that this applied to most classroom activities.

Among many imaginative activities favoured by this teacher was the use
of metacommunication tasks, in which pupils had to convey precise information to listeners whose needs they had to understand and make allowance for.

In this typical example the pupils have made cheese boats and are giving
verbal instructions to the teacher who enacts them before writing them down
for another class.

> *T:*   OK. I'm going to test your instructions and see if they
> work . . . 'And then stick cocktail sticks into the boat.'
>
> *Pupils:*   No . . . no. That's wrong. Stick it on.
>
> *T:*   So there's something missing isn't there?
>
> *Pupil:*   Stick it on the cheese.
>
> *T:*   Right.
>
> *Pupils:*   Oh (laughter).
>
> *T:*   Right. Tell me what to write so that it makes sense.

Pupils finally agree on complete and comprehensible instructions.

Mrs Law also told of how she had come to see the value of drama, where
the value was in the fun and allowing pupils to get caught up in the action so
that they overcame feelings of inadequacy and being wrong, and where a real
and immediate, rather than abstract, context was created that provided far
superior thinking.

> The quality of thinking is just in a different class altogether, because
> it's meaningful and immediate to them, and in a context that, however
> momentarily, was a real one, in terms of their imagination at that time.

Mrs Guthrie endorsed the values of creative activities, citing specific techniques like guided imagery in artwork, 'you are taking them into the situation,
where it will go from here, they are engaged in it'. And she added that activities like drama gave pupils a sense of worth and value, that 'leads them to a
greater sense of self-awareness, "what I have", "what I do", "what I, how I
think", is important — and it's not a matter of right or wrong'.

She also practised and valued:

> a lot of the cognitive sort of open-ended stuff. I love that kind of area
> where they are looking at things happening, and having to think about
> why it's happening, and what kind of logic you know is happening
> and why.

She believed that her pupils were motivated to know and understand, and that
she was just: 'hooking in to their natural curiosity'.

News sessions were especially lively and productive in this classroom. The following illustration was typical: Mark had brought in a magazine on dinosaurs.

T: What happens to the body of a dinosaur Mark? Can you see? What happens to it under the water?
Pupil: Bones.
T: Sh. Let Mark answer.
Mark: Turns into a skeleton.
T: That's right. What happens to the flesh? And the skin? And the parts that are soft? Sam?
Pupil: It crinkles away.
T: It crinkles away. What's another word?
Mark: Rots.
T: It rots away — and all you're left with are the bones.
Mark: The bones.
T: Then thousands and thousands of years later the sea has disappeared and more land has come on top. And this man goes out for a walk. What does he see sticking out?
Pupil: A head.
T: People called archeologists come along and they chip away very carefully and they discover the bones and the teeth — think about it.

The conversation continued for a long time with the introduction of new ideas and new vocabulary, and with all the pupils appearing engrossed, enthusiastically involved in planning a dinosaur project and a museum visit.

This session is a good illustration of the kind of cognitive involvement and advance that Mrs Guthrie described in her interview.

I just love that excitement when you get, when you — you know they're there. They've got it or they've brought something to it you never expected.

In the interviews teachers were asked for their opinions on one-to-one teaching and on peer groups, and whether these encouraged reflection in pupils.

Mrs Macdonald saw her teaching as being 'on-call' all the time as pupils were not often able to work independently. She said that more time for one-to-one work with pupils would be wonderful but was not practicable, as with ten pupils who were all demanding there were constant interruptions. She would be wary of setting up peer group teaching because of the danger of pupils being shown up or bullied. Again her sensitivity to concentration difficulties and pre-adolescent vulnerability was highlighted.

Mrs Stevenson emphasized the value of individual teaching for all pupils and especially those who were nervous and withdrawn. She also said that there were benefits in peers explaining to each other and in joint problem-solving. Both could help their learning and understanding.

As noted in chapters 3 and 5, Mrs Macdonald's and Mrs Stevenson's pupils were in fact occupied in individual work for over half the total recorded class-room time, and this was considerably more than in the other two classrooms.

Mrs Guthrie said that the large proportion of individualized work in her classroom was a result of classroom management constraints. She would have preferred more group work but would need a helper to monitor a group: otherwise the pupils were unlikely to achieve anything purposeful because they did not relate well together. She felt they were able to achieve something constructive in individual work. But she highlighted the dangers of isolation and dependency in pupils working alone, and felt that group work was much better for them; they would be working collaboratively and learning to be social beings. Her pupils spent equal proportions of time overall in whole class and individual activities; and a greater proportion of small groupwork than was experienced by Mrs Law's pupils, whose commitment to whole class activity was clear in her interview and in practice occupied over half the class time recorded, being much the highest of the four.

Mrs Law said that in an ideal world nothing except care should be one-to-one, but that in practice some pupils were likely to feel exposed in group work, and like Mrs Guthrie she said that the availability of help determined the feasibility of small group work. She believed that group activities were more stimulating for pupils, although their differing abilities meant they very rarely worked absolutely together. Her solution was to teach the class as a whole for much of the time with lots of changes of pace and activity. Mrs Law's experience of peer teaching was mixed. The potential gains for teachers were great. They could be illuminated by seeing one child teaching another, understanding their thinking, seeing their self esteem rise and their learning being reinforced. But she had experienced some pupils being very bossy and managing with their peers to the extent that they could impede rather than assist learning.

Teachers' feelings and expectations for their pupils

Mrs Law was aware that she reacted to pupils' behaviour more strongly than many other teachers dealing with special educational needs and said that she felt comfortable in doing so because she treated her own children in the same way.

> And that is from a position of great love, but also the knowledge that I am responsible for them, and that I must not let them do things which are going in the end to be wrong, or lead them into wrong ways. So because I have that great love I also have that great responsibility.

Love for the pupils is not commonly discussed in educational writing but this was not the only teacher who expressed a deep emotional bond. Mrs Guthrie also said: 'I find I gravitate towards the children who really are showing quite different behaviour, behaviourally disturbed, emotionally disturbed children.' She said she had worked with some pupils who were 'absolutely floundering' and this had made her feel desperate and she felt she couldn't cope with seeing children struggling in a situation where resources would not allow her to help them.

> There's always this dissonance I find in myself as to what I'd like to be doing or having my children be or do, and the constraints in which I am working, which are caused by the education system of which I am part.

This teacher said her approach was that everyone has something to give and it helped her feel open and responsible to the pupils. 'I suppose because I am a Christian I look for the good.'

Her empathy with the pupils was expressed when she said:

> I think our schools are quite bleak places . . . I feel quite miserable going into school every day and I'm not surprised the kids do.

Remarkably this teacher's classroom sessions were notable for their bursts of pupils' delighted laughter.

She explained that she had greatly enjoyed teaching where there was a sense of value all round, everyone felt that what they had to say was of value and worth, and there was a great deal of respect for one another, parents and children.

Mrs Stevenson also indicated her emotional commitment to her pupils when she expressed her worry that at school 'we criminalize children . . . (they are seen as) "bad" children therefore we must punish. Instead I feel they are "sad" children who need help.'

She stressed that regardless of academic achievement many pupils will grow up to be lovely human beings and 'we can help them to be self disciplined and responsible, confident, adults' and again she used the family analogy. 'Respect, communication, (are important) it's like any family.'

The fourth teacher, Mrs Macdonald, expressed her pessimism for the future of many pupils alongside her sympathy with them. 'They have quite a sad life and, you know, school is one of, probably, their mainstays in their whole life and they probably will never get anything like it again' and 'I think some of the homes they come from, the lack of parental support, the lack of any kind of support for them, the lack of them being developed at home . . . and they see the kind of lives their parents or maybe their family have and they think that's the way they're going to live for the rest of their lives . . . And I think that's outwith any teacher's control', and later, saying how depressing an experience it had been when she carried out a small follow up study of some of her former pupils.

One didn't even recognize me, was in her nightie still at lunchtime, that was the way the family lived. I mean, just no sparkle at all, nothing to live for, nothing to really have a reason to get up for in the morning. It's very sad.

The pessimism this teacher expressed so honestly about her pupils' future and about the effect that schooling might have in mitigating or ameliorating this was very striking and may have related to her conviction that bright cheerful lively classes which helped pupils to concentrate, and entertained them, were all important.

This view contrasted with that of the three other teachers who all admitted feeling frustrated or depressed with their work at times but nevertheless had a fundamentally optimistic view about their pupils and their potential: this was illustrated by such comments as 'I believe there's a way with every child', and saying that teaching is exciting in feeling that 'you have moved a human being on a bit': 'I do get a real buzz from kids coming on. Their minds fascinate me', and 'The aims (for special education) are the same for all children, to help them develop their full potential'.

The teachers whose classroom talk consistently contained a high proportion of Category 2 talk were aiming to encourage reflection in their pupils. Their classroom practice is clearly associated with their views about their pupils' learning difficulties and about education generally.

All the teachers were very aware of the importance of self-esteem in their pupils, and of their vulnerability in this respect, and all believed in variety and interest and the importance of lessening their distractibility. But these aspects of pupils were seen as primary, by Mrs Macdonald and Mrs Stevenson, as prerequisites to achievement; by the two other teachers they were also believed to be fostered by appropriate classroom experiences: if pupils were challenged cognitively and their opinions and ideas taken seriously and listened to, then they would increasingly feel more confident and more knowledgeable about themselves as learners, and they would be more likely to be engaged and attentive. In other words if pupils were treated with respect as classroom participants by being held to account for their judgments, being expected to be accurate communicators and being given increasing responsibility for decision-making and planning then they would automatically become more confident and competent.

The other striking aspect of the views of the teachers whose own classroom talk particularly emphasized and encouraged reflection by pupils, was their endorsement of the importance of immediacy in their responses to pupils; clarity, 'pointing out what's happening and why', and seizing opportunities and interest as they arose, while crucially, also having the confidence and flexibility to:

go off with something, when the opportunity arises, go with it — because that's come from the child, it's come from the source, it's a response to the environment, it's meaningful, it has potential if something took off then I would abandon whatever was planned for the next day and just let it go. I think you have to strike when the iron is hot with any children and if something is going well, you know, stick with it. And if something is not going well, then just chuck it out. There's no point in labouring against, you know, you have to be responsive all the time to what's in front of you.

Mrs Law also expressed her view that teachers need to give clear messages, that they are often too cautious and tentative for pupils to understand.

Whereas in many special schools I think people give ambivalent messages without meaning to. They say 'now, Johnnie, that's naughty, you're not supposed to do that, now nobody else will be able to play with that toy because it's broken, what a shame' (gentle tone). Now the words are there, but the body language, the voice is all saying 'what a nice boy you are', and I don't think the child gets the messages. I don't believe they are able to extrapolate that.

Some features of special schools make them particularly favourable contexts for the kind of responsive flexible approach which involves a deep understanding of individual pupils and their particular difficulties in learning, and the creative ability to 'take off' as described by these teachers. Small classes and until recently, at least, considerable teacher autonomy concerning the curriculum, together with their skills and experience in analyzing and meeting individual pupils' educational needs favour a responsive approach which should enhance pupils' real and self-perceived effectiveness, and enable them to at least sometimes 'stun and amaze' their teachers.

Classroom Ethos

This chapter concludes with a discussion of classroom ethos and its role in facilitating learning, by engendering confidence, value and respect for all pupils.

Examples from two of the study classrooms were chosen for their illuminative nature out of many possible ones from all the four schools studied. They were selected and are discussed by Judith Scott, the researcher whose wide ranging approach and sociological training was especially valuable in this task, and from whose fuller publication the extracts are taken (Scott, 1994).

After many hours listening and transcribing the tapes, it became more than apparent that the dialogue that was written on the page was less than half the story, the important bits that were missing were the unseen and unheard past, the bit that had gone before, and the 'feel' of the classroom. In other words the context from which the written dialogue had been extracted was such an important part of the story that it could not be ignored. In this section we attempt to put some flesh on the abstract notion of the classroom environment or culture . . . or ethos . . . or 'feel'. This brings us to the first difficulty which is one of defining what exactly is meant by this abstract notion of ethos or culture. Each person tends to have their own idea of what they mean by this 'feel' or sense of the atmosphere, and any definition tends to narrow the concept. It is, however, the breadth of the concept that is both its strength and its weakness.

The subjective nature of the concept is raised further when attempting to define a 'good' or positive ethos or culture within a classroom. In general terms this has been taken to be an atmosphere that appears to promote the self-esteem of all the pupils in the classroom, where they are encouraged to see themselves and each other in a positive light, where they feel that they themselves and their ideas are valued, where there is a non-judgmental acceptance of each pupil's worth, where there is a relaxed, but controlled, sense of purpose, calmness and security.

This chapter looks at teacher talk and pupil talk from classrooms with this positive ethos, where there was a good 'feel' within the classroom, and discusses examples and incidents that would appear to promote, control and maintain the atmosphere within the classroom.

In looking at episodes of teacher and pupil talk this chapter is taking a very narrow perspective on the climate of a classroom. The atmosphere in the classroom itself is influenced by the school environment in which it rests, there are physical and material aspects to a school and classroom climate, there are organizational aspects, there are wider social and economic influences; in short the atmosphere or ethos in a classroom is a product of a full range of micro and macro influences. Rutter *et al.* (1979), in his seminal work, suggests that the 'cumulative effect of . . . various social factors was considerably greater than the effect of any of the individual factors on their own', and he continues, 'the implication is that the individual actions or measures may combine to create a particular ethos, or set of values, attitudes and behaviours which will become characteristic of the school as a whole'. Teacher and pupil talk is therefore only one particular aspect of this 'ethos, or set of values, attitudes and behaviours', but the examples investigated later in the chapter perhaps indicate at the same time the presence of wider influences and approaches within their school settings.

Within the educational field there is an increasing interest in the ethos of schools, involving a variety of disciplines and approaches. Rutter's work initiated the idea that the 'school effect' was a significant factor in pupil behaviour and attainments. This may seem a commonplace assumption now, but at the time when his study started there was 'widespread acceptance among academics that schools made little difference' (*ibid*). Research attention then focused on the extent to which ordinary schools vary in their effects on children's cognitive performance.

Within the child development and the psychological fields there has been a similar move towards acknowledging the importance of the context in which development was occurring. Nisbet (1990) points out that, within research on teaching and learning to think, the most interesting trend has been the recognition that thinking is not purely cognitive, but involves affective factors — feelings, values, attitudes and motivation.

The promotion of good management within education has led to the development of a set of performance indicators that include a number of indicators relating to school ethos. Her Majesty's Inspectorate, who developed these indicators, have commented on the 'good tone, atmosphere, spirit or ethos' in schools which are 'well led and where teaching and learning are effective and relationships are well handled' (SOED, 1992). The twelve ethos indicators they identified refer to the whole school experience and although none stands on its own, the focus in this paper is on three of them: pupils' morale, the learning context and teacher-pupil relationships. In an interesting slant, it is suggested that pupil morale is the most significant ingredient in the success of a school; it may equally be suggested that this is important for the pupils themselves. The focus is on the degree to which 'pupils enjoy school and feel that what they are learning is interesting and relevant'. Within the learning context, with the implication that this means the classroom, focus is on the expectations that both teachers and pupils bring to it, and on how they relate to one another within it. This overlaps with the indicator that addresses teacher-pupil relationships.

Harmonious relations between teachers and pupils and the degree of courtesy and respect are evidence of the 'ethos' prevailing in the learning context.

The topic is complex, and much of it cannot be explicitly illustrated by examples of classroom talk, but the quality of the teacher-pupil relationships and the degree of respect and courtesy involved are arguably both explicitly and implicitly illustrated in them.

Classroom Interaction and Ethos

The following excerpts of teacher and pupil talk are taken from classrooms where the ethos or culture appeared to be positive for pupils and teacher, and at the same time the whole school ethos or culture appeared to include many of the criteria discussed in the previous section. One of the striking aspects of these classrooms was the degree of respect that the teachers had for their pupils as individuals in their own right; this respect was shown in many ways, but from the point of view of gathering data and being able to provide an illustration this can only be shown by verbal communication taken from the transcripts. Respect in this sense involved the teacher encouraging the pupils to have consideration for each other, and modelling how to be considerate by her own approach to her pupils. Respect in a wider sense was approached through discussion of gender and race issues and also in a discussion on death. Respect is what Smith identifies along with interest as one of the two characteristics of classrooms which can facilitate thinking and learning, in his wide ranging analysis. 'There must be respect for those who are taught, and also for what is taught' and 'when teachers respect the feelings and opinions of their students then teachers and students become partners in whatever is thought about, to the advantage of both parties' (Smith, 1992).

Another noticeable factor within these classrooms was the consistency of approach of the two teachers, Mrs Guthrie and Mrs Law.

The first examples are all incidents selected from one morning session of normal classroom activities, and are placed in the order in which they occurred. The issues appear without being planned and it is interesting to note that the teacher is prepared to take all the opportunities to address issues as they arise.

The first short excerpts occur while the teacher and the majority group in the classroom are having a discussion: the teacher asks the permission of the pupils to interrupt their discussion in order to control and manage the two other pupils in the classroom.

Discussion between teacher and group of pupils:

> *T:* Can we just stop a wee minute while I sort Claire and Malcolm out.
>
> Teacher moves across room to sort out problem, before returning to continue discussion with the group.
> Discussion continues.
> And again a few minutes later:
> *T:* Claire, what are you doing. (Raised voice)
> *T:* Excuse me. (Quietly, to group she has been talking to.)

Teacher then moves across room to deal with the problem.

In asking the pupils' permission to interrupt the group work, the teacher indicates both respect for the pupils and that what they have been doing is important. As it is, the group sit quietly and wait while the disruption is being dealt with.

Later, during the course of the same morning, the issue of respect for others emerged involving the social aspects of race and gender, interspersed with the teacher encouraging pupils to respect each other within the classroom.

Pupils and teacher have been looking at four different pictures of people eating a meal and discussing what they saw. A pupil pointed out that the people in one picture had black hair:

> *P:* They're Paki.
> *T:* Could you use the word Pakistani that Karen used, 'cos it's nicer. Would you like us to call you a 'Scottie'?
> *P:* Nuh.
> *T:* No, you're Scottish, that's the proper word. So let's use the word Pakistani or Indian. They might be Indian.
> Discussion continues . . .
> A few minutes later . . .

T: I'm sorry.
T: It really is very hard to hear what Rachel says, and it's especially hard if other people are talking at the same time.
T: Rachel sat very quietly when you were talking Patrick . . .
Pause.
All silent.
T: Thank you.
Discussion then continues . . .
A few minutes later . . .

Discussion about the pictures of people eating meals continues

T: OK, another question. Let's look at the green picture. I'd like everyone's ideas on this. Who cleans this kitchen?
Louise: The lady.
T: Umm. (Pause) Hands up.
T: Who cleans this kitchen, Patrick?
Patrick: The mum.
T: The mum.
T: What do you think, Kirsty?
Kirsty: The mum.
T: Linda?
Linda: The dad. (Laughter)
T: He cleans the kitchen.
T: Why did you laugh?
Louise: Dads don't . . . some dads don't clean the kitchen. It's always the mum.
T: Some dads don't clean the kitchen. It's always the mums?
T: What do you think, Helen. Who do you think cleans this kitchen?
Helen: The mummy.
T: Rachel, who cleans this kitchen?
Rachel: The mum and the dad.
T: The mum and the dad.
Rachel: Yes.
T: Do they do it together?
Rachel: No.
T: Tina, who cleans this kitchen?
Tina: The lady in the house, the dusting and that . . .
T: So what do you think about that? Louise laughed when Linda said the daddy cleans the kitchen. (Laughter)
T: Your daddy and mummy both clean the kitchen?
Linda: Yeh.
Tina: Ma dad and me clean the kitchen. Ma mum and my sister clean the living room.

131

T: Right, so your dad does help clean, right. So what do you think about that?

Louise: Fine.

Tina: No bad.

T: So you think that's fine.

The discussion continues, and in a gentle way the issue has been seriously addressed and examined and all pupils have been included in the discussion.

On another occasion the following discussion took place. This arose during a game of 'musical telephones' which was to encourage the pupils both to communicate with each other and to communicate using the telephone. Two pupils were left holding telephones when the music stopped, the pupil with the red phone had to think of a person or organization such as auntie, friend, police, local 'take-away', to ring, and pupil with the black phone had to pretend to be that person, and between them they had to construct the conversation.

Pupils and teacher playing game of 'musical telephones' . . .

Tina: Hello, is that the hospital please?

Louise: Yes, it is.

Tina: I've phoned to see if my wee girl is OK.

Louise: No, she's died.

Tina: Ah.

Silence.

T: Louise would you make this like a real phone call, would you do that on the phone to somebody . . .

(*Linda:* You've said your daughter's died.)

T: Just put the phone down a minute please while we talk about this. Would you do that to somebody? (*Louise:* No.) No, I hope you wouldn't and I hope nobody ever does it to you, what a terrible thing. That does happen to people sometimes that their children are getting very ill and sadly sometimes they do die. What do you think people in hospital do if they have a child who dies, how do you think they tell the mums and dads? They don't phone up and tell them.

Helen: They wait till the mum comes in and then they tell her.

T: They would phone up and say please come to the hospital, we need to talk to you. You would never, ever talk like that on the phone, Louise. Can we start that phone call again. Right, start from the beginning.

Tina: Hello, is that the hospital?

Louise: Yes, please come down, I'd like to talk to you and your husband please.

Tina: Is it important?

Louise: Yes it is.

Tina:	OK, I am just coming.
T:	Good. (Music starts)

Again in a gentle, but firm, manner, respect for people's feelings was addressed and discussed; the issue was not ignored.

In another situation and classroom, respect is created and maintained in a more implicit rather than explicit manner. One way that demonstrates this is in how knowledge about home and family is put on an equal footing; it is not a one-way process of teacher expecting pupils to tell her about their family doings and news on demand, it is a give and take process which is genuine, voluntary and non-judgmental.

Class news time, where pupils and teacher are sitting around in a circle . . .

T:	. . . Good, is there anything else that has been happening last night that you want to tell us about?
T:	Did I tell you that Rory got a mouse this weekend, remember I told you we got a cat and a little kitten? Do you think it is a good idea to have a mouse as well if you've got a cat?

Discussion, about what might happen if you have a cat and mouse in the same house, follows.

The teacher has given her news as part of the class news time. Her news is part of a longer-term dialogue, where she had obviously talked about the cat before, and there was also no need to explain that Rory was one of her family, so that basic knowledge about family backgrounds was assumed to be shared by everyone.

With this background of having revealed a glimpse of her own family the teacher later on in the same session is able to ask about the people at the home of a pupil and to probe mildly, without any sense of threat or demand.

Talking about models they have made in the classroom . . .

T:	Did they like your car when you took it home?
T:	What did Alastair say?
Pupil:	He says, he went . . . (indistinct)
T:	Did he? That's super.
T:	And what about Stuart? What did your mum and your . . . what's his name, John, is it John?
Stuart:	Joe.
T:	Joe. What did he say about the car? Did they like it?

In this case the teacher is also indicating awareness and acceptance to the pupil of their particular home circumstances.

Humour and fun were an important part of the communicating process in this classroom, and again the fact that it was part of a two-way process took away any sense of threat to the pupil. The following example was part of a long session in which, building on a story the pupil had read in his reading book, the pupil had to think up and draw items to put into a cauldron in order to make up a witch's spell, and then make up magic words to accompany the spell. The teacher encouraged and cajoled the pupil to do this on his own, but he did not find use of his imagination and free thinking easy; the time span shows the degree of his difficulty, in that he has been set his task approximately thirty-five minutes before the following interaction occurs.

T:	I'm going to see Mark for a minute. How are you doing?
T:	Right, so what's your magic words?
Mark:	Uh . . .
Pause.	
T:	Goodness me, all this stuff will have boiled away to nothing by the time you have said your magic words. Let's leave the magic words for a minute if you're not sure. Is it because you can't think of any? Well do you want to put down some words that you know?
T:	What magic words do you know?
Mark:	Abracadabra.

A few moments later, after the teacher has dealt with another pupil.

T:	Good. Abracadabra.
T:	What's your spell for?
T:	No what are you going to do with this spell? Is there anything you would like to get rid of or change?
Pause.	
T:	Apart from magic the teacher into a frog, is that what you would like to do?
Mark:	What?
T:	Magic your teacher into a frog.
Mark:	Aye.
T:	Would you? Oh, then where would you be without me I wonder?
Mark:	We would do all the work.
T:	You'd do all the work would you?
Mark:	I'd finish all the books.
T:	So you would magic the teacher into a frog and you would do all the work with the magic spell would you? You would tidy up the room as well would you Mark?
(*Pupil:*	That's a good idea.)
Mark:	. . . and water the plants . . .
Mark:	. . . and change the classroom.
T:	What would you change the classroom into?

The conversation continues in this vein.

Here, gently teasing the pupil, by suggesting that everything 'will have boiled away to nothing by the time you have said your magic words', doesn't spur him on. However, when the tables are turned and the teacher puts herself at the receiving end of the humour, the pupil's imagination is fired and suggestions come pouring out. The fun also emerges in the next excerpt, where the teacher and pupils laugh together over the pupil's efforts to read sentences from his workbook.

Teacher and pupil going over sentences in work book . . .

Mark: I know what to do.
T: What is that word?
Mark: I know.
T: What . . . does it say, the word . . .
Mark: Don't . . .
T: Rubbish. (Mock stern voice)
Mark: (Laughs)
Mark: Dragon.
T: Oh . . . Oh . . . no . . . (laughs)
T: Let's read the sentence to see if that helps.
Mark: Right, I know.
T: Read the first sentence.
Mark: The book was about . . . about . . .
T: y-e-s . . . about, about . . .
Mark: . . . a . . . dragon. (Funny voice)
T: or . . .
Mark: The book was about a tr. . . . (laughs) a tree.
Teacher and pupil laugh together.
Mark: Now, now . . .
Mark: This . . .
Pause
Mark: (Tries again) Pirates.
T: Come on, read the sentences.
Mark: I know.
T: You don't know.
Mark: I do.
Pause.
Mark: There, that . . .
T: What is the right sentence then?

Conversation continues, then Mark works on his own. A few minutes later his teacher returns to look at his work . . .

T: What does that say?
Mark: Tail . . . belt.

T:	A what?
Mark:	. . . round a tree.
T:	. . . and a?
Mark:	. . . a dr . . . tail.
T:	. . . a belt round a tail, right?
Mark:	Aw naw . . . Tick them (laughing)
T:	This is . . .
Mark:	Tick them.
T:	What does that say?
Mark:	A trip . . . what have I done here?
T:	(Laughing)
Mark:	(Laughs) It isn't funny.
T:	(Laughing)
Mark:	I've done that . . . funny.
T:	What should it . . . what does it say?
Mark:	A dragon under a tree.
T:	Uh ha. (Conversation continues . . .)

Within the fun Mark is able to see that he has made a mistake and to admit that he has 'done that . . . funny'.

These few examples may give a flavour of the type of exchanges that are taking place in classrooms where there is a positive ethos, where respect between teacher and pupil exists, and where the self-esteem of the pupil is encouraged. These exchanges cannot be taken in isolation; they would not be effective if they were not part of the whole school approach, and also if they were not part of the historic process of the individual classroom. In other words, these examples are both the result of a positive ethos as well as the means of creating this indefinable 'ethos'.

The indefinable ethos or climate or context appeared to be a significant factor in the effectiveness of pupils' classroom experience.

8   Along the Continuum: Mainstream Contexts for Reflection

The research described so far involved no intervention and no specially designed programmes for pupils: rather, their usual planned curricular experiences were sampled to obtain a picture of the amount and nature of their reflective activity, and their teacher's facilitation of this.

The three initiatives in mainstream city schools which are described in this chapter complement and enrich this picture. All were long-term imaginative and ambitious attempts to enable pupils to think more deeply and effectively in the classroom. All were designed and implemented by experienced teachers of pupils across the ability range and each focused on an important and challenging area: pupils' access and handling of written information: spatial representation on maps: and in pre-schoolers, phonic awareness.

The three accounts, for the most part in the teacher-researchers' own language, describe ideas and activities which are appropriate for a broad range of pupils across the age and ability continuum, like our research findings on classroom processes. Even on a more restricted view, many pupils in mainstream have considerable difficulties in learning, and many of those now in special schools will be taught in future in mainstream settings.

Common features of the special and mainstream school research are identified and discussed in the final chapter.

The Factfiler Programme — Finding and Using Information

Introduction

Pat Mackenzie, now a teacher educator, describes the Factfiler, a programme she designed to help 7 and 8-year-olds in a city primary school to find and use information more effectively in cross curricular environmental studies projects.

She evaluated the effectiveness of the programme with a mixed ability group of eight pupils within one class. After familiarization visits she took charge of the whole class for one hour weekly over eight weeks. During this time she worked through the Factfiler programme with her intervention group and the rest of the class worked in the usual way on their project.

During this period a range of evidence, videos, checklists and fieldnotes were collected. Comparisons were later made with a new project worked on by the group of pupils with Factfiler experience (the Badger group) and those who had worked in the usual way (the Squirrel group).

Implementing the Programme

Having prepared the Factfiler and visited the classes several times with my puppets, the programme was ready to be tried with the Badger group. The initial day set the scene, provided the general rationale, spelled out the overall goals and intentions and established the right ethos for a healthy partnership.

I explained the collaborative teamwork approach and the partnership roles for learning to become independent researchers for the Woodland Project. It was put to the class that we could find out more if we divided up the work into three teams so that each team researched a different animal. The class accepted that I could work with only one group as trainee researchers while the others worked on other tasks. Each team, however, would present their work to the rest. The trainees would have to explain what they'd learned about being a researcher as well as presenting their information.

They knew that I was a researcher and were excited when the idea of the Young Researchers' Club was introduced. To their delight, badges were issued for their respective roles as trainees. In this session we only had time to form our five key research questions which we thought the other children would like to know about. These questions later formed the basis for putting our brainstorm words into organised categories and these were subsequent headings for note taking: habitat, food, families, habits, appearance. I then read over the text to them to familiarize them with new topic words and suggested they did some personal search for further information in their spare time. The enthusiasm was high and the time flew past.

Each subsequent week followed a similar pattern which fell into five stages. At each session, the badges were issued, and resources were ready to hand for the children to collect themselves before starting. The puppet MacFact was then helpful in focusing their thinking on the day's task in hand and asking them to remind him of our good work motto. On a wall poster this was spelled out: talk: do: check: review. This wall poster and the Think Trail (figure 6) were referred to at the outset in preparation for getting ourselves organized.

We referred to our overall plans, pointed up the value of collaboration, the social skills for teamwork, and how a team should be prepared and organized. The review discussions took place after every stage so that the pupils were very clear about each part.

The first stage, establishing the learning to learn process was part of the preliminary talk and involved recapping on progress, engendering enthusiasm for gaining further skills (and therefore more independence), setting realistic targets for the day and negotiating criteria for success which were linked to the review afterwards.

Stage 2 centred on the text as a whole group activity with shared reading

Figure 6: Think trail — pupil reminder

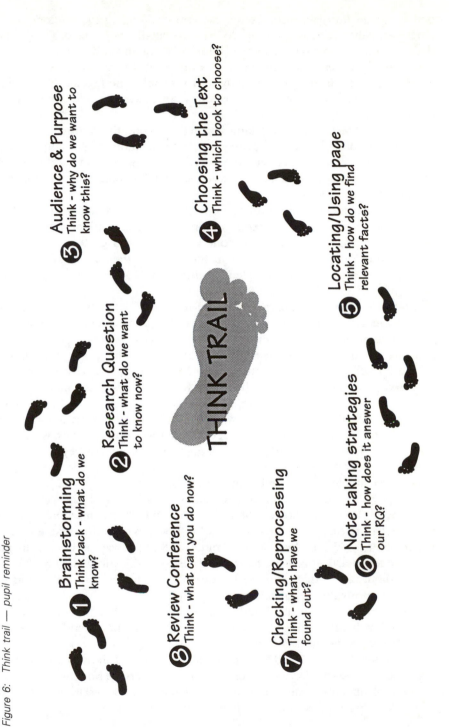

THINK TRAIL

1 Brainstorming
Think back - what do we know?

2 Research Question
Think - what do we want to know now?

3 Audience & Purpose
Think - why do we want to know this?

4 Choosing the Text
Think - which book to choose?

5 Locating/Using page
Think - how do we find relevant facts?

6 Note taking strategies
Think - how does it answer our RQ?

7 Checking/Reprocessing
Think - what have we found out?

8 Review Conference
Think - what can you do now?

and language fun games for examining and challenging the author's use of language. New terminology, introduced incidentally as I talked aloud when demonstrating, was repeated by the children. Rereading and dipping back into texts already covered was emphasised during all the sessions, as this is an essential process in reflective reading and research. The familiar text also reduces the level of cognitive demands and frees readers to reflect more easily on meaning.

Stage 3 centred on note taking and reprocessing the information in two parts. We used the first Factfiler sheet which focused on transferring the highlighted points onto the sheet and organised the notes under agreed headings. Sheet 2 was generally used the next week so that the children had to rely only on the notes from sheet 1.

This sheet focused on rewriting from their own notes in their words. After a demonstration the team worked in pairs, reading and taking notes for the different headings. Each pair chose one heading then used the notes to draft two information sentences. The team then shared their findings, discussed them in relation to the agreed criteria and these were used for the poster and book.

Stage 4 centred on collating their information for the Badger poster and considering layout and presentation for their intended audience. Factfiler sheet 3 was a summary of the poster task and there was a procedural checklist and a simple evaluative set of criteria for producing a quality poster for the team to use for self-monitoring and for evaluation at the review discussion. They were to use the five headings with the two research questions which were also illustrated to give the reader extra information.

Designing the poster also allowed pupils to use the organisational features of information writing. Help sheets with larger outline writing were available to use as headings. They could choose, cut out words they needed and colour these to make their own attractive headings. The group then eagerly designed a simple quiz using Factfiler quiz draft sheet 5 to go with the poster.

Stage 5 centred on the organizational devices and special pages in information books. This task allowed them to decide which organizational features they needed to make a realistic information book. We used the same collated information for the Badger Book in much the same way as before, to give them added practice in using their newly-learned skills in a slightly different task without taxing them too much, and to let them see that they could use the same information in a different way.

The pages were headed and ordered identically but this time the new learning involved deciding what was necessary for the book, and then designing contents, index and glossary pages.

Factfiler sheets 6, 7 and 8 were drafts for these and showed a strategy for ordering their lists in alphabetical or page order. When the book was compiled, we then planned our team presentation and each pair agreed to describe parts of the learning process and how they conducted the task.

Discussion

Throughout the weeks we observed a growing confidence in the group. Although we had to read and reread the text each time we discussed different aspects, depending on the stage of the process: this turned out to be a great confidence booster for the hesitant readers as they were working with familiar texts without feeling they had to read it again by default!

Yet, possibly through pressure of time, we rarely encourage this. I noted early on before it was pointed out to them, that when I stopped to question during reading, children seldom, if ever, referred to the text, and I wondered if inadvertently we give the notion that comprehension is merely a memory test.

I always modelled procedures first, encouraging interaction by getting the puppet to ask them what to do next. For example, they soon could remind me to refer to our research question to help us find the information to answer it. 'Wait. Our research question, our question. You've not done it.' As they gained in competence, more responsibility for decisions was handed over to them, and with prompting they were able to talk me through the Think Trail.

The use of new terminology in natural relevant contexts seemed to support their understanding and eventual personal use of these terms. It proved extremely helpful to have this shared language for reflecting on our progress as children referred more easily to specific issues: 'See on the last line of the text, we could highlight that bit about . . .' suggested James. 'I can make the heading for the glossary in a different colour and, em, can I make it bigger, so you can find it better?' asked Sam.

At the review session the children swapped over the sheets to check each other's work. They were particularly enthusiastic about the highlighted words and they could see how this helped them locate the relevant facts. It had the added benefit of supporting them as they related a summary of their piece of text to the others. Highlighting was always extremely popular but some found it easier than others. At first everyone merely transferred the individual highlighted words. When they went to use these notes the following week, they realized that words on their own didn't always make sense. Some children easily latched onto annotation, but two pairs needed careful guidance whenever they attempted this themselves. Although they could explain why we highlighted words and appeared to understand which facts we needed in discussion, it was a difficult concept that required a lot of experience before it was mastered.

The review conferences created interest in the process and with a little encouragement the children began to offer suggestions for refining strategies. For example, we noted in week four that the badgers' food was a mixture of plants and grubs or small animals. Nick suggested using two colours to separate these and the others clapped spontaneously saying 'brill, yeah, good'. This created fairly keen competition to 'invent' other strategies. Laura suggested grouping the two types and the notion of sub-headings was born. Transferring the highlighted words did not prove too difficult but it was tedious for those who found writing laborious and they were pleased that this task was shared out. Each week, we reflected on the notes and swapped them around so that everyone used each others' and had a good knowledge of the different areas.

We also had a few minutes' oral practice in using them and being real authors. The two criteria were to make the sentence sound like book information and to choose useful points that other children would be interested to know. The pairs swapped around regularly and were shown how a team should comment constructively at the review meetings.

When we helped each other refine our efforts, drafting was mentioned so that the notion took root before they saw it as tedious rewriting. They saw the value of note taking. 'It's dead easy, writing, eh?' 'You just look at the notes and get your ideas.'

Writing in their own words now appeared less daunting and with guidance and discussions at the drafting stage, the pairs managed their tasks quite well. When it came to the actual writing, they talked about what they wanted to say, were willing to listen to others' views and make changes to their work. 'Right, OK, I can easy change it.' The oral practice, together with the language awareness raising games and discussions all contributed to their confidence. As detectives, we spent a few minutes each week examining some of the author's more complex sentence structures. Children also became more confident to challenge the published text. In week 5 the two Davids, usually reluctant readers with writing difficulties, brought out their own rewritten version of a sentence we had discussed earlier.

Original text	Pupils' own words
'Nearby there may be a tree marked with long scratches.'	'There might be a tree near the set.'
'This is where badgers have stood on their hind legs to clean and sharpen their claws on the trunk.'	'It might have big long scratches on the trunk because the badgers might use it to sharpen their claws.'

The other children preferred the pupils' version to the author's one which was 'too complicated' and 'old fashioned as well'. Their confidence soared and it made everyone keen to try to be real authors and write in their own words. They enjoyed checking each other's writing by listening and their comments indicated that some awareness of genre was emerging. Sam attempting the glossary himself wrote:

'Tunnels — little corridors under the ground.' The text was 'The earth was dug out when the tunnels and rooms were made.' Neil's notes 'Very clean and tidy. Eats outside.' The text was 'Badgers are the tidest of animals and never have a dirty home. They always eat outside.' It was also clear from their suggestions for the final poster and book that they were considering their audience.

'I know let's make the title in black and white stripes like a badger, everybody will like it.' They wanted their book shaped like a badger 'because it would make people want to read it.' They also reminded me about putting their names on the cover and were keen to include the date of publication and a dedication to their teacher. The children displayed great pride in this work and were seen showing it to others. 'It's brill, eh? D'you like it? See that's my bit.'

Even the shy ones were willing to take part in the oral presentation and the team discussed quite readily what they would say. All the pairs appeared confident as they made their contributions and could describe how they had worked and what they had learned as trainee researchers. They were able to respond to the close questioning from the rest of the class, helping each other out where necessary. They clearly were well aware of the process and had enjoyed following the 'think' steps and having responsibilities in the 'talk, do, check, review' process. The next stage was to return the following term to see if the metacognitive guidance strategies had any lasting effect.

Long-term Effects

In term 3, after a fourteen-week lapse, I was able to return to the class. The class's new project was health and the groups had already been assigned to investigate blood, bones and teeth. I had prepared the Factfiler sheets and resources and intended to compare the approaches of the Badger group and of one of the non-intervention groups (Squirrels).

First, I interviewed each group to see whether their original perceptions had altered. The Badger group were able to articulate emerging awareness of the task requirements and revealed several interesting insights about their role. When one child spoke it seemed to spark off other contributions.

They were asked how they would make an information book:

You would put in pictures and information, but you've to write it yourself 'cos you're the author now.

Em, make it nice and put good headings and pages to find things . . . eh like an index.

You would get an information book. Yea, and photocopy it and get those pens . . . yea and, em, highlight facts and put them in notes on those on those mm sheets contents . . . eh . . . and index and (pause) a glossary and publishers and everybody signs its contents.

They were aware of their learning about process as well as content.

We learned about badgers' food, families and habits, and we were good detectives 'cos we could find information in tricky bits. We could highlight and write good notes.

em, we learned how to make a book properly just like a real one
. . . only ours is better. Ours looks like a badger. We've kept it. It's in
the class.

They could also describe some of the differences between fiction and non-
fiction texts a little more specifically.

. . . no it's not the same 'cos it's wrote different. It tells you lots of
information. It's not a story. It's harder . . . You have to think more.

The comparison group had researched squirrels during the previous term.
They had been very interested in the Badger presentation when all the strategies and resources (including the Factfiler sheets and highlighting pens) had
been described. Their replies, however remained vague.

We put in pictures and stories.

Mm we have to cut out pictures or draw.

. . . and write stories underneath.

Make it nice especially the cover.

Their perception of the learning was entirely content based.

. . . em about squirrels' food, and what they eat . . .

. . . their houses and how everyone cuts trees.

. . . they'll have nowhere to live.

Now the new tasks with the same outcome as before were presented to the
two groups. The Badger's group was researching 'blood', and the comparison group 'bones'. Both groups were given exactly the same guidance, and
instructions, and shown that the Factfiler resources, highlighting pens, paper
etc. were at their disposal. They were told that we wanted to see how the
groups worked together in pairs as a team, and how they helped each other.
The sheets and other resources were explained and left accessible to guide
their work. They should only ask the teacher if their partners couldn't help but
we would always be there if they wanted.

It was apparent on analysing all the collected evidence in consultation
with the teachers, that the intervention programme had effected positive changes
for all the children in the Badger group. For example, the children seemed to
have greater awareness of the project demands, how to tackle them and when

it was appropriate to ask for help. They also seemed better motivated, as their attitude and attention was more positively directed towards the task in hand. They could articulate (sometimes with prompting) most of their learned strategies, and seemed more confident, competent and better organized in setting about the various tasks. Each member demonstrated in varying degrees an emerging metacognitive awareness of the demands involved in the project tasks and how to proceed.

The Badger group displayed behaviour that manifested some development of metacognition, an awareness of effective learning processes and knowing when they genuinely needed help from the teacher. For example, they made some attempt at organizing themselves before starting, collecting resources and discussing who needed what. They collected the photocopy sheet, pens and the note making sheets 1 and 2. They ticked off items on the checklist on sheet 4 and arranged everything at their table. Concentration was higher and most of their talk was task specific. They consulted the Think Trail poster, attempting to follow it, and could be heard trying out the questions on each other. They collaborated well, frequently prompted each other, and often offered or asked opinions. Joanne leaned over at her partner's query and pointed, showing how to note take. With support they all coped remarkably well with transferring to the note form. Joanne in particular worked confidently, transferring her own highlighted words without help.

The pupils selectively asked the teacher about genuine issues relating to reading and note taking. All pairs spontaneously wanted to use drafting and even though they asked for help, they showed signs of reflection and evaluation, for example when they argued over the best way to do things as they tried to recall the strategies to refine their writing.

No, I want to write the words first on this paper — it's easier that way.

But we could just make it up in our heads and try it on the paper. You can change it can't you?

With prompting they continued fairly methodically and when their own notes and sentences were ready for making the new project book, they consulted the Factfiler sheets to check their progress, before checking with the teacher. They even made some attempt at using the competences within the group.

What will we do now (both look at the sheet) . . . Oh yea we've to do the other page. I'm doing the writing . . . You're doing the heading.

Often they recognized how to fulfil the tasks successfully, and could set personal standards.

I'd better check my spelling and fix that bit at the end before I do it in pen.

When the group were almost ready to put the book together, they showed awareness of appropriate procedures and needed very little help. They were well motivated to use the accumulated information. Lorna took over leadership. 'Right we've got all the headings (holds them up). Well let's get them in order first. I did it last time so I know how. Who's got the contents and index? You should keep all your notes in your folder, Martin. Researchers should be organized or you'll get mixed up.'

The Squirrels, the comparison group without experience in using Factfiler, showed an unthinking, unquestioning approach with no organization, although both groups had been given the same prompts and reminders. For example, after collecting the resources and settling to read they flicked through the books, stopped at pages that caught their interest, and proceeded to copy the pictures along with the information.

Here's a good one Anne, it might look nice, eh? I'm going to do this one.

No one looked at their guidance sheet or attempted to make use of the photocopied text or the other Factfiler sheets. There was no real collaborative talk indicating any clear perception of the task. Their cooperation consisted mainly of sharing pens, or books, talking about what the poster would be like and telling their partner what they were doing.

We'll make really nice big coloured in ones and ours will be best.

Requests for teacher help were generally about what they were allowed to do.

Am I allowed to cut this out?

Can I stick this on now?

There was very little evidence of self monitoring as they tended to keep asking the teacher for reassurance.

'Is this ok?' or 'what'll we do next?'

Their finished work showed that they had copied the information rather than write for themselves and no one had tried note taking even though techniques had been suggested and the Badger group had talked a lot about it.

It was interesting to note that this group did not mention any of the process techniques, even though they had shown great interest when the Badger group had given clear explanations in term 1. It would appear that unless children experience the process for themselves and understand what is involved then the learning has no significance for them.

Discussion

The educational dialogue central to the programme seemed to fulfil a number of interrelated functions. By engaging in reflective discussion about the rationale and thinking behind each process before attempting it themselves, pupils were better informed to make sense of their learning. Trying things out, then relating them to the main intentions to help them see how each contributed to the final product, helped them understand the need to work methodically through each step, reflecting on their activities.

The reviews where children listened to each other explain and justify their actions, seemed to clarify understanding, and helped self-confidence as their views and opinions were listened to, acknowledged and valued by each other as well as the teacher.

The constant practice and referral to their growing list of personal competences raised the level of awareness of pupils' capabilities and gave them the foundations for selecting appropriate strategies. This enabled them to approach learning as a problem-solving activity, and consider how to call upon their strategies. The discussions also provided opportunities for eliciting diagnostic information, by tracing the source of misconceptions and gaining intimate knowledge of each child. The teacher was able to empathize more readily with the children's viewpoint and recognize when to generate greater motivation to learn.

The kind of context for reflective discussions was also an important factor in achieving success. With young children, reflective talk needs to be contextualized in a believable age-appropriate way if they are to appreciate its significance and understand how it relates to them. The role play within the Young Researchers' Club provided a meaningful enjoyable setting for them to reflect on the nature of their insights. The talk which focused on each step of the Think Trail provided a range of relevant contexts for reflection.

The reading support strategies of familiarizing, priming or cueing, and paraphrasing, seemed to facilitate access to understanding information texts and thus provided them with relevant linguistic experiences for literary development.

Attending to the language used by the author to convey information seemed to guide the pupils towards comparing and identifying the genre of information texts, glossaries, indexes and notes, thus helping them to consider that language in text can be organized in different ways to suit the writer's purpose. By concentrating on relevant features and discussing how these related to the writer's aims, children had the means to recognize the genre and thus were beginning to gain greater control over their own reading and writing. Discussing and working from the various perspectives of reader, writer, editor supported deeper understanding. Alternative viewpoints provided them with intellectually challenging ways of looking at learning.

The complexity of the project task provided the range of opportunities for reflective discussions that seemed to support pupils' metacognitive development. The final stages of producing the information book seemed to be the anchor point which enabled them to see how separate skills fitted together meaningfully, and the perspective of real researchers provided the bridging platform for helping the children appreciate the validity of their procedures.

In conclusion, in the Factfiler programme, where learning was a collaboration between adult and child, the reflective discussion acted like a scaffolding within the zone of proximal development. That is to say, the partnership approach helped children go beyond that which they already knew.

Too often the abuse of topic work has left children bewildered by the task in front of them, to muddle along without knowing why. With guided discovery, children can be encouraged to formulate their own hypotheses about the nature of their learning. The collaborative approach can ensure that children feel valued and respected by sharing with them in decisions about their own learning, whilst providing the necessary support for each to gain success. Once self-confidence is established, the teacher can enhance the learning through positive constructive feedback.

We cannot ignore the mounting research evidence on the benefits of allowing children to be a responsible respected partner. We should seek to include many opportunities for reflection to ensure that all learners are given the chance to develop to their optimum potential.

> *Note*: The results of this study formed the thinking behind Pat Mackenzie's Teachers' Guide for the Oxford Reading Tree Factfiler, a programme for teaching information handling from books, published by Oxford University Press (1994).

Challenging Thinking through Mapping

Introduction

Linda-Jane Simpson, teacher of 5–6-year-olds in a city primary school, describes her work on developing their spatial and symbolic understanding through maps.

Two things greatly raise children's thinking levels — interaction and positive expectations. This reflective description outlines challenging theme work with a primary one class. It highlights the exciting results when a mixed ability class of children and afforded these two vital elements.

The ideas and techniques which this section contains originate from actual work done in a number of my infant classes. My own learning and understanding has developed and improved with each successive experience shared in the classroom. Involvement in various in-service courses is to blame for my becoming something of a reflective practitioner. I am very interested in, and do reflect on, what is happening within the work I provide for the children. Present and future work is informed by past experience. Like a good wine, I am improving with age and maybe I now have something to offer other teachers. Young children of wide ranging abilities can be challenged and supported in work, such as mapping, previously unexplored because it was generally considered to be beyond their understanding.

I feel any account of my work should be preceded by a brief outline of the core ideas on which it rests. First, role play is the central ingredient in most of my theme work because there is no better way to get myself and the children right into situations, all actively contributing to the thinking aloud process. Everyone is linked by the purpose which the drama context provides. Ideas for the context can be 'of the moment' or tentatively planned beforehand. I develop the work both in response to these context ideas, and the needs of the children. Everyone contributes something to the brainstorming and all offerings are accepted without judgment. Those children with a higher level of thinking skills will have a greater grasp of the issues and therefore much to contribute. It is important though that the awareness of all the children be raised, through involvement and seeing the strategies being role-modelled within the interaction. Each child will take from the experience whatever is relevant to their particular stage of development.

> I finally understood that I should let the work be my focus, not my
> fear that the child may not be involved . . . Trust the work, and the
> children will give what they can give, and the teacher will give what
> she can give. (Booth, 1994)

The second basic idea underlying my work, is that for me, teaching infants involves reducing concepts and skills into progressive constituent steps, and varying the degrees of support to guide them through those steps.

Thirdly, first-hand experience has shown that the more children see and grasp the interconnected nature of knowledge, the better their learning will be. This is confirmed in Fisher's research

> When materials, activities, and discussions develop from the interests
> of the children, curriculum remains whole, not broken into bits and
> pieces; meaningful, not irrelevant; functional, not artificial and con-
> trived; and engaging, not boring. (Fisher, 1991)

I would now like to describe the stimulating venture we took into mapping. With hindsight, and through analyzing what was achieved, I can now discern a progression of three key stages in any such work with young children.

The first stage I have labelled 'on the ground', because here the children need to go to, and return from, places in a real environment. They make accompanied journeys and are encouraged to observe things and places they pass on the way. Making some kind of three dimensional representation of those journeys in sand, in compost or with boxes, is the second stage in the development. The landmarks noted on the physical journey are now represented on the 'model map' with actual objects or constructions. The third stage is a difficult transition and one for which the first two stages prepare. It is the move from three-dimensional model maps into two-dimensional drawings, with increasing symbolic representation required. Within a drama storyline theme, the same three stages into mapping are followed, with one important difference. At stage one the 'ground' in the drama is imaginary. There are various techniques which I go on to describe, to define the space and to make the imaginary journey just as real.

School, My New Environment

School, my new environment was the first designated topic for Primary 1 and I gave it added purpose with the arrival of a letter from their nursery teacher. She wanted them to find ways of explaining what school was all about, which she could use with her current nursery children. With the need to research and collect information obvious to everyone, the children started on a programme of accompanied visits to various locations in school.

When referring to people and places, I used the commonly used terms, and the children with minimal adult help were to get themselves there and back, as well as delivering a message of some kind. My aims here were firstly that the children would start to associate certain people with places around school. Secondly I wanted people in a certain role to be identified with certain equipment: for example the janitor with keys, the auxiliary with plasters, and the secretary with letters.

I started using little pictures to represent particular people. These early symbols then appeared in a little recording book 'I can find my way to . . .', designed for the children. It consisted of a lengthwise section of paper with arrows, boxes and pictures representing people, or their symbols, and places such as toilets and cloakrooms. The boxes were for recording successfully reaching that place or person. The little book represented the children's first experience of a checklist; symbols to represent places and people; entering their own symbol to register a 'yes'.

Once the active work 'on the ground' around school was under way, the children thought about, and investigated, the sizes of rooms in the infant block, beginning very simple measurement and estimation, using their eyes and the language of comparison: big, bigger, biggest. They then helped to find appropriately sized boxes to make rooms on a model map. Once we had labelled their choice of boxes with room names, there was a great deal of debate as to where to position them in relation to each other. I encouraged the children to go out of the room to check for themselves, and commented on their role as researchers.

My next challenge was for the children to consider the uses made of the rooms, and they discovered that some were used for the same purposes. We could have written word labels on the map, but I wondered if the children could come up with other ways to show the similar usage of some rooms. I had to lead the children into suggesting the use of colour.

When discussing the revised model map, I challenged the children; 'How will other people looking at our map, know what the colours mean?' It became obvious that the map makers would have to explain that to any map users. I introduced the idea of a key, to unlock the box of answers often found beside a map and we constructed a key together, with word labels, symbol pictures, and colours, and attached it to the large map.

It was remarkable how even the least able children were able to take puppets directly from place to place on the map as instructed. These 'school people' puppets began as black pen drawings which were enlarged, with card and handle added. The children loved using puppets and I realized, from the way they talked out their journey on the map, that all of them had moved on from working 'on the ground' to understanding a three-dimensional model of that space.

The transition from the three-dimensional 'box map' to a two-dimensional map was done as a collaborative exercise. The children's task was to compile a 'pathway map', on a long strip of paper. With a teacher acting as a scribe, the group were asked to note and record everything they passed on the way from the classroom to their destination, quite a complex journey involving right and left turns. In order to simplify the task I had first to lose my own adult need for total accuracy. So the task was narrowed to recording the landmarks, working from one end of the paper to the other, as the journey progressed, using the children's own ideas, such as a rectangle with fish inside it, for the fish tank. The pathway map produced was a very good attempt at symbolic representation, to which written labels were added. Some members of the working group helped to explain the finished product to the rest of the children.

Leading from the collaborative to the individual task, each child was given a sheet of symbols. These were pictures we had devised together, to represent each of the following — dining room, cloakroom, toilets, the deputy head-teacher's room, and classroom. Groups were asked to cut and paste the symbol pictures in their relative positions on a large coloured sheet of paper.

A visit to the local library yielded surprising and encouraging information about the connections the children were making in their thinking. As we toured the library, recording on our sheets, an information board caught and held their interest. Alan had spotted a key of symbols used to categorize the adult fiction, and in certain areas of shelving we found books with the same symbols on their spines. When the children were to go and draw 'things I can see at the library', he and a number of others worked at copying the symbols on to their sheet. I had overlooked that information board completely on my preparatory visit and it showed how important it is to let the children take charge of their own learning.

In the final week of the topic I gave certain able children, including Alan, a test of their understanding. In groups of three, with a parent helper, they were to make different journeys around school and draw their own symbols on an individual 'pathway map' as they went. The adult was to compile a key of their symbols. Alan's group had the most challenging journey since it was the reverse of previous 'pathway maps'. In forming a map for the journey the boys borrowed from symbols used before, but also came up with one or two of their own.

Next term I managed to continue the use of symbols and keys, this time on charts rather than on maps. The children chose their own symbols from a selection we compiled together. When Chris told me that he was going to stay in a cottage near a loch, I asked him if he would draw us a map. With his mother's help he returned with a wonderful picture map complete with key, showing how challenged he had been by the mapping work, and that he had progressed through the three key stages and understood two dimensional representation beyond the context of the school environment.

Mapping in Drama

Wolf Paw, Wise Man of the Woods, was the drama storyline I wrote to lead very naturally into map work. The basic idea was formed before theme work started, but then elements were added as work developed with the children.

Having defined the space of the drama and familiarized the children with features of that space by exploring it Indian file, I moved them into the next key stage of the mapping process using a letter from Wolf Paw, containing a request for sunflowers and maps, to guide us in the role of visitors, from our homes to his cave. We had been making sunflowers: the children were immediately focused by this direct request for maps and no one hesitated about being able to supply them.

We all sat around a large piece of green cloth to make a model 3D map. I led the children's thinking by asking them questions, for advice, and to be reminded of facts. It is important to keep up the pace to maintain their interest without denying them the important space and time for reflective thinking. The cloth map is a progressive process of building up a three-dimensional relief map, with known landmarks. To give a feel for the interchange of questions and thoughts, a sample of classroom dialogue is provided. I hope to convey the way I question, and depending on the children's reaction, how I may then reshape the question or statement and repeat it in a different form.

> *T:* This model map does not look like the woods, it's too flat, we need some bumps.

Chris suggested a big stone. Although not the answers I was looking for, I was pleased that other children called out landmarks remembered from the Indian file game.

> *T:* We'll keep all those in mind. What could we crush up?

Someone said foil and then another person said paper. I gave several sheets of newspaper to Joe and John, and they loosely crushed it up and laid it on top of the green material.

T:	What are you going to do? Put it like that?
Joe:	All in the middle.
Andrew:	Not all in the middle, at the side.

I remarked that they were not green bumps and when I asked for suggestions on how to make them green, I got several answers ranging from painting to colouring them in.

T:	Is there a quicker way?
Ricky:	Put it underneath.
T:	Underneath the carpet? Ricky show us what you mean.

Ricky took a lump of paper and put it underneath the green fabric.

| *T:* | Ah . . . look . . . wonderful. No one would know that was newspaper. And because we've put that bump, now we've got a hill. |

Later, four children drew pictures of their homes and put them on the map.

T:	Now then, let's think of some of the things we see on the way to the cave. Close eyes and think. (Visualization to aid recall) I don't really remember.
Gary:	Water.
T:	Is the water a pool . . . a stream . . . or a big wide river?
Joe:	A stream.
T:	I wonder how we could show a stream on our map . . . on our model? We've already got our hills where Wolf Paw's cave is, and the flat space where our homes are.
John:	Get some blue paper and cut the shape of it.
T:	Blue paper? Why blue?
Ricky:	Because the water is blue.
T:	If you're looking down on a stream, what sort of shape does it make, as it goes along the ground?
Chris:	It makes a thin line.

I showed them a selection of varying shapes and types of blue paper and we eventually settled on a thin strip of blue crepe paper. (Choosing appropriate working materials is important).

Alan:	You could cut it.
Gillian:	Get pieces of paper and pencil and colour it in quickly.
T:	Red?
Gillian:	No, blue.
T:	Kate have you an idea of where the stream might go? Could you help us with the stream?

Kate pointed to an area on the map.

> *T:* You think it goes there, right? Does the stream go together like that?

I bunched up the blue crepe strip into a bundle.

> *T:* Kate you'll have to show me.

She then lay the blue strip straight across, from one edge of the fabric to the other.

> *T:* Does a stream go straight like that?
> *Jamie:* Cut a bit off. It's too long.
> *T:* I'll pull it out like that ... Hands up those who've seen a stream? Think back to the stream that you've seen. Did it go straight like that? (Visualization to aid recall).
> *Alan:* It went a wee bit bendy.
> *T:* Could you show me?

Alan put some curves into the first section of the crepe paper. Chris took over and put more bends into the strip, this time all the way along it. We continued to add further landmarks, thinking hard to get them positioned in the order we encountered them.

A video recording made of the map making process showed how engrossed the children were, concentrating for at least thirty minutes. It also showed that the children who did not contribute directly were all watching and listening. Everyone observed the proceedings and was part of the experience at their own level. I had made a general request for some children to draw maps of our cloth model, so that we would have a copy of it on paper.

On completion of their work, they were each able to point out, on their own maps, many of the landmarks we had discussed. That of Angus is typical. Later when I examined the maps more closely I discovered that both John and Chris had produced something more akin to a cross-section. This may have been because of their working positions and the relief nature of the map.

Two other techniques, which I used to get my least able group more actively involved, included replacing the sand with compost and putting rocks, stones and twigs in the tray as well. The children brought in small plastic animals of their own to add to their compost models of the wood and Wolf Paw's cave. This group also made individual maps on paper after I modelled the technique and provided them with pre-written instruction labels.

On a prepared large size map the children collaboratively decided on the vital instructions needed at various points on the journey, like 'go right', and 'jump' and I stuck those on to my map. Once they had completed their individual maps by sticking on the instruction labels, we left them out to guide Wolf Paw's visitors.

Wolf Paw had asked us not only to make maps, but to also find a way of getting the maps to his friends. We had a collaborative talking session, a

Figure 7

Map by Chris

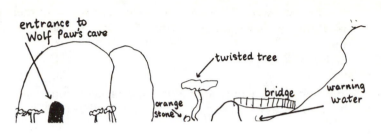

Map by Angus

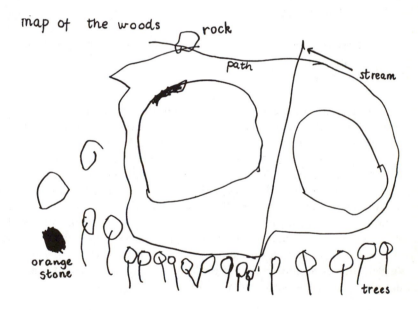

brainstorming, to work out a solution to this second challenge. The children suggested leaving maps on the doorsteps.

> T: Would I know to pick that up, or would I think someone had been untidy with litter?

They gave me various suggestions 'write your name on . . . put names on it . . .' and then someone said 'write Wolf Paw's visitors'. I wrote that on the outside of one of the maps and in the role of visitor came along, read the writing and said 'Ah that's me!'

> T: What do we want the visitors to do to that? We want them to
>   pick it up . . . Is it enough to write Wolf Paw's visitors? Hands
>   up.
> John: Write 'pick it up'.

John wrote the sign and teacher came along and picked up the sign but left the map behind. Andrew was heard to say 'there's another one', meaning the map.

> T: What can we do to make them pick up both things?

I got various sensible suggestions including writing another sign, 'The map will help you' from John. This time the 'visitor' picked up the two messages and left the map saying 'I wonder where the map is?' Several of the children called out 'The map's there.'

> T: They've picked up the two messages. How can we point them
>   to the map?
> Chris: An arrow.

I continued the mapping work where I could in the drama. During a performance to parents, a number of children used their bodies to form the path, the landmarks and the cave, for Wolf Paw's visitors to follow.

One day John spoke about the other path, the path off to the left, which sparked off another idea. I took the children on a guided visualization up the other path until we came to the crystal clear waterfall of every rainbow colour. The children later drew the waterfall in the colour that they had seen in their imaginations. 'Thinking with images can be a powerful aid in all aspects of the school curriculum, in language work as the stimulus to imagination, . . . and in art as the inner representation of creative experience.' (Fisher, 1990)

Visualization is an important yet underused technique, which is an aid to thinking on a much deeper creative level.

Discussion

The experiences which this work provided gave the children the opportunity to develop their thinking, not only in purely mapping terms, but also in ways of solving problems. It was exciting to observe how they began to connect concepts learned inside the classroom with aspects of life outwith school.

Building up the model map on cloth helped the children bridge the gap between the real and the symbolic in their own thinking. It also provided me with an opportunity to talk collaboratively with them.

Proof that many early mapping techniques were internalized is observable in the purely symbolic pathway maps which they produced. They continue to present me with colourful imaginative maps complete with relevant physical features and the beginnings of a storyline.

Our experience together in all the work clearly shows that you are more likely to move the children's thinking on if you: break the concepts down into progressive visual steps: use role play to experience situations and problems first hand: talk and think together, and role model how a thinker works things out.

Young children often think aloud naturally. They need to see that it is a respected adult strategy too.

Rhyming, Reading and Reflection

Introduction

As part of the region's commitment to the expansion of nursery education, Linda Watson was appointed as teacher to a newly-established nursery class, two years ago.

I was involved (she writes) from the outset in a project-based on the emerging research evidence regarding the precursors of literary development (Adams, 1990). With the approval and support of the Headteacher, I worked with the Principal Learning Support Teacher and Educational Psychologist for the school; this reflected the recommendations for collaborative ventures in the epilogue of Bryant and Bradley, (1985).

Rationale for the Study

'Early Intervention', 'Recovery Programmes' and 'Phonological Awareness' are now familiar concepts in our classrooms, but they seem to be initiated after a child has experienced some degree of failure. Despite the very convincing evidence related to phonological skills in pre-school children, our nursery classes are not realizing the implications of the research. Logic tells us that if an intervention is to be 'early', it must start in the nursery. If young children are aware of alliteration and rhyme before starting school, then we should capitalize on this phonological awareness by fostering, promoting and extending it. If, as a result, reading difficulties are reduced, then recovery programmes will be needed for far fewer children.

Much guidance has been offered on the form, structure and pacing of interventions designed to help children with reading difficulties. With the exception of Lundberg, Frost and Peterson (1988), little guidance has been offered on the form, structure and pacing to enhance phonological awareness, letter identity, and knowledge and concepts about print in the nursery, and certainly nothing to match the degree of clarity and specificity offered for work with older failing readers.

Thus the aim of this project is to develop within the framework of sound nursery philosophy and practice, a range of activities and approaches which children will enjoy and which will involve them in playing with words and sounds. It is hoped to develop children's sensitivity to sounds to a level which will prevent or greatly reduce reading difficulties at the primary stage. The development of practice to improve phonological awareness will be accompanied by activities to develop awareness of the forms, functions and uses of print and to develop letter identity knowledge.

An initiative such as this in the nursery class should create a very sound foundation from which to approach beginning to read in the first primary years. It should also assist, concurrent with other indicators, in the early identification of children with specific learning difficulties. In our case there was an extremely interesting bonus: evidence that the children were becoming reflective and questioning in a range of situations. This was revealed in their activity and spontaneous comments.

The First Year of the Project

In the nursery school half of the forty 3–5-year-olds attended in the morning and half in the afternoon.

August–October

All the children sang nursery rhymes at least once a day, concentrating on five of the best known, like 'Baa-baa Black Sheep', and 'Hickory, Dickory, Dock.' They also learnt action songs like 'Ring a Ring a Roses', poems, and counting games, such as 'One, Two, Buckle my Shoe'. Wherever possible the daily story contained rhymes or alliteration, as in 'Each, Peach, Pear, Plum', and 'Terrible, Terrible, Tiger'.

These are just a few examples of what were used. There are poems, songs and stories for every subject topic which arises in the nursery setting, so there is no difficulty in providing children with a supply of material which fits into the ongoing curriculum.

The results of this were that children were singing or reciting nursery rhymes almost all the time, giving us the opportunity quite spontaneously to join in. We were then able to encourage development either on to other rhymes in related topics or to look more closely at the rhyme itself.

November–December

At this stage we decided to work with children in smaller groups, chosen randomly, to carry out more specific work on rhyme. We divided the children into four morning and four afternoon groups of five. Each group was given at least two ten-minute sessions every week, with the opportunity to work with the teacher and nursery nurse alternately.

During these sessions, the children chose nursery rhymes for their group to say or sing together; they filled in missing words and completed rhymes that had been started. They also thought up rhymes for particular words, and identified rhyming words in books and pictures.

There were varying degrees of success and interest within the groups with some children managing to remember the rhymes and others at the stage of making up their own rhymes like 'a log and a sog in a bog', and 'a bug and a dug eat a slug'.

Throughout this period, stories, poems, and rhymes continued to be read to the class as a whole. A similar line was pursued with games, clapping out sounds, and dancing. We played games like 'Snap' and 'Happy Families' with picture rhyming cards. 'Animal Lotto' was popular, in which the child named the animal card picked up and then everyone thought of other words which sounded the same. Art work was done very successfully around rhymes like 'Hickory Dickory Dock' and 'Twinkle Twinkle'. Children in the early primary classes were also doing art work around nursery rhymes and the nursery children were taken to look at it and try to identify the rhymes.

By this stage it was obvious that the older children were moving ahead of the rest and beginning to identify words in books and in pictures displayed on the walls. They were also beginning to ask questions like 'What does that word start with?'

January–April

We now separated the 4-year-olds who were shortly due to start their first primary year and decided to carry out specific work with them. We revised nursery rhymes and rhyming words, establishing that the children really knew some rhymes by heart and had some understanding of words which sound the same. We also looked at their ability to supply missing words, and to identify the odd one out in a list of words like cat, sat, mat, table — using Bradley's three conditions. Either the last sound of the odd one is different — cat, hat, fan, rat, the middle sound is different — pat, fit, bat, hat, or the first sound is different — rod, rot, box, rock. Initially, the children found this hard going, but the more often they played, the better they became. They certainly learned a lot in the process and one child called it the 'Problem Words Game'.

The second main activity was clapping out syllabic rhythms. Children liked especially to clap out their own names. This led to the discovery that names were of different lengths, and we therefore began to investigate word length. The children were very keen on this and were searching everywhere for words to see if they were wee words or big words, long or short. They then started counting how many letters were in each word, which required some understanding of where a word began and where it ended. One child reported to me that he told his mum that 'not all words were the same size' and his mum said it was 'amazing that he knew that!'.

Finally, having started to identify words, we began to find words in sentences. Children counted words in sentences and again were fascinated that some sentences were longer than others, some with just a few words, and others with many.

At the same time as this was going on, children were still frequently being given stories, poems, and rhymes, continuously increasing their repertoire. This always fitted into the ongoing work of the class without difficulty.

April–June

We continued all of the above work with particular emphasis on letter recognition and letter sounds, using alphabet books to teach the children the name and sound of each letter, finding out what letter their own name started with, with continual emphasis on the format and function of print and understanding the language of books: beginning, end, title and author, and knowing about reading left to right. Most importantly this was showing children that reading has its rewards in providing information and giving them immense joy and satisfaction.

The Second Year of the Project

The year began with about half the children returning to nursery and the introduction of new children, mainly 4-year-olds, into the class. We began as in the first year with a large input of nursery rhymes. Obviously, the children who had already been at nursery were very familiar with these and the new children less so. Those who know the rhymes well began asking questions like 'What was Humpty Dumpty made of?', and 'Was the wall not very strong?'. A long and sustained interest in this rhyme led us in all sorts of directions. We put out large and small wooden bricks for children to build walls. We gave them real bricks, and they experimented with building walls, roads and pavements. We went to a building site and watched bricks being used to build homes, and we investigated various uses of brick in buildings around the school, including the school itself. We also boiled eggs for snack time, so that the children could examine and discuss the eggshells. All the while, the rhyme was being repeated, read, and discussed. The children were able to read it from the wallchart and with different texts and illustrations.

'Baa-baa Black Sheep' was given similar treatment and investigation. They became very interested in wool and how it got from the sheep's back into their jerseys. Again they had access at all times to the rhyme on the wall and in various texts so that they could read it, repeat it and find it whenever they wanted. Some of the children began to identify initial letters, for example 'H' and 'D', and we talked about the letter with which their names began. They were soon able to recognize not only their own names, but also names which started with the same letter. Interestingly, at this time, Primary 1 teachers in our school were reporting that the children who had gone from our nursery to theirs knew their nursery rhymes very well, and were able to take part in discussions on them.

During January, I was able to observe over a four-week period, for one hour per week, the areas of the classroom which allowed children in an informal way to develop their literacy and this helped nursery staff to develop these skills further.

For example, in the music area, Lorna read out loud, 'What's the time, Mr Wolf?', and Nicky tapped out the rhythm on a wooden block. In the writing area, Anna wrote her name in capital letters and covered the page with different capital letters. In the cookery corner, Andrew said 'My name begins with "A" and Diane's begins with "D": a number of children then talked about names and numbers, and Liam selected all the names which began with "L" '. Cathy drew a big 'C' in the sand, and in the book corner Richard saw the word Renoir on a print above the books and commented 'that's a word like Richard. It starts with "R" '.

Discussion

One of the interesting and unexpected side-effects which I observed during this time was the development of the children's thinking. There was evidence of children trying to make sense of situations and asking questions about them. There was evidence, too, of children considering other people's contributions to a discussion and taking them on board.

One example is of an activity set up with two of the boys, Steve and Andrew, who had shown curiosity about melting candles the previous week. One initially had thought that the melted wax was water or paint but now concluded that it must be wax and deduced that it resulted from the heat, and that when further away from the flame it hardened.

A second was when a group of four solved the problem of a three-seater car being inadequate for all of them, in which they spontaneously and repeatedly used counting.

The third example is of a long sustained conversation between Andrew and the teacher while looking at books and pictures of space shuttles.

In all these situations the children asked many questions, and used much reflective language, often relating knowledge from elsewhere to the topic of interest 'I've heard about' and 'you need oxygen to breathe', and reminding each other to 'listen', or commenting on another's 'great idea'.

The pupils' reflective behaviour appears to have been facilitated by the detailed discussion of nursery rhymes and stories, and the focus on language and meaning and small group experiences in which the staff were responsive to their ideas and able to help them extend and reflect on consequences and implications.

In the final term, I introduced the Oxford Reading Tree rhyme and analogy card game series. The children had shown how much they enjoyed playing games with rhymes, the most accessible sounds of language. They seemed
to find it easy to analyze words by their initial sounds, the onset, and by the
final part of the word, the rime, (so that in 'cat', 'c' is the onset, 'at' is the rime).
Focusing on the link between rhymes and shared spelling patterns in this way
helps children to develop the ability to use the spelling pattern of a known
word to read a new word with the same spelling pattern, as in hat, cat; that
is, it helps the children to make analogies. Knowledge of letter: sound correspondence and the ability to make analogies are important decoding skills
related to reading and spelling ability.

Cards and games of the Oxford Reading Tree (Hunt and Franks, 1987)
provided a flexible resource to help the children develop the ability to categorize words on the basis of their constituent sounds and to further develop their
awareness of alliteration and rhyme, and they had great fun doing so. Throughout the two-year project, regular meetings were held to evaluate each stage
and plan the next one. It became increasingly obvious that understanding of
the philosophy and rationale behind the intervention is essential for staff to
make informed decisions on a daily basis, in recognizing and using opportunities offered by the children and using effective pacing and grouping.

According to Adams (1990), 'Along with phonological awareness, basic
print awareness, word awareness and letter recognition are capacities which
we should seek to develop in kindergarten school. Collectively, the research
shows that, if we could do so universally, we would enormously reduce the
rate of primary school failures'.

We realized in our project that if we were to persuade other pre-school
teachers to undertake this work, we would need convincing evidence to show
that activities related to print and phonological awareness can be infused into
normal good practice. We must be able to show that a pre-school teacher can
guide, direct and respond to opportunities without losing the child-centred
ethos on which is based the philosophy of nursery education. We must also
be able to show the puzzlement and wonder an appropriate response can
produce, the fun, enjoyment and sense of worth which children achieve in
group work and whole class work, where the focus is on chanting, rhyming
and rhythm.

To achieve this, we decided not only to draw teachers' attention to the
research findings which underpin the work, but also to produce a video to
illustrate some of the work in progress. The video was made in the third term
of the second year, and, we hope, combined with the literature, this will provide the impetus for other teachers.

'Earnest commitment to pre-school literacy support may be the soundest
investment we can make for the future . . . educationalists, psychologists and
policy-makers should do all they can to ensure that all our children are headed
towards the future they deserve rather than being locked into the one which
their parents got' (*ibid*).

Conclusion

What features of these three different projects were instrumental in helping pupils to move forward in their thinking? At this point I identify and discuss some common elements before considering their general relevance in relation to pupils with learning difficulties in the next and final chapter.

All three programmes were long-term and embraced a range of curricular areas, although they all had a clear focus on important aspects of cognitive development. These comprised: understanding the links between spoken and written words and the sounds within words: the relationships between real space, landmarks and their symbolic representation, and for the oldest pupils, the use of information in texts in their own writing.

Each approach was developmental, with teachers planning and adapting learning experiences and challenges on the basis of their pupils' current understanding. This is particularly clear in the work on maps, where initial real life exploration was succeeded by symbolic representation on a map based on a story. Powerful reminders of the focus of pupils work were present in the classrooms: the Think Trail and good work motto in the Factfiler programme, the use of symbols to remind groups of their day's programme of work, and the numerous nursery rhymes and related pictures on the nursery school walls.

However, to quote Mrs Law from chapter 7 'you can put up displays for all you like but they (the pupils) will very often never see it, just walk past'. It was the teachers' provision of stimulating experiences and contexts that ensured this did not happen, and their child centred approach was always responsive and receptive to pupils' contributions and ideas. All three teachers stressed the importance of helping pupils to advance in their own learning, by responding to their ideas, pointing out links with other experiences and helping them to monitor their own learning. For example the nursery children made up their own words and rhymes and their teacher developed activities on the basis of their interests and ideas: the first year primary pupils invented their own symbols for landmarks and in Factfiler pupils devised a poster to monitor their progress. The teachers were especially alert to evidence of spontaneous reflection, like noticing a library coding system, the different lengths of words and the effect of highlighting printed extracts for a reader. Their accounts demonstrate the value they attached to the many indications of pupils' independent reflective activity, and how they scaffolded this in their classroom interactions. These show how assistance to pupils was reduced over time: for example in Factfiler they were reminded to check facts with the text before asking the teacher, or at another stage, to ask their partner questions first, in the knowledge that the teacher would help if really needed. Linda Watson's comment that 'we must be able to show that a preschool teacher can guide, direct and respond to opportunities without losing the child centred ethos' applies way beyond the nursery and beautifully describes the process whereby teachers can help develop pupils' potential through a combination of sensitive contingent responding and appropriate challenges as described in chapters 1 and 2.

The process is best seen in the kind of reflective episode identified earlier in the special schools. In responding to pupils' questions, ideas and initiatives, the three mainstream teachers also used a lot of Category 2 talk. This was often embedded in lengthy dialogues involving a teacher and several pupils, like in the reflective discussions integral to Factfiler, where pupils explained and justified their actions, and in map work where working groups explained their work to their peers.

The teachers also made many contributions which often introduced new vocabulary. The 7 and 8-year-olds using Factfiler began to talk of texts, glossaries, facts and notes, and the nursery children learned concepts such as title, beginning, end, and author.

In all three projects, and most with the oldest pupils, metacognitive awareness was observed and encouraged by their teacher by means of appropriate Category 2 talk, which made this explicit. Teachers did this for example, by pointing out writing strategies to help information to be made prominent and clarified, the use of visualization to help remembering, the likelihood of misunderstanding in other people, the making of analogies through analyzing written and spoken words.

The findings from the Factfiler programme, however, show how necessary participation and active personal use of metacognitive and strategic behaviour were for these to be internalized and used on a similar task. Those pupils who simply were told about them, although they listened with interest, did not choose to employ them. Knowing and doing were both necessary.

The two primary developments fitted well within the flexible curricular guidelines for 5–14-year-olds in Scottish schools. The guidelines emphasize and recommend group work, problem-solving and discussion, in all areas of the curriculum. They were positively helpful in planning these projects and certainly did not act as constraining straitjackets. Two features of the projects reported in this chapter appear to be important contributors to their success: pupils' work with their peers, and role play activities.

Group activities, in which cooperation and discussion were prominent, occupied much of class time. In the two primary programmes there was emphasis on pupils reporting to each other on what they had done, answering questions from their peers, and listening to one another's ideas. These were also encouraged in the extension work which the nursery staff built on the spontaneous questions and enthusiasm of their pupils. As their teacher reports, these 3 and 4-year-olds were beginning to consider each others' contributions and 'great ideas'. Awareness of their own and others' understanding was enhanced in the Badger group's production of a self-monitoring aid in the form of a poster, and in the first year primary pupils by the task of helping a nursery teacher explain to her young pupils about their school's layout and personnel.

The power of role play to help children to reflect was spelled out by Linda-Jane Simpson when she said, 'there is no better way to get myself and the children right into situations, all actively contributing to the thinking aloud process. Everyone is linked by the purpose which the drama context pro-vides.' She provides convincing evidence of its powerful facilitating effect in enabling pupils to some extent at least to get into the mental position of other people, their likely confusion, misinterpretation, and lack of the knowledge that they, the pupils, possess.

She repeatedly and skilfully reminded them of these complexities in her own role playing and she also modelled thinking aloud, as when she closed her eyes and said 'close eyes and think. I don't really remember . . .' In the Factfiler programme in the roles of researchers, writers, editors and detectives pupils gained a deeper understanding of concepts, of genre, audience, and the usefulness of annotation and subheadings. Both primary programmes used puppets, MacFact as a reminder to pupils of their thinking and to highlight possible misunderstandings, and in mapping, those made by the pupils to walk over routes in their maps, and thereby enhance their understanding and memory.

A progression can be seen from the nursery school children's participa-tion in action songs, and nursery rhymes whose meaning and implications were explored in depth with their teacher, the 6-year-olds' participation as map makers, and guides in an imaginative story, to those in Factfiler who were taking on sophisticated tasks of research and writing. In all three classrooms the teachers modelled reflection in thinking aloud, planning, and encourag-ing reflection and contributions such as 'can you help me' and 'I don't really remember'.

What of the slower learners? All three classes were in city schools with pupils of a wide range of ability. In Factfiler the familiarity and repeated refer-ence to a small number of texts reduced cognitive demands and helped the slower learners, who were reading for a purpose rather than to practice some-thing at which they were unskilled. In map work the slower learners bene-fitted from extra concrete experiences with a three-dimensional representational model: their teacher comments that those mainly watching and not directly joining in the group construction of the map were also concentrating and learn-ing. 'Everyone observed the proceedings and was part of the experience at their own level.' And in the nursery school the familiarity, explicitness, repeti-tion and subsequent developmental work of the nursery rhymes was ideally suited to facilitate deep learning in all the pupils. All the teachers' expectations for all their pupils were high: they were confident that the slower ones bene-fitted, and both they and their pupils were not hampered by a history of past failure.

There was ample evidence that real learning had taken place in all three settings. It persisted over time and was generalized to new tasks and contexts. Evidence from the nursery of informal comments by parents of their children's talk at home, and the primary teachers of those children who had experienced the nursery phonic awareness programme, add to their teachers' classroom observations of increased curiosity and awareness in that setting.

In the mapping programme the pupils showed their understanding of spatial relationships and symbolic representation in the imaginative drama setting which built on their earlier work on maps in the school. Outside the classroom these pupils demonstrated their new awareness, in the library and on holiday. More formal assessment provides clear evidence that the group of pupils who had Factfiler experience spontaneously used strategies, language and cooperation in a new task in a way that was radically different from those of a comparison group, who had been told of these but had not directly used them. As Pat Mackenzie says, the latter showed an unthinking, unquestioning approach, in which copying dominated, with very little evidence of self-monitoring, and they relied heavily on their teacher for reassurance.

The very positive conclusion from this chapter must be that in the mainstream classes described, young pupils are being helped to be reflective. High pupil:teacher ratios, curricular guidelines and a wide ability range are not preventing this. In the final chapter these encouraging results are considered along with those from the research with pupils who have learning difficulties.

9 Classrooms for Reflection

We cannot enter pupils' heads and read their minds, but we can observe their behaviour, examine their work, and listen to what they say. And all teachers do this continuously.

In the special school research one fruitful way of studying pupils' reflective behaviour was during the periods of time when they were 'absorbed, taken up in what they're doing', in the words of one of our teachers. The nature and contexts of such reflective episodes provide useful insights into ways of helping pupils to think well and to make intellectual progress.

Private, hidden reflection was obviously not available to us: reflective episodes were embedded in verbal interactions, 'ways of talking that have special value at specific moments' (Cazden, 1988). The kinds of episode illustrated in chapter 6 were regularly experienced by the target pupils in two classrooms, but were almost absent from a third and were often not satisfactorily resolved in the fourth. The episodes in which pupils made intellectual progress were those in which teachers were responsive, explicit and worked with pupils to encourage reflection.

Encouraging Reflection in the Classroom

Responsiveness

Ideally a teacher's role in an episode was to respond and tune in to a pupil's current focus of interest and level of understanding, and to support and extend this by expert scaffolding.

There were many examples of this, like when Samantha was reading and her teacher repeatedly probed her understanding and emphasized her (Samantha's) mental activity, with 'so what do you think? . . .', and 'that's a good guess', and 'remember to check'.

In such situations teachers were making fine judgments on how much assistance pupils needed in order to avoid any sense of failure, but at the same time to foster their feelings of competence and independence, the essence of scaffolding. 'I mustn't push too fast, could jeopardize success so far', and 'I think he will either call out for help constantly or give up and need coaxing' were typical comments.

One of the teachers was very successful in leaving a pupil with a problem to think about, with specific instructions and reminders, as for example with Mark:

I want you to think very carefully what the difference is between a square and a rectangle. They've both got four corners and they've both got four sides, but there's a difference between them. Why are some squares and some rectangles? I want you to have a little think about that while you're colouring in. It's to do with the sides . . . (Mark laughs).

The importance of responding to the pupil's current interest was stressed in the teacher interviews in chapter 7, particularly by Mrs Law. 'If something took off you should go with it because it's meaningful and has potential'. Conversely there was no point in 'labouring against' when things were not going well, she said.

Explicitness

When teachers were engaged with pupils in successful reflective episodes, their own attention was focused and their language explicit, far removed from the detached vagueness that has been repeatedly found to increase pupils' frustration and reduce their levels of achievement. A series of studies have shown that the vaguer a teacher's classroom talk, (for example, containing 'somehow', 'just about', 'thing' and 'kind of'), the fewer and shorter pupils' initiations will be. (Dunkin, 1987) In our research, target pupils' frustration was sometimes very apparent when what a teacher said revealed how she had not succeeded in tuning in to their thinking.

In chapter 5 general non-specific feedback from teachers was commonly found in some of the less satisfactory classroom conversations, where the target pupil and teacher did not share the same focus of attention, and such Category 3 talk was not common either in longer classroom conversations or in reflective episodes.

Pupils need to know how they are doing and where they are, both in the narrow contexts of episodes and in the longer ones of complete classroom sessions. Research on classroom practice has begun to consider pupils' understanding of what they are to do and why, and has revealed what probably would surprise many parents and teachers, that this understanding is often hazy and may be quite wrong. Parker-Rees (1996) found that teachers of primary pupils between the ages of 5 and 8 never discussed with them the purpose of their classroom activities but spent a lot of time and effort on telling them what they had to do. And their pupils never asked their teachers for such reasons. Getting the task done was the overriding concern of both, rather than the processes of negotiation and achieving understanding, with their potential for enabling true progress in pupils' thinking. Our target pupils found it very difficult indeed to tell the researcher about their classroom work in any kind of detail. Coming to school on the bus and getting up for breakfast figured almost as much as references to their work in school. It is all the more important, then, that their teachers try to create with pupils a familiar mental framework for introducing and closing sessions that would help pupils to know what to expect and why, a kind of generalized event representation which could facilitate the focussing of their attention (Nelson, 1986). The aide-memoire used by Quicke and Winter (1994), and the Think Trail described in the last chapter are excellent examples of constant visual reminders to help reflection. In the classroom sessions we studied, all the teachers made introductory remarks about their planned activities, and in those where reflection was most emphasized this was accompanied by teachers' specific focusing of pupils' attention, by saying things like 'we will just read them, so everyone knows what they are', or, to a pupil, 'explain to Paul what we are doing'. In this they were emphasizing that their pupils should particularly attend to and understand their initial instructions. In classrooms 2 and 3, work often began without this attention to pupils' readiness or current understanding, but with practical instructions about materials which in effect often distracted them.

Marked differences were found too, in the ways in which the teachers brought sessions to a close, and these were very consistent. Figures 2 and 4 show how some sessions simply came to a halt at break time, and in classroom 3 there was rapid tidying up for the next teacher, in the relatively short sessions which ended quite abruptly with remarks like, 'Oh glory, it's that time again, tidy up time. Can you put your things together and it will be the first thing we start next time.' Perhaps the published curriculum programme was assumed to enable pupils to develop a sense of continuity and of their progress, but this was never made explicit. In the more reflective classrooms teachers always drew a session to its close by involving all the pupils in the class, either with comments on their hard work or helpfulness, telling them what was to follow their break, or, most frequently in classroom 1, with a brief class discussion including a demonstration or description by pupils of their work to their peers, as in the following example:

T: Mark, would you like to tell us what you've made?
Pause
T: What did you join the wires to?
Pause
T: Start with the battery.
Mark: We joined the wires to the battery and then we joined them to that bit there.
T: What's that bit called?
Mark: The bulb.
T: Right, carry on . . .
Mark: And then we put the drawing pin in and we put the wire bit round the drawing pin, and it can go on and off.
T: Mark's made a path for the electricity. Look carefully . . .

In the mainstream classwork described in chapter 8, there was a great deal of explaining and discussion by groups of pupils of this kind, which was often integral to their work. As we have noted, cooperative group activity was not a common feature of many of the special school sessions we observed: consequently there was less need for pupils to give each other an account of what they are doing. Such reflective discussion may, however, as in Factfiler, be an important vehicle for reflection, particularly for pupils who do not verbalize their thinking very readily.

Teacher Talk

Category 2 talk was much more common in the two classrooms where most of the satisfactory reflective episodes were identified. Such talk is responsive and explicit and has the potential to extend pupils' thinking through tuning in to what they say, asking them for explanations and justifications, pointing out analogies, consequences and inconsistencies and raising their metacognitive awareness. It was also noticeable in the more informal observations of the mainstream settings described in chapter 8.

At the risk of labouring this important point, Category 2 talk is not simply checking on pupils' knowledge, like Category 1, but extends and explores it, and demonstrates a teacher's interest. All the teachers used Category 1 talk including several direct questions at the outset of their sessions in the classroom, but as the work progressed, in classrooms 1 and 4, they addressed more probing challenging talk to their pupils. Our audiotapes recorded marked changes in tempo at this point, with frequent and long pauses within and between episodes of reflection.

Cazden (1988) reported on research findings in mainstream schools showing that when teachers waited longer for pupils to reply (at least three seconds) then the quality of their classroom interactions improved in several ways. Pupils' responses became more varied, and teachers reacted to these with more variety themselves, asking fewer but more complex questions, sustaining the development of ideas more successfully, and with raised expectations of the pupils. Teachers of pupils with learning difficulties often find it particularly difficult to wait while they struggle for an answer, and sometimes report that they have had to train themselves to do so. A mixture of impatience, sympathy and emotional tension along with expectations about a person's ability, leads to a well supported generalization about interpersonal communication: that cutting short the communicative efforts of those who find it most difficult to articulate their thoughts is a common response which is likely to compound their difficulties further. And in reading McNaughton and Glynn (1981) found that teachers' correction of the lowest ability groups was immediate, much quicker than for better readers. Again, with a longer delay, pupils' self-corrections and accuracy increased.

In the special school classrooms teachers did not always wait long enough for pupils' replies. The taperecordings included a number of occasions when pupils' replies or contributions were lost as the teacher had moved on, and this was most evident, as would be expected, in the classroom with a strong emphasis on finishing the work. In this classroom too there were few breaks in the high level of talk and activity in which pupils could engage in reflection.

Modelling

Modelling by teachers is a powerful and effective influence on their pupils, particularly where the classroom ethos is warm. Non-verbal indications of puzzlement and concentration form a significant part of this but are not part of our evidence. Category 4 talk comprised teachers' own problem solving, thinking aloud, planning and checking and was present at times in the talk of all four, as shown in table 4: although such examples were infrequent, they were usually responded to by pupils. For example, when teachers expressed puzzlement, pupils often came up with explanations. Used judiciously this is an effective way of helping to draw attention to ambiguity or inconsistency. A more deliberate approach which also could be effective would be along the lines of Ashman and Conway's (1989) work reported in chapter 2, which could emphasize a teacher's own planning in addition to practice in joint planning with the pupils. Other good examples of more specific strategies are verbalisation and visualization to help memory. Chapter 8 contains many striking examples from the mainstream work, of teachers modelling reflection very effectively, particularly in role playing and discussion, and the use of drama was warmly endorsed by staff in both mainstream and special settings.

In summary, teachers can be effective in encouraging reflection though classroom interaction by providing pupils with contingent responses which explicitly encourage them to reflect, and by modelling reflection themselves. What should we be looking for and helping to develop in pupils?

Reflection by Pupils

Indications of pupil reflection will include those cited in chapter 5: their spontaneous and appropriate use of the language of reflection, their asking of hypothetical questions, their requests for explanations and noticing and correction of inconsistencies. Examples occur throughout the data, although they were sparse, and were sometimes barely audible, and could not be responded to by the teacher. Moreover some target pupils only ever used more complex language like hypothetical statements, in chatting to their peers, and not in class activities. However, there was sufficient evidence to judge that they were familiar with the less complex kind of reflective language that would be expected for their general level of development. With further experience in meaningful contexts they would be expected to understand and use more complex terms like 'however', and 'necessary'.

There were very few references to strategies by the special school pupils. However, as figures 1 and 5 make plain, they were seen to be using strategies in their practical activities like experimenting and testing. With more emphasis on talking about what they had been doing, and explaining to their peers how they had tackled complex problems that truly engaged their interest, pupils could in time become more proficient and comfortable with metacognitive language, with summarizing and planning and prediction. This kind of activity was reported by Powell and Makin (1994) (and referred to in chapter 2) as leading to improvements in their pupils' ability to verbalize about their work at a deeper more reflective level. Practice in listening to their peers' accounts of what they had done was a less frequent experience for the special school than for the mainstream pupils, but it has the potential to enlarge their understanding, and to understand different viewpoints, as well as highlighting likely misinterpretations and ambiguities. One teacher, as reported in chapter 7, planned many focussed communication and role play activities to enhance her pupils' awareness of other people's perspectives, but there was additional potential within the whole range of curricular activities for helping pupils share other perspectives than their own, by talking and by planned cooperative activity. Palincsar's (1986) impressive results from reciprocal tutoring in groups highlights its potential for slow learners, provided that feedback is explicit, and the group maintains its focus on meaning. A different approach, also described in the first chapter, is that of Lipman (1988), emphasizing democratic discussion of imaginative, logically challenging materials. Both have reported particular success with children who were relatively unsuccessful in school.

In chapter 5 we remarked on the infrequency with which pupils linked other experiences in or out of school with their current classroom activity. Their teachers did make such links in Category 1 talk quite frequently, particularly at an early stage in a session when outlining pupils' work. Often such links were brief and simply to the effect that pupils had done the same kind of thing before, a process of consolidation and repetition rather than extension. Pupils in the special schools rarely spontaneously made such linking, and this surely indicates their need for more explicit awareness of its importance, like that emphasized by Quicke and Winter's research with teachers and reported in chapter 2.

In chapter 8, nursery school children often introduced ideas and knowledge they had developed at home into conversations with their peers and teacher. Andrew displayed considerable knowledge about space, explaining 'I know a lot about these space shuttles because I've been watching programmes' and 'my Dad taped it', and 'I've got Space Lego', as he talked confidently about oxygen, planets and orbits, and planned to write off for more information with his parents' help. This kind of conversation in nursery school is far removed from those rather sterile, limited, ones which have been reported by researchers such as Tizard and Hughes (1984). They are strikingly different, too, from the classroom talk of our much older, much more experienced pupils in special schools. For them, to judge from our evidence, outside and previous experiences did not automatically feed into their current ones, in the smooth and confident way shown by some of the much younger children at nursery level.

As pupils with learning difficulties often do not spontaneously generalise their learning to new but similar tasks and situations it is important that they are encouraged to habitually make connections, and look for similarities. This could be highlighted more by teachers, particularly in group situations.

Intellectual Challenge

We would also wish to see pupils' absorption, engagement and perseverance over time on challenging activities. Our observations often lent support to the common generalization concerning pupils with learning difficulties that was foremost in the minds of the teachers referred to at the start of chapter 2, their liability to be distracted and difficulty in concentration. However, there was also evidence of sustained periods of attention when pupils became caught up in a challenging task, both as individuals and when working with their peers. One of the teachers in our study was especially skilled in her timing of specific and positive comments about her pupils' good thinking, hard work and attentiveness, and interspersed periods of concentration with physical activity like rhythmic clapping games which refocused their attention and relaxed them.

This introduces the final and probably most desirable feature of pupils' experience to be considered in this section — their enjoyment, enjoyment of problem-solving, of challenging intellectual experiences, and their growing curiosity, eagerness, and responsiveness. In chapter 5 an example of how the different classes reacted to the presence of the recording apparatus, microphones and research assistant demonstrated how the effects of a teaching style which gave explanations and reasons, and encouraged pupils to ask for these, showed in the spontaneous curiosity shown by some pupils, and was also very evident in the mainstream settings. In the depictions of classroom sessions in chapter 6 are recordings of laughter, smiles and excited exclamations which are associated with reflective episodes. The audiotapes contain many examples of pupils' laughter, some embarrassed, some teasing, and some delighted. Pupils laughed readily at teachers' jokes and were easily upset if frustrated or shown up in some way.

Our target pupils' enjoyment was certainly not less during the sessions when they reported that they had been really working hard and that they had found their work difficult, but their dissatisfaction was very clear on occasions when they had met with challenges which were not concluded in a satisfying way. Pupils' reactions then were negative and emotional, as they also were when given work that they found too easy or childish.

Emotional Aspects

Pupils' extreme sensitivity and feelings of inadequacy when they were not successfully coping with their classroom activities were very apparent. They were all extremely reluctant to ask for help and to admit their difficulties, even with the most tactful of teacher support.

Admission of confusion and being able to ask for help and knowing what help is needed is a characteristic of effective and mature learners as the initial quotation in chapter 5 indicates.

Its importance is often underestimated in the classroom behaviour of pupils with learning difficulties. There are several possible contributory factors that lead pupils to make the kind of emotional outburst of Mark in classroom 1: 'Go away, Miss. I'm not doing this until you go away. Move your damn chair.' One is the sense of exposure in one-to-one situations with a teacher. This was never shown by Mark in small or larger group situations, where he was an active, cheerful and confident contributor.

Being a member of a group has many potentially positive aspects in relation to reflection. One that is often overlooked in discussions of provision for pupils with learning difficulties is the reduction of their feeling of emotional exposure. Our observations did not lend support to the view expressed in interview by one of the teachers in a special school: 'They don't want to lose face in front of their mates and they don't want to be seen as needing special help.' Mrs Macdonald was always very sensitive to the potentially negative aspects of group work:

> For a secondary aged pupil, if you had someone that was more able even trying to read with someone who was less able, there's all of the emotions and it's a very sensitive area. It would be alright if they were able to take that but I think that you would have to be aware of the sensitivity of the situation, and it's not just the reading, it's the emotions, you know, what might go on in the playground afterwards, the bullying or badgering that someone might get from that.

There is, however, a case for claiming the opposite: that group work, certainly when sensitively handled, can help reduce the likelihood of teasing and increase pupils' appreciation of each others' individuality and contributions. We have reports of this from the literature and from our own research in the special and mainstream classrooms.

It would be a mistake to deny that many pupils with special educational needs show great reluctance in admitting confusion and a consequent avoidance of this by playing safe. They often have little faith in their own judgments and readily agree with and rely on those of other people. When they are mistaken they may believe that this is a situation they can do nothing about, that their lack of ability is the cause, and they may act in a very passive manner, dependent on their teachers' step-by-step prompting, not investing much effort and missing out on challenging experiences that could boost their confidence and feelings of control. Chapter 2 indicated that some teaching methods within special education may have unintentionally fostered such dependence.

The risk of this is reduced in classroom activities which give pupils responsibility for decision-making and where there is not necessarily a right answer, but where the consequences are apparent. Group tasks in which they have to accommodate the different views and contributions of their peers reduce the likelihood of passivity. The examples in chapter 6 of successful activities such as model construction, communication tasks and role playing in an imaginary problematic situation all shared these features, and they are important constituents of the mainstream programmes described in chapter 8.

The importance of a general ethos of warmth and positive expectations in helping pupils to feel valued and accepted was highlighted in chapter 7. At a more specific level within classroom interactions there is also enormous potential for enhancing pupils' positive feelings.

Mrs Law's skill in detecting and lessening feelings of inadequacy was shown in a session involving Isobel, who had shown unexpected difficulty in a simple counting game.

Her emotional tension was shown by her inability to stop counting at the appropriate point.

T:	Ah, that was too many. Let's all help Isobel. Let's count to two and then stop. Are you going to join in, Isobel?
All:	One, two, stop!
T:	You do it.
Isobel:	Stop.
T:	You've got to count first.
Isobel:	One, two, three, four.
T:	Thank you.

Some ten minutes later, she deliberately praised Isobel's work and attitude.

T:	Isobel tries hard to be sensible. She's good to play with. She's a good typist. Isobel's a good swimmer. She knows the days and she knows what she wants to do and she knows what she likes. She's good at 'tig' and she's a good person.

Such explicit focussing on a pupil who was temporarily vulnerable was a characteristic of Mrs Law's approach, who was always aware that even in a very supportive and positive classroom ethos her pupils' feelings of worth as thinkers and learners were readily undermined.

Another way of raising pupils' confidence is for teachers to deliberately foster their unique and individual contributions, particularly in group settings. One of our special school teachers repeatedly stressed the value of pupils' ideas that were different from those of others, and she had no hesitation in telling pupils how boring it was when they copied each others' contributions, and would respond to original contributions with comments like 'That's interesting! I hadn't thought of that.'

The same teacher in her interview showed her awareness of the importance of pupils' attributions concerning their classroom work, acknowledged in
chapter 1 to be very salient for those pupils who have most difficulties with
their work. 'It's part of the way I talk to children', she said, 'Whenever they
come up with a good idea I say "You were really thinking hard", and if they
have not succeeded, "that's because you weren't trying hard enough"'. The
effectiveness of this depends on teachers' accurate judgment of their pupils'
current understanding, which Mrs Law certainly possessed. She had a central
concern that pupils should be stretched, and she observed that 'in a lot of
special schools nobody makes real demands, everybody is nice to the pupils
and pats them on the head and they are never seriously challenged.' This view
went hand in hand with her conviction that distractions in the classroom were
often due to pupils' fear, all about 'I can't do this, I'm terrified that you're going
to expose me.' She saw the classroom work as the place for raising pupils'
confidence, self-esteem and understanding of their own and their peers' feelings and ideas, automatically at the same time with the effect of reducing any
difficult classroom behaviour. This is an important contrast with teachers who
sometimes avoid making intellectually challenging demands on their pupils
because of their emotional volatility. However, as we saw in chapter 6, our
target pupils made negative comments about 'easy' classroom activities and
their comments and observed non-verbal behaviour were much more enthusiastic when they had engaged in work that was quite hard but had some kind
of positive outcome.

For these target pupils positive attitudes towards hard work were modelled by their teachers, and helped by their teachers' sensitivity to their individual, sometimes idiosyncratic ways of working, their discussion of helpful
strategies, and their explicit contingent scaffolding to aid pupils' understanding. Repeated emphasis on these aspects of classroom experience can facilitate
a shift in pupils' focus from finishing the task in hand, to attending to their
own learning and reflecting on it, thereby increasing the chances that it will be
retained, consolidated and generalized.

What about Mainstream?

Our 11-year-old target pupils in their classes of no more than ten to twelve,
did experience classroom interactions when their thinking was supported and
extended. Earlier chapters have identified a number of factors associated with
such experiences: these range from a relatively narrow focus on talk by teachers,
through their planned activities, to more general aspects such as classroom ethos.
Individual chapters and the first part of this concluding one include suggestions
for the enhancement and emphasis of such potentially facilitating experiences.

Our focus has been on classroom interactions in which pupils' thinking is
encouraged. In these interactions, a teacher, as Mrs Law said, has 'to be responsive all the time to what's in front of you', to a pupil's current awareness, likely

misconceptions, interest, and emotional state. And to help pupils to extend their thinking in reflection, teachers often have to do more, to scaffold interactions sufficiently but not too much, in order to promote pupils' independence and awareness of themselves as thinkers. This is differentiation and support for learning at their most effective, and teaching at its most skilled.

What are the implications of these findings for mainstream schools, which have become increasingly the preferred placement choice for those pupils traditionally described as having moderate learning difficulties? Chapter 2 emphasized the heterogeneity and complexity of this, the largest group of pupils with records (in Scotland), or statements (in England and Wales) of special educational needs.

In chapter 8 all three mainstream settings were clearly facilitating and enhancing reflection in their pupils, by well planned, focused and imaginative activities in which role play, group activities, and, especially in the nursery class, the children's own spontaneous curiosity were much to the fore. While all three classes included children from a broad spectrum of ability, they were much younger than the pupils at the special schools, and none of them were currently experiencing such learning difficulties that they were being considered for the recording process.

Another major difference at the time of research was that the special schools were only beginning to follow the guidelines of the Scottish 5–14 curriculum, whereas for the primary schools these were clearly established as a framework within which teachers planned and evaluated class activities. Both the primary school developments, as reported in chapter 8, were in tune with the requirements of the guidelines which emphasize the processes of learning, and activities such as problem-solving, finding out and group work.

Bennett's research on low attaining pupils who were transferred from special to mainstream schools showed that they did not automatically then experience a broader curriculum, and that in any case curricular change alone would not necessarily improve their learning experiences. In line with the thesis of this book, Bennett (1991) says 'Teachers need the skills and knowledge to effectively implement that curriculum', in order to improve the quality of pupils' learning.

Bennett's conclusions in many respects resemble the findings reported here. Pupils and their parents commonly claimed that the special school work was too easy and boring, and some pupils, especially shortly after transfer to mainstream, were stimulated by a more varied and demanding curriculum. But detailed analysis of their mainstream classroom experience showed how in many respects it remained very unsatisfactory. Pupils who had moved to mainstream were very dependent on their teachers, asking for frequent checks; they took longer than other pupils to settle and adjust to activity changes, and were involved in their work only at a superficial level for relatively short periods of time. They were found to often fail to understand their teachers' instructions (which were also judged to be unclear and inadequate by the researchers) and their tasks were often incomprehensible to them.

The most essential element of classroom interaction, the teacher's awareness of a pupil's understanding and misconceptions, 'creating a window into the child's mind' was found by Bennett to be deficient. His comment that 'teacher educators have some explaining to do about a general absence of courses on the diagnosis of learning at either pre-service or in-service level', may sound harsh and unreasonable to those targeted, like myself, but it is supported by his evidence, and to a lesser extent, by some of our findings. Alarmingly, Bennett reported the worst diagnostic assessments in special schools and classes where they had 'naively' expected to find the best practice. The conclusion, if this is generally true, would be that for pupils with moderate learning difficulties, special school experience is sometimes repetitious, undemanding and uninvolving, but that there is also a serious risk in mainstream that they will gain little understanding from inappropriate tasks.

Positive suggestions from Bennett's work are similar to those in this book: the role of social group activity in learning, the critical role of talk, and the need for teachers to optimize classroom dialogue. Many of our examples of classroom interaction show that teachers did at least some of the time succeed in understanding their pupils' thinking, and in helping them extend it in reflection.

This applies equally to special school and mainstream settings. Good educational practice is good educational practice in both. The features that were highlighted in the mainstream programmes and were judged to help pupils to advance in their thinking were also among those that the detailed analysis of special school classrooms indicated were important, and have been discussed earlier in this chapter.

What remains to be noted and not ignored are some additional factors which appear to be important and helpful for pupils with a history of difficulty in learning. These need to receive emphasis whatever the pupils' educational setting and whatever curriculum is being offered.

First, the pupils' self-esteem, emotional vulnerability and sensitivity to others' expectations have to be constantly borne in mind. Teachers in special schools become accustomed to a range of emotional, volatile, behaviour and may indeed, as in our study, expect it. While we had evidence that such expectations might lead teachers to play safe with a consequent reduction of excitement and challenge, they cannot and should not be ignored.

Second, as the teachers in the special schools stressed, their pupils benefit from clear, explicit responses, rather than more general encouragement. They need a teacher's clear framework and rationale for their classroom activities, interactions that encourage reflection, discussion of their own individual learning styles, and practice in self-monitoring. There is considerable evidence from research over the past decade and a half that 'pointing out what is happening and why', in the words of a special school teacher, is necessary, because it cannot be assumed that they will learn by picking things up casually and incidentally. Teachers need to help pupils to see links between their current and past experiences, between home and school, what they see on television and what they hear about in class discussion. The more this happens the more they will spontaneously begin to generalize their understanding. Contingent responding in the form of scaffolding by a teacher is instrumental in helping pupils to make intellectual advance during reflective episodes. But this need not be during individual teaching. Small groups may be less threatening and peers can be effective tutors.

But for this to work pupils and teachers need to be able to recognize at least some of the episodes in which pupils with learning difficulties are challenged, and pupils need the confidence to ask for help, discuss their progress and monitor their reflective activity. These essentials can be facilitated by the kinds of experience discussed in earlier chapters, but they certainly cannot be assumed. Metacognitive awareness is known to be relatively delayed and difficult for those with learning difficulties and has to be actively fostered, by classroom practice, modelling and by the prevailing ethos. Teachers may choose to make relatively minor alterations to their practice which can have quite significant effects. Collaborative, extended, classroom research into such **changes** in practice has a great deal to offer, in increasing our understanding of the potential benefits of maximising pupils' opportunities for reflection.

Perhaps most important of all are the expectations and attitudes of both the teacher and their pupils, in any classroom. As we saw in chapter 7 these determined the ways in which teachers interacted with their pupils, the conveying to them of a sense of respect for them as individuals, with valid ideas and interests which could and should be shared with others. Category 2 type talk by teachers expresses this underlying belief in teachers and encourages reflection in their interactions with pupils.

What is very clear is that whether in mainstream or special school settings teachers who provide intellectually challenging experiences for all their pupils are more likely to enable them fulfil their potential as reflective learners, and, in the words of one of our research study teachers, they may 'surprise you, just stun and amaze you if you give them the opportunity'.

References

ADAMS, M. (1990) *Beginning to Read: Thinking and Learning About Print*, Cambridge, MA, MIT Press.

ALEXANDER, R. (1992) *Policy and Practice in Primary Education*, London, Routledge.

ASHMAN, A. and CONWAY, R. (1989) *Cognitive Strategies for Special Education*, London, Routledge.

ASHMAN, A. and CONWAY, R. (1993) 'Teaching students to use process-based learning and problem-solving strategies in mainstream classes', *Learning and Instruction*, **3**, pp. 73–92.

BENNETT, N. (1991) 'The quality of classroom learning experiences for children with special educational needs', in AINSCOW, M. (Ed) *Effective Schools for All*, London, David Fulton.

BENNETT, N., DESFORGES, C., COCKBURN, A. and WILKINSON, B. (1984) *The Quality of Pupil Learning Experiences*, London, Lawrence Erlbaum Associates.

BONNETT, M. (1994) *Children's Thinking: Promoting Understanding in the Primary School*, London, Cassell.

BOOTH, D. (1994) *Story Drama*, Ontario, Pembroke Publishers.

BORKOWSKI, J. and KURTZ, B. (1987) 'Metacognition and executive control', in BORKOWSKI, J. and DAY, J. (Eds) *Comparative Approaches to Retardation, Learning Disabilities and Giftedness*, Norwood, NJ, Ablex.

BORKOWSKI, J., PECK, V. and DAMBERG, P. (1983) 'Attention, memory and cognition', in METSON, J. and MULICK, J. (Eds) *Handbook of Mental Retardation*, New York, Pergamon.

BOUD, D., KEOGH, R. and WALKER, D. (1985) *Reflection: Turning Experience into Learning*, London, Kogan Page.

BRENNAN, W. (1974) *Shaping the Education of Slow Learners*, London, Routledge.

BROWN, A., BRANSFORD, J., FERRARA, R. and CAMPIONE, J. (1983) 'Learning, remembering and understanding', in MUSSEN, P. (Ed) *Handbook of Child Psychology*, 3, New York, Wiley.

BRUNER, J. (1973) *Beyond the Information Given: Studies in the Psychology of Knowing*, New York, Norton.

BRUNER, J. (1983) *Child's Talk*, New York, Norton.

BRYANT, P. and BRADLEY, L. (1985) *Children's Reading Problems*, Oxford, Blackwell.

BURDEN, R. (1994) 'Trends and developments in educational psychology', *School Psychology International*, **15**, 4, pp. 293–347.

References

CAMPBELL, R. and OLSON, D. (1990) 'Children's thinking', in GRIEVE, R. and HUGHES, M. (Eds) *Understanding Children*, Oxford, Blackwell.

CAMPIONE, J. (1986) 'Reaction time and the study of intelligence', in WADE, M. (Ed) *Motor Skill Acquisition of the Mentally Handicapped: Issues in Research and Training*, Holland, Elsevier.

CAMPIONE, J. (1987) 'Metacognitive components of instructional research with problem learners', in WEINERT, F. and KLUWE, R. (Eds) *Metacognition, Motivation and Understanding*, Hillsdale, NJ, Lawrence Erlbaum Associates.

CAZDEN, C. (1988) *Classroom Discourse*, Portsmouth, NH, Heinemann.

CRASKE, M. (1988) 'Learned helplessness, self-worth, motivation and attribution retraining for primary school children', *British Journal of Educational Psychology*, **58**, pp. 152–64.

DANIELS, H. (1990) 'The modified curriculum: Help with the same or something completely different?', in EVANS, P. and VARMA, V. (Eds) *Special Education: Past, Present and Future*, London, Falmer Press.

DEY, I. (1993) *Qualitative Data Analysis*, London, Routledge.

DOCKRELL, J. and McSHANE, J. (1993) *Children's Learning Difficulties*, Oxford, Blackwell.

DONALDSON, M. (1978) *Children's Minds*, London, Fontana.

DONALDSON, M. (1992) *Human Minds: An Exploration*, London, Allen Lane.

DUNKIN, M. (Ed) (1987) *International Encyclopaedia of Teaching and Teacher Education*, Oxford, Pergamon.

EDWARDS, D. and MERCER, N. (1987) *Common Knowledge: The Development of Understanding in the Classroom*, London, Methuen.

EDWARDS, D. and WESTGATE, D. (1987) *Investigating Classroom Talk*, London, Falmer Press.

FISHER, B. (1991) *Joyful Learning*, Portsmouth, NH, Heinemann.

FISHER, R. (1990) *Teaching Children to Think*, Oxford, Blackwell.

FLAVELL, J. (1981) 'Cognitive monitoring', in DICKSON, W. (Ed) *Children's Oral Communications*, Orlando, FL, Academic Press.

FLAVELL, J. (1985) *Cognitive Development*, Englewood Cliffs, NJ, Prentice Hall.

FLAVELL, J., GREEN, F. and FLAVELL, E. (1995) *Young Children's Knowledge About Thinking*, Monographs for the Society for Research in Child Development, 60, 1, Chicago, IL, University of Chicago Press.

FREEMAN, J. (1991) *Gifted Children Growing Up*, London, Cassell.

HARRIS, P. (1989) *Children and Emotion: The Development of Psychological Understanding*, Oxford, Blackwell.

HENWOOD, K. and PIGEON, N. (1995) 'Grounded theory and psychological research', *The Psychologist*, **8**, 3, pp. 115–18.

HUNT, R. and FRANKS, T. (1987) *Oxford Reading Tree: A Teacher's Guide*, Oxford, Oxford University Press.

ISTOMINA, Z. (1982) 'The development of voluntary memory in children of pre-school age', in NEISSER, U. (Ed) *Memory Observed: Remembering in Natural Contexts*, San Francisco, CA, Freeman.

JACKSON, B. (1968) *Life in Classrooms*, London, Holt, Rinehart and Winston.

KAIL, R. (1990) *The Development of Memory in Children*, New York, Freeman.

LANE, N. and LANE, S. (1986) 'Rationality, self-esteem and autonomy through collaborative enquiry', *Oxford Review of Education*, **12**, 3, pp. 263–75.

LIPMAN, M. (1988) *Philosophy Goes to School*, Philadelphia, PA, Temple University Press.

LUNDBERG, I., FROST, J. and PETERSON, O. (1988) 'Effects of an exercise program for stimulating phonological awareness in pre-school children', *Reading Research Quarterly*, **12**, 2, pp. 263–84.

McNAUGHTON, S. and GLYNN, T. (1981) 'Delayed versus immediate attention to oral reading errors: Effects on accuracy and self-correction', *Educational Psychology*, **1**, pp. 57–65.

MEADOWS, S. (1993) *The Child as Thinker*, London, Routledge.

MEICHENBAUM, D. (1985) 'Metacognitive assessment', in YUSSEN, S. (Ed) *The Growth of Reflection in Children*, Orlando, FL, Academic Press.

NELSON, K. (1986) *Event Knowledge: Structure and Function in Development*, Hillsdale, NJ, Lawrence Erlbaum Associates.

NISBET, J. (1990) 'Teaching thinking: An introduction to the research literature', *Spotlights*, **26**, Edinburgh, Scottish Council for Research in Education.

NISBET, J. and SHUCKSMITH, J. (1986) *Learning Strategies*, London, Routledge.

PALINSCAR, A. (1986) 'The role of dialogue in providing scaffolded instruction', *Educational Psychology*, **21**, 1, pp. 73–98.

PARKER-REES, R. (1996) 'Pupil voices on the curriculum', in POLLARD, A., THEISSEN, D. and FILER, A. (Eds) *Pupil Perspectives and the Curriculum*, London, Falmer Press.

PHILLIPS, T. (1985) 'Beyond lip-service: Discourse development after the age of 9', in WELLS, G. and NICHOLLS, J. (Eds) *Language and Learning: An Interactional Perspective*, Lewes, Falmer Press.

POWELL, S. and MAKIN, M. (1994) 'Enabling pupils with learning difficulties to reflect on their own thinking', *British Educational Research Journal*, **20**, 5, pp. 579–93.

QUICKE, J. and WINTER, C. (1994) 'Teaching the language of learning', *British Educational Research Journal*, **20**, 4, pp. 429–45.

QUICKE, J. and WINTER, C. (in press) 'Autonomy, relevance and the National Curriculum: A contextualised account of teachers' reaction to an intervention', *Curriculum Studies Journal*, **2**, 2.

ROBINSON, M. (1986) 'Children's understanding of the distinction between messages and meanings: Emergence and implications', in RICHARDS, M. and LIGHT, P. (Eds) *Children of Social Worlds*, Oxford, Blackwell.

ROGOFF, B. (1990) *Apprenticeship in Thinking: Cognitive Development in Social Context*, Oxford, Oxford University Press.

RUTTER, M. *et al.* (1979) *Fifteen Thousand Hours*, Cambridge, MA, Harvard University Press.

SCOTT, J. (1994) 'Communicating context: A tangled web', in WATSON, J. (Ed) *Working with Communication Difficulties*, Edinburgh, Moray House Publications.

Scottish Office Education Department (SOED) (1992) *Using Ethos Indicators in Primary School Self-Evaluation*, Edinburgh, HMSO.

Scottish Office Education Department (SOED) (1994) *Support for Learning*, Edinburgh, HMSO.

Sebba, J., Byers, R. and Rose, R. (1993) *Redefining the Whole Curriculum for Pupils with Learning Difficulties*, London, David Fulton.

Simpson, M. and Ure, J. (1994) *Studies of Differentiation Practices in Primary and Secondary Schools*, Edinburgh, Scottish Council for Research in Education.

Smith, F. (1992) *To Think: In Language, Learning and Education*, London, Routledge.

Smith, P. and Meux, M. (1970) *A Study of the Logic of Teaching*, Urbana, IL, University of Illinois Press.

Sugden, D. (Ed) (1989) *Cognitive Approaches in Special Education*, London, Falmer Press.

Sugden, D. and Newall, M. (1987) 'Teaching transfer skills to children with moderate learning difficulties', *British Journal of Special Education*, **14**, 2, pp. 63–7.

Tharp, R. and Gallimore, R. (1988) *Rousing Minds to Life*, Cambridge, Cambridge University Press.

Tizard, B. and Hughes, M. (1984) *Young Children Learning: Talking and Thinking at Home and at School*, London, Fontana.

Todman, J. and McBeth, J. (1994) 'Optimal mismatch for transfer of learning', *British Journal of Developmental Psychology*, **12**, 2, pp. 195–208.

Vygotsky, L. (1978) *Mind in Society: The Development of Higher Psychological Processes*, Cambridge, MA, Harvard University Press.

Wang, M. (1991) 'Adaptive instruction: An alternative approach to providing for student diversity', in Ainscow, M. (Ed) *Effective Schools for All*, London, David Fulton.

Wells, G. (1981) *Learning Through Interaction: The Study of Language Development*, Cambridge, Cambridge University Press.

Wells, G. (1985) *Language Development in the Pre-school Years*, London, Cambridge University Press.

Wishart, J. (1991) 'Motivational deficits and their relation to learning difficulties in young children with Down's Syndrome', in Watson, J. (Ed) *Innovatory Practice and Severe Learning Difficulties*, Edinburgh, Moray House Publications.

Wood, D. (1988) *How Children Think and Learn*, Oxford, Blackwell.

Wood, D. (1992) 'Learning through talk', in Norman, K. (Ed) *Thinking Voices*, London, Hodder and Stoughton.

Woods, P. (1993) *Critical Events in Teaching and Learning*, London, Falmer Press.

Wragg, E. and Brown, G. (1993) *Explaining*, London, Routledge.

Index